A PENGUIN HANDBOOK

THE
WILD GARDEN

Violet Stevenson, one of Britain's best-selling
gardening authors, has been flower and vegetable
grower, florist and home gardener. She has
gardened in urban plots – even on city roofs – and
for thirty years has maintained a country garden,
where her theories and beliefs about conservation
and natural gardening have been applied. Close
companionship with many forms of wildlife has
brought her to a sharing attitude, where people,
plants, insects and animals have equal
occupational rights.

THE
WILD GARDEN

VIOLET STEVENSON

PENGUIN HANDBOOKS

PENGUIN BOOKS
Viking Penguin Inc., 40 West 23rd Street,
New York, New York 10010, U.S.A.
Penguin Books Canada Limited, 2801 John Street,
Markham, Ontario, Canada L3R 1B4

First published in simultaneous hardcover and paperback
editions by Viking and Penguin Books 1985

Published simultaneously in Canada

The Wild Garden was conceived, edited, and designed by
Frances Lincoln Limited, Apollo Works,
5 Charlton Kings Road, London NW5 2SB.

ISBN 0 14 046.710 6

(CIP data available)

Printed in Yugoslavia by Mladinska Knjiga, Ljubljana
Set in England by Chambers Wallace, London

CONTENTS

FOREWORD

In some ways when we create a wild garden we return to our beginnings, for the first gardens were made from plants brought in from the wild either because they were not to be found locally or so that they were near at hand when required for healing, medicine, cooking or some other purpose.

Those gardeners who created the first romantic wild gardens had no need seriously to consider conservation. Except where industrialization had wantonly trespassed, roads, woodlands, heaths, meadows, marshes, ponds and streams were still much the same as they had been for centuries.

Now, however, there is a need for consideration, not only for many familiar and beloved plants, but also for the myriad creatures dependent upon them which are no longer commonly seen. Many of us who grew up in a less industrial world and a less farming-efficient countryside miss them. For a number of reasons we realize that we should not allow these plants to disappear. I hope that this book will show that it should not be difficult to stay the loss, indeed, that it will help increase their numbers.

Until quite recently, making a wild garden or a patch in a larger plot offered problems of its own. For example, since no conservationist should entertain the thought of lifting plants from the wild to bring home, where were the native plants needed to stock it to come from?

When I wrote *A Garden Full of Flowers* in 1968 I included a list of wildflowers worth growing and selected particularly only those which were listed among garden flowers in the seedsmen's catalogs and so were readily available to the gardener. There were 82 names! The list included many garden favorites such as wind flower, *Anemone nemorosa*; pasque flower, *Pulsatilla vulgaris*; Pyrenean lily, *Lilium nyrenaicum*; and snake's head lily, *Fritillaria meleagris*.

It is now possible to buy all manner of seeds and plants, too, of truly native species, even of those that have become very rare in the wild. Using wild-flower seed and with surprisingly little work, a dull and demanding lawn can be transformed into a flowery mead. Any piece of poor, unproductive land can be converted to a place of beauty.

A shrub border or a wooded building-site can become a flower-carpeted coppice. Prefabricated shapes and easy-to-handle plastics enable the gardener to make a pond, the most quickly created form of wild garden one can hope to have, and a sure magnet for a wide variety of wildlife.

To create and run a successful wild garden, a change of attitude to both plant and garden beauty is demanded. When I was last in Australia, I was interested to find that gardeners there had begun to reject cultivars in favor of native plants. Even though some are not so showy, they have a natural beauty of their own.

Apart from the interest and joy of having native plants at hand and watching them grow, and the satisfaction of having found an easier way to manage the plot, the wild gardener also has the added pleasure of sharing it with a number of fascinating tenants, the number of which increases as the garden becomes wilder. For instance, once their season arrives, there are always butterflies and moths in my garden. As one would expect, since their caterpillars and many other insects are plentiful, birds also abound. The many nests we find and fledglings we see are evidence that all parts of the garden are their territories. That there are also many other little creatures present is shown by the unmistakable traces left here and there, noted as one walks by or disturbs soil and heaped leaves in a border or hedge bottom. Only small traces, but important proof that there is yet another bonus worth noting – no-one is alone in a wild garden.

Violet Stevenson

WHAT IS A WILD GARDEN?

INTRODUCTION

Today's concept of a wild garden differs greatly from that of a century or so ago. A wild garden then was not a place for the care or protection of native plants for, after all, these still abounded in the countryside around. It was instead a contrived and romantic wilderness, a selected spot for those plants both novel and familiar, homesprung and exotic which, in spite of their beauty, would not fit into the precise gardening styles which then prevailed.

For centuries the vogue had been for controlled and very formal gardens. The plants, selected both for beauty and use, and later for novelty value, were grown in well-defined beds, which were most usually shaped to fit an overall geometric pattern, such as in the parterre. Although at first the plants within the beds were diverse, the ultimate ideal was that the decorative kinds should conform, for example be of uniform height, and that they should be ornamental at about the same time, flowering plants in spring and summer, to be replaced by evergreens in winter.

William Robinson and the wild garden

The man who tried to change this, and who indeed revolutionized British gardening by calling for informality in design and natural planting, was William Robinson (1838-1935), an Irish-born gardener of great imagination, drive and perhaps a certain opportunism. In 1870 he published *The Wild Garden,* where he wrote: 'My object . . . is now to show how we may have more of the varied beauty of hardy flowers than the most ardent admirer of the old style of garden ever dreams of, by naturalising innumerable beautiful natives of *many regions of the earth* in our woods and copses, rougher parts of pleasure grounds and in unoccupied places in almost every kind of garden.' (The italics are mine.) The gardens planted as Robinson advised were created in the grounds of great houses as a conceit, devised rather in the manner of the contemporary ferneries and grottoes to delight and amuse guests. They were intended as an attractive and pastoral contrast to the disciplined bedding and seasonal displays of the 'trim' garden which Robinson so criticized.

Robinson used plants considered too coarse for the trim garden, and curiously many of those he cites – peonies, delphiniums and lilies – are in fact favorites of today's trim gardens. Moreover, many herbaceous borders and island beds in the average garden are assembled in the way visualized by Robinson for his wild areas. The great difference is that these are not tucked away in some glade but stand revealed in the middle of a lawn or by a house.

RIGHT *A leafy corner of a garden originally designed by Gertrude Jekyll, continues to typify her style. Apparently informally grouped, in fact each plant has been carefully considered. Under a canopy of native trees, among exotic conifers and others, including on the left the Japanese angelica tree,* Aralia elata, *the South American* Gunnera magellanica *rises majestically above a carpet of ferns.*

LEFT *Ground under trees cleared of too dense and coarse undergrowth offers an area in which some of the most charming wildflowers can be encouraged to grow. Little labor is required, other than in the removing of those interlopers such as brambles which would smother the smaller plants. There are subjects suitable for all kinds of soils, but local plants can best guide the new wild gardener. William Robinson might well have approved of this particular scene, as he wrote: 'a pretty plant in a free state is more attractive than any garden denizen'.*

Significantly, Robinson's influence was felt at a time when exotic plants were being introduced, many of them plants which could not be expected to conform to the garden fashions of that time. Furthermore, the plant hunters brought back vivid descriptions of the terrain and settings in which they had found their trophies growing. The plantsman, standing spellbound before an imported lily growing in a pot, imagined it in its native setting, and tried to create the nearest thing to it. True, in his own plot the trees overhead, the shrubs below and the ground cover beneath might be comprised of subjects of different genera from those of the immigrants' home land, but would they fundamentally be so different? Was it not possible to reach some compromise? And, of course, it was.

In native woodland and coppice the would-be owners of wild gardens set about creating delightful areas for the cultivation of exotics. Soon, with the import of plants ever-expanding, on the right soil and in the right climate, rhododendron, eucryphia, pieris, kalmia, magnolia and others either took the place of native oak and birch or mingled amicably with them. Thus the romantic wilderness became an important part of the great gardens. Some still exist and are still known as 'wild' gardens.

Gertrude Jekyll and the hardy flower border
Gertrude Jekyll (1843-1932) had great influence on the breakaway from the overly formal. She admired the sweet simplicity of cottage gardens and her innovation was to bring new plants and old cottage favorites together, in borders away from wild areas, which she also planted in the Robinson manner. But with her painter's eye (for that was her training), she saw the pitfalls of the new gardening fashion, 'because it is understood to mean the planting of exotics in wild places, unthinking people rush to the conclusion that they can put any garden plants into any wild places . . . I have seen woody places that were already perfect with their own simple charm just muddled and spoilt by a reckless planting . . .'

On the whole she thought it better to leave the wood alone, but where it joined the garden to allow some bold planting of flowering plants 'as of Mullein in one part and Foxglove in another; for when standing in the free part of the garden it is pleasant to project the sight far into the wood, and to let the garden influences penetrate here and there, the better to join the one to the other'. But, her great contribution was to reinstate native plants to flower borders, planting them alongside newer cultivars and exotics.

Wild gardening in the grand manner
It is worth considering that except for the energetic and enthusiastic Miss Jekyll, few of the people who had their gardens restyled did the actual work

LEFT *The original concept of the wild garden was that it should delight and amuse, and should display plants not as they are found in nature but in a contrived natural setting. If indigenous plants were not spectacular enough, then certain others should be imported and set down among the most attractive of our native plants. Lilies such as this* Lilium giganteum, *one of Gertrude Jekyll's favorites, and many other species were to be seen in a woodland setting, framed perhaps by imported shrubs and fringed by both exotic and native ferns.*

themselves. This was left to the professional land-scaper and afterward to the gardener (who by nature and training usually found it difficult to be anything other than precise and tidy). Miss Jekyll, in her wooded area, among other devices had a pit dug 1.2m/4ft deep and about 3.5m/12ft across so that it could be filled with a carefully selected soil mixture, brought there by many donkey cart-loads, each holding three wheelbarrow loads, for her to grow to perfection her precious *Lilium giganteum*.

Even today many of the famous and great 'wild' gardens of the traditional romantic style are in fact intensively cultivated mainly because they contain or are intended to contain many exotics, the original habitats of which were in areas of rich, very humusy or acid soils which must be provided if the plants are to grow happily. So although the flowery areas were informal when compared with those of the past, they were seldom if ever really relaxed. It was not, I suggest, until professional gardeners became fewer and owner gardeners more plentiful that the majority of gardens took on as much 'sweet disorder' as they have today.

The ecological garden

Although the romantic wilderness is still an important, and desirable, part of the garden scene, some gardeners are moving into a rather different wild territory. In almost every country there now exists a lively interest in conservation and in providing a haven for native flora and fauna, rather than the display area for exotics and cultivars.

In my own garden, the native plants which I especially treasure are plants which once were common locally, many of which appear spontaneously in the garden, while others are rescued from the center of a rough farm road, from a building site or a field about to be sprayed with herbicide. I like to think that here in our garden is a little credit bank ready to pay out with interest if and when the time comes. These plants are symbolic of my personal concept of a wild garden, which is not just a wild place but which has become a place where wild plants and creatures are encouraged. The garden

ABOVE *The modern wild garden may take many forms, but all include those plants which may be considered to be labor-saving – those which on the whole can be left to grow their own way, layer on layer, nestling close together or even entwined, as they do in the wild. Informality is the rule. Straight lines are avoided or eliminated. Path and border edges are softened by an embroidery of sprawling and creeping plants.*

is very much under control, yet I believe it to be more wild than tame and it grows wilder all the time as yet another plant appears to have established itself and each day brings new sightings of wild creatures. I identified around 300 native plant species at the last rough count, and that did not include the many grasses and ferns.

Wild gardening – a more relaxed attitude

Since the time of Robinson's wild garden and Jekyll's mixed borders, the number of plants under cultivation has multiplied so considerably and the hybrids and varieties have so improved that few people wish to banish them. So where the gardener is more interested in the general appearance of the plot rather than its content, and where the cultivation of exclusively native species does not greatly appeal, then there is no reason why exotics and cultivars should not grow happily alongside native species, especially if the exotics are also attractive to wildlife. But, it is not generally realized that many of our familiar garden plants are in fact

BELOW *To convert a traditional garden to one with a wilder appeal, only a few touches are necessary in the beginning. For example, stately foxgloves will mingle agreeably with other plants, both native and exotic, and will seed themselves. Some garden shrubs can be supplemented by natives. Bushy and leafy perennials, creeping, climbing and trailing plants, will provide cover for wildlife.*

native. This point should be stressed, in case the novice gardener believes that 'wild' plants are limited to those seen around in great quantities at certain times of the year, such as dandelions and cow parsley, and often referred to as 'weeds'.

Furthermore, many 'exotics' are naturalized and some have been adopted by wildlife. For example, princess tree, a nectar plant for bees and a native of east Asia, is found growing on waste land in numerous cities, and rhododendron, of uncertain origin, provides excellent cover. The Kenilworth ivy, *Cymbalaria muralis*, which takes a hold in the smallest crevices of town walls and appears in country roads in some southern and western states, was introduced from southern Europe as a plant for hanging pots and baskets. The curious houseleek may have 'escaped' from rooftops where it was sometimes planted as a ward against fire.

A NATURAL OASIS

Even the smallest of formal gardens, kept well groomed and constantly tended, will be demanding of time, labor and money. Unfortunately, there are other things, some less tangible perhaps, but to many people more precious, which are inevitably sacrificed in a perfectly maintained plot. So often, in spite of the wealth of bloom and color, there is a feeling that something is missing. I sympathize with the three-year-old child, standing on the threshold of an immaculate billiard-table lawn, who turned to his hosts and told them kindly, 'We have daisies on *our* lawn.' And I have come to agree with the friend who told me, 'If there is no moss, for me there is no magic.'

Only gradually are people realizing that herbicides and insecticides used in the perfectly maintained plot lead to an all but sterile environment. And not only in gardens: so often in city parks and so-called environmental improvement areas the ground is sprayed to clear wild plants, only to be replaced by a monoculture – a single species of grass relieved by perhaps one or two species of trees – not as time-consuming as rows of bedding plants, but certainly more dreary.

No one really knows what the long-term effect of persistent herbicide use will be, and this is perhaps the most important reason for discouraging that use. Once the gardener makes this decision, he or she will soon learn that it is extremely satisfying to leave nature to her own devices and see a succession of wild plants gradually introduce themselves, soon followed by a whole range of wildlife.

Bringing nature back to the garden

A wild garden depends very much on the personality of the gardener, and on his or her locality. Many urban dwellers will want to bring the countryside to town and fill their small gardens and backyard plots with a mixture of wild and exotic species, or perhaps produce a synthesis of wild species to remind them of their favorite stretch of countryside. Small urban gardens can be made to look striking, with ferns sprouting from shaded walls and different mulleins or clovers, for example, seeding among pavement stones. In the suburbs, where there is usually more space available, the gardener can plan for continuity and mix plants of varied sizes, using a more casual blend of native and exotic.

If you have the motivation and the space, then you could create the ultimate wild garden – several different habitats merging into one, a situation that would be hard to find in real countryside. For example, a large garden could support a grassy meadow area, a small woodland coppice or natural

RIGHT *No matter how small or how urban, it is possible to create a wild garden in which water, living green leaves and a succession of flowers not only attract many forms of wildlife but provide also a delightful and restorative retreat.*

BELOW *Few places hold more charm than a flower-filled grass plot and few places are so easy to create. A mixture of grass and cornfield annuals sown in autumn or spring will become a delight the following summer.*

hedgerow, a butterfly border which could effectively simulate the side of a road, with its multiplicity of plant species, and perhaps a pond. Depending on local conditions, the site might lend itself to a heath, limestone or rock garden. The possibilities are endless but the opportunities are there with so many nurseries now producing more native plant stock and seed.

As more and more of our countryside is taken over for agriculture or is buried under the concrete of expressways or industrial developments, gardens, in terms of the space they occupy, represent important potential sanctuaries for both plants and animals. This applies especially to small discrete habitats such as hedgerows, ponds and meadow. By creating and knowing how to encourage such habitats, the wild gardener plays an important ecological and conservational role. What may start as a hobby may even become an obsession, albeit a fascinating and worthwhile one.

A neighbor, a keen cottage gardener, shocked to find herb robert in one of my borders, commented in her country burr, 'Fancy *you* growing they!' When I explained that I was not growing them, simply allowing them to grow, she shook her head, uncomprehending. To her these were weeds, common wild plants, and she had not noticed that they were no longer common outside the boundaries of our gardens. This is the case with many wild plants in many localities. So what, indeed, is a rare plant?

At one time only plants with extremely specialized requirements – native orchids, for example – were considered rare. Gradually as more and more wood and grassland have been turned into agricultural land, roadways and housing developments, even a relatively unspecialized plant has become scarce. The biennial fringed gentian, for example and trailing arbutus, *Epigaea repens*, are now extinct in most localities where they formerly occurred. Appalachian trilliums are still abundant in localities where protected but in other areas have been decimated by collectors for the wildflower trade. Some rarities have been in cultivation so long that they are found in many nurserymen's lists. Sometimes they are to be found on sale in gardens open to the public and on roadside stalls.

If those urban or suburban gardeners have doubts on the wisdom of growing wild plants because of the likelihood that they will be too 'weedy'-looking and will cause a nuisance to neighbor's gardens, compare the names in a flora with those in a seedman's or nurseryman's list. It should then become evident that there is a great range of beautiful wild species to draw upon, which have inhabited our gardens for centuries. Some of them are known affectionately as cottage flowers, plants such as cornflowers, columbines, loosestrife, heartsease and maiden pinks.

The wildlife bonus
A wild garden should be aesthetically pleasing and at the same time attractive to wildlife. Even people who cannot tell one bird from another and who

LEFT *Hibernating butterflies will stir in early spring. After so long a fast, once on the wing they seek energy-providing nectar. Few suitable garden plants blossom early enough, but there are some native species which do. The goat or pussy willow's catkins offer nectar to the butterflies and pollen to early foraging bees. Salix caprea, one of the commonest willows in the garden, is widely naturalized in North America. Similar native species are* Salix discolor *and* S. humilis.

consider that most insects are pests will find that encouraging wildlife into the garden can open up new vistas and stimulate new interests. The garden will take on a new life of its own, not only during the spring with its surge of nesting activity. If you provide the right kind of food and shelter you can continue to attract wildlife through the year with groups of finches feeding on seed heads in the autumn, followed by waves of winter migrant birds that will gorge themselves on carefully planted berry-laden trees and bushes.

You will be amazed how quickly animals of all kinds will respond to selective planting. Even the addition of one native species can make a lot of difference, such as an early-flowering goat or pussy willow which will provide a rich source of nectar and pollen to insects newly emerged from hibernation. A single cluster of pussy willow catkins may contain an assortment of syrphids, bees, moths, and butterflies. Later in the year the willow's fluffy seeds provide a fine lining for nests.

Not everyone in town welcomes the country invasion. Where for neighborly harmony's sake or perhaps for other reasons the gardener wishes to present a well-groomed garden, it is still possible to help in the maintenance of wildlife. In my own 'trim' borders near the house, many kinds of native and naturalized plants grow happily with the more cultivated kinds, so easily in fact that they often have to be pointed out to visitors. A butterfly border of native plants can be both pretty and neat (see pages 50-51). It can also be supplemented by nectar-rich exotics so that it conforms to the general idea of a flower border.

The wildlife aspect of wild gardening is especially satisfying for those people who spend a good deal of time at home – young children or the elderly, as well as the infirm who may be confined for long periods.

A change of approach

New gardeners may have few problems in setting to and starting a wild garden, but more traditional gardeners like myself may need consciously to

encourage a more relaxed frame of mind. Think of it this way: if, during a normal working day, one is continually subject to a strict routine, then why impose a similar pattern on a place which has nothing to do with one's work? It certainly can be very invigorating to mow the lawn or hoe after a day at the office but all this energy can, with a wild garden, be channeled into more constructive rather than destructive occupations. There is always plenty to be done in creating a wild garden before you arrive at the right aesthetic and ecological balance; and if you are to attract wildlife, you must set up as many nooks, corners, shrubs, climbers and shelter belts as you can. But, while introducing native species, there is really no reason at all why you should dig up favorite cultivars which can easily fit into your design.

LEFT *Many garden perennials, like these lupins, will quite happily become naturalized. If they are left to seed them-selves, they gradually revert to type, which of course presents no problem to the wild gardener. Umbellifers push their way into many gardens. Beautiful but invasive, they grow quite well among other plants and are most effective where they can be given an area to spread and colonize.*

ABOVE *The beautiful Wild gladiolus,* Gladiolus illyricus, *a plant that is a near relative of the cottage garden G.* byzantinus.

A solution to poor soil

Frequently the creation of a wild garden, however romantic the term may sound, may in fact be the most practical way of dealing with a fallow piece of land. Not all houses are surrounded by a plot of best top soil. In the traditional flower garden, and certainly in a vegetable or fruit plot, the gardener often sets about altering the type and quality of the soil in order to grow favorite plants or a greater range of them, or to produce heavier yields of food crops. In wild gardening we should not be so concerned with altering the soil; rather we should be more concerned with finding plants to suit it and in maintaining its condition for as long as possible. This means that we avoid going against the grain by adding fertilizers or artificial manures, and leave it, as much as is practicable, to nature.

Do not be despondent, therefore, if your soil is poor and you cannot afford to enrich it. Many wild plants flourish best where the soil is poor. Take, for example, the management of grass in a flower meadow. When the long grass is cut it should not be allowed to lie. It should be cleared by raking and removing it from the site as soon as possible. This is because when mown grass is left to rot it is gradually incorporated into the soil below and becomes a form of organic manure which will increase the nutrient value of the soil. This will suit some plants, especially grasses, but other meadow plants will find enriched soil unsuitable and their numbers will decline. While some species die out, others, not always so welcome, are likely to appear in great numbers. (See pages 56-67 on wildflower meadows.)

Soil quality can be tested in the first year by roughly broadcasting some of the cheaper seed bought from traditional seedsmen rather than from wildflower specialists. Shirley poppies, a variety of the wild red one, and cornflowers are examples. Once it is appreciated how well these grow and how profusely they flower by this rough and ready method, the gardener is likely to be encouraged to go to a little more trouble on the same soil.

ABOVE *Dappled shade, rather than the dense canopy offered by some trees, provides ideal conditions for many plants which have handsome, long-lasting foliage. To avoid competition with any tree roots near the surface, before planting raise the area in which they are to grow.*

LEFT *Where the ground of a new garden is well covered with vegetation, wait to see what plants flower or thrive before completely clearing it.*

ABOVE *The lady's slipper orchid,* Cypripedium calceolus, *is almost extinct in the wild in Britain. The American form,* C. pubescens, *is threatened by collectors.*

New ways of seeing wild plants

While some may think that a plant in seed is drab, others see beauty in its new form, texture and fecundity. Certainly a truly wild garden will never give the months-long display of floral color expected from, say, petunias and begonias. It is often possible to plant in such a way that the eye can be taken from fading spring-flowering plants and directed to those that bloom in summer or autumn. In winter, especially in frosty weather, spent stems take on a new beauty and significance, being either covered with sparkle or visited by seed-seeking birds.

Some plants will go through their annual cycle very attractively and usefully if their seeds and fruits are of value to wildlife. Others may not please the more tidy-minded gardener. Those of mine which grow alongside cultivars and other garden plants and are likely to become straggly are usually trimmed, often with pleasing or unexpected results. Red campion and toadflax, for instance, after seeding stems are cut away, will usually continue to bloom, albeit less luxuriantly, sometimes deep into winter. However, a permanently tidy or disciplined plant such as a large fern or some berried shrub will always divert attention at the critical season. Late-blooming nectar plants are also good for this purpose, plants such as *Sedum spectabile*, michaelmas daisies or golden rod are all extremely attractive to late-foraging butterflies and other insects.

A garden to relax in

Conservation and sentiment apart, there is another valid reason why more people are turning to a less formal way of gardening and from there to wild gardens. House owners are not automatically skilled gardeners, and there are many people with gardens who actively dislike gardening chores but nevertheless want to have attractive plants at hand. Such people are obvious candidates for wild gardens, for upkeep can be kept to a minimum. This view may run counter to expectation, but, once set up, a wild garden can be almost self-

maintaining. And if your plot is not as tidy or well-groomed as visitors might expect a garden to look, you can always say with honesty, 'It's supposed to be wild.' Instead of censure, usually a genuine interest is aroused, especially if the gardener can then point to an interesting butterfly or nesting bird to show the benefit of non-interference.

With imagination, your garden can be transformed into a tranquil oasis, not only for wildlife, but for yourself. There are few things nicer than to relax in your own garden, and if it has a wild feel about it, you get additional satisfaction – perhaps from a shaded corner with foxgloves busily visited by bees, or from the wonderful confusion of the twining stems of hops and bryony rambling over a hedge or fence. It is easy to forget, too, just how much children like wild patches of garden to play in, where there are places in which they can hide. Perhaps many of us need this, a modern counterpart to the old medieval walled garden, with its arbors and secret places, a garden that shuts off and is a respite from the cares of the world.

ABOVE *What might be an eyesore in a neat, well-groomed plot can prove to be an asset in a wild garden. A tree stump often houses a diversity of wildlife. This one will soon be hidden from view as the fern fronds extend and as the honesty seeds itself. But why go to the trouble of cutting down a dead tree? Leave it and drape it with attractive climbers, to provide nesting and roosting sites.*

PLANNING THE WILD GARDEN

AN UNHURRIED APPROACH

The great thing to remember about creating a wild garden is that it should not be hurried. Take time. As with any garden, one is well advised to spend the first year taking stock and planning gradually. Too often, when confronted with an uncultivated building plot or an established but overrun garden, the new owner impulsively sets to work, clearing it of all vegetation that he or she considers to be ugly or that is labeled 'weeds' by popular opinion. These plants are often purposely and ruthlessly destroyed by the application of some virulent weedkiller, or a great deal of hard labor goes into eliminating them by hand. When making a wild garden, these impulses should be subdued. Many of the plants that are despised or even feared horticulturally are essential to the lives of living creatures. The stinging nettle (see page 52) is just one example. If the gardener is not familiar with wild plants it is a good plan to spend a season or two identifying those which grow spontaneously, and then checking their usefulness in both bird and insect books. If the plants prove to be unattractive visually yet are well worth saving, allow them to grow somewhere out of sight. The bramble is one example. Spread over an area it can be an unsightly nuisance, but its importance for wildlife (see page 48) means that you should try to retain it if you can.

Similarly, if you acquire a site that has been newly cleared, whether it once sustained shrubs, trees, grass or was waste ground, wait and see what appears in the spring. Since the topsoil will have been disturbed, and especially where subsoils have been raised, there will be an upsurge of growth from seeds which have lain dormant, possibly for years. Once light and moisture reaches them, the seeds will germinate and the seedlings grow vigorously, often in great numbers.

This is why where new roads have been built the sides are often covered with scarlet poppies; their oily seeds remain viable for many years. A similar spontaneous show once happened in my own garden when we purchased an adjoining piece of land. When it was worked for the first time, the ground was smothered with a crop of corn chamomile, *Anthemis arvensis.* An unexpected show of this kind might be welcome in a new garden, for it has in it the beginnings of a flower meadow. However, not all seedlings that appear in this way are as attractive or as welcome as poppies and daisies. If you are unlucky there may be one or two dominating species only which will need to be cleared or at least drastically reduced.

If, on the other hand, the soil is very poor and unproductive, and the site has little to commend it so far as beauty and special features are concerned, consider taking a short cut. You could establish a water and waterside garden. Aquatic plants will grow rather more quickly and luxuriantly than land plants in a similar situation. Alternatively, especially where the soil is either exhausted or unresponsive, cover the area with a good layer of gravel and make a gravel garden. Surprisingly, but as all who own a gravel path or drive will know, a great variety of plants elect to grow in the medium. Purposely planned and planted as a wild garden, it can be used to great advantage. Stone could be used instead of gravel, especially if you live in an area where flat local stone abounds. Pave some areas informally, and fill the spaces with plants, which will soon spread to color and cover the stone. See also chapters on water gardens, rock gardens, pages 108-113 and on 114-120.

RIGHT *The introduction of a selection of distinctive foliage and flowering plants into a town or paved garden need not lead to an untidy or unkempt appearance. Yellow-flowered corydalis in the left foreground readily grows in cracks between stones. Thyme, opposite, which will self-seed freely in pavings or gravel, scents the air and attracts butterflies and bees. The variegated flag growing in the little pond is a variety of the yellow water flag.*

Besides the all-important matter of soil type (see pages 32-33), there are other site factors that you need to take into account before deciding what kinds of plants to grow and how to distribute them. These include aspect, sun and shade, wind exposure and shelter, drainage and the general lie of the land, such as whether it is flat or sloping.

A windy site offers problems. Take note of the direction of the prevailing wind. If trees grow in the vicinity, these should give a guide, for the treetops inevitably become sculpted by a strong prevailing wind. It is important to establish shelter in a windy site: in a small garden even one large shrub or a group of trees will help in this respect, and evergreens are particularly useful. Take care not to shut out the sun when you plant windbreaks and shelter screens of trees or shrubs. If this is likely to happen, plant the trees and shrubs in interrupted groups rather than a single dense line. And these trees and shrubs play more than a weather-protective role: they give birds cover and nesting sites. (See also native plants for shade, page 42.)

If you live in an area subject to frosts, try always to avoid the creation of a major hollow or valley in your landscaping. Frosts tend to roll downhill and will settle in and fill a dip in the land to create a frost pocket. With a sloping garden always try to leave a gap in fences, walls and hedges or other boundary at the lowest point, so that the frost can continue to roll downhill rather than becoming trapped and causing damage.

Adapting a traditional garden

Where a gardener's aim is to change the nature of the existing plot and create a wild garden instead, obviously it will not be possible to start from scratch. Existing plants, particularly trees and shrubs, may have sentimental value or may deserve respect because of their age. Or, if you live in a town, there may be prohibitions on felling mature

trees. But it should not be difficult, whatever their country or origin, to fit trees into your wild garden design. Some trees can be suitable as supports for climbing plants, and so provide a quick means to a more natural and informal scene, especially if native climbers are used.

The substitution of a native shrub or tree for an exotic species can make a remarkable difference, especially if the native is common in the locality. There is a fine range of native shrubs and trees, all of which have an important ecological role, often one which an imported species cannot understudy. On the other hand, exotic climbers may prove more effective in terms of fast growth and cover than a native species. *Clematis montana* is especially vigorous and has the bonus of masses of pink flowers in the spring.

However large or small the garden, the transition from traditional to wild can be stepped, beginning with concentrating the garden plants near the house, and then designing the rest of the garden so that you are led gently into a wild area. You can begin by introducing some natives into the borders at a point further from the house so that they grow among the exotics and the cultivars – columbines, red campion, Jacob's ladder and many campanulas.

The grass areas can follow a similar theme, that is, mown frequently near the house, a little shaggier and mown less frequently father away, perhaps embroidered with white clover for honey bees and prunella and speedwell for delight, and then on to full flower meadow (see pages 56-67), cut just twice a year. This is much the method followed in my own garden.

If there is space, a little group of shrubs and trees can be constructed, accompanied by suitable herbaceous plants, ferns perhaps, or, if there is enough shade, Solomon's seal, lily-of-the-valley, forget-me-not and London pride. There are also ways of extending the wild area visually. A shrub

ABOVE *Solomon's seal,* Polygonatum multiflorum, *also known as David's harp, is a woodland plant.*

RIGHT *Where a traditional garden exists, the gardener is advised to take time over its conversion. Many of the existing plants can be left to grow alongside any native species to be brought in. Some, like yellow potentilla, may be indigenous. Fruit or other trees can support native climbers and also be attractively underplanted with native and exotic ferns and other shade-loving plants.*

border, screen or hedge can be made to take on the semblance of the margin of a wood, where ferns and woodland plants can reach out into the more formal garden areas, fringing them discreetly.

A patch of wild garden

Where a driveway leads to a house, the land on either side could be used as a wildflower border. There is something very refreshing about turning off from a busy road to find oneself immediately among cool, leafy climbers and country flowers. Much will depend upon the width of the drive borders – there may be space for a series of levels, with trees, shrubs and ground covers. Or, the border may be wide enough only to house a colony of ferns and, say, bluebells in spring, foxgloves in summer and perhaps colchicums and cyclamen in autumn and winter.

In most gardens there is a compost pile and a utility area tucked away out of sight. Visitors' steps are usually steered away from it. If this portion were to be enlarged, it could become a wild area where the more informal plants, nettles perhaps or long grass, could be allowed to grow. It could be hidden by one or more native shrubs – a holly, black haw, high-bush cranberry or flowering dogwood growing on a leaf-littered ground.

Sometimes it is possible to annex a strip of land to use as a wild plot. Often there is, or could be, a little piece of no man's land outside the garden proper, even flanking the road or pavement, perhaps at the foot of a boundary hedge, wall or fence. In my own case there is such a strip out in the road which leads to the house, on the far side of a wall. In this overspill strip are allowed to grow a great assortment of plants, most of which were originally selected because they are the food plants of certain butterflies. These were brought from other parts of the garden and transplanted. Others, such as the garlic mustard, *Alliaria petiolata*, host among others to the orange tip butterfly, have just dropped in. Each year the range of plants increases as the native species, their seed dispersed by wind, birds or some other natural means, become established among those that were planted. Most are welcome. Thistles, for instance, attracted masses of beautiful goldfinches one year. But one finds that borders of this kind, which are very much on view to those who visit or pass the house, may need a little more grooming than most wild plots, mainly because certain plants which find their way there are very invasive and become dominant, *Alliaria petiolata* and couch grass, *Agropyron repens*, for instance.

Banks and ditches

Where a grass bank lies either outside or inside the perimeter of the garden consider whether or not it should be kept carefully mowed and groomed. Hot and sunny or cool and shady, it can prove to be a splendid habitat for a varied range of plants, and need not present an untidy appearance. A cool, shady bank can hold many of the little early-flowering spring bulbs: aconites, snowdrops, crocus, scillas; miniature daffodils, bluebells, fritillaries, combined with violets, primroses, self-heal and other low-growing meadow flowers.

On a sunny bank other meadow flowers will flourish, those with the shortest or sprawling stems usually being most suitable. Whether for acid or alkaline soils, lady's bedstraws, clustered bellflower, cowslip, harebell, self-heal, field scabious and oxeye daisy are examples.

A ditch, which by its very nature is likely to be moist at certain times of the year or in some cases certain times of the day, offers yet another site for improvement and exploitation. Fern-lined sides topped with carpeting, moisture-loving plants, will transform what is usually intended as a utility feature into a charming one without diminishing its purpose.

Accommodating existing garden features

A wall, particularly if it is an old one, can become a wild plantation in its own right, for it will support a wealth of plants if encouraged to do so. Such a wall garden also offers a safe haven for many forms of wildlife. A dry-stone wall can be a good setting for alpine plants and will prove to be an attractive

ABOVE *The tallest of all the bellflowers, the giant bellflower,* Campanula latifolia, *is found naturalized in New England. Its shoots may be cooked like spinach.*

and interesting feature the year through.

In the same way a hedge can be made to play a more important ecological role. If it is already a 'wild' hedge – that is, made of natives, hemlock or osage-orange perhaps, it should not be difficult to transform it into a more fecund hedgerow, with many plants growing at its foot and some creepers within it. As in so many cases, the local flora is a

FROM TRADITIONAL GARDEN TO WILD

This garden is being gradually transformed from traditional to wild, and favorite exotics and garden plants mingle happily with the native species. Plants grown in tubs near the house are selected to attract butterflies and moths, and make the link from house to garden. The potted plants here are thyme, nicotiana, geranium and petunia. From the steps, you go down past the rock garden where alyssum, thrift and campanulas grow among the heathers. The lawn here is kept fairly short, with some meadow flowers grown around the edges and opposite the pond. A bird feeder is attached to an overhanging branch from the next door garden, and buddleia and lilac attract insects. From the pond area, the garden takes on a wilder aspect, with the grass becoming meadow-length and, at the end of the garden, quite long, where it offers a haven for insects and small mammals. Here also grow plants to provide food.

1 Wild Cherry, *Prunus avium*
2 Cornflower, *Centaurea cyanus*
3 Buddleia, *Escallonia macrantha*
4 Species rose, *Rosa* sp.
5 Sweet flag, *Acorus calamus*
6 Bog arum, *Calla palustris*
7 Marsh marigold, *Caltha palustris*
8 Holly, *Ilex aquifolium*
9 Smokebush, *Cotinus coggyria*
10 Russian vine, *Polygonum baldschuanium*
11 Hazel, *Corylus avelana*
12 Brambles, *Rubus* sp.
13 Lilac, *Syringa vulgaris*
14 Lawson cypress, *Chamaecyparis lawsoniana*
15 Rowan or mountain ash, *Sorbus aucuparia*
16 Foxglove, *Digitalis purpurea*
17 St John's wort, *Hypericum* sp.
18 Crab apple, *Malus pumila*
19 Nettles, *Lamium* sp.

good guide to what to grow, but it is also pleasing to introduce some species which are not so common, perhaps violets, spring beauty, cranesbill for early spring, creeping jenny for summer, tall Solomon's seal and wild phlox for butterflies. Ferns and troutlilies will provide an evergreen mixture.

If there is an existing hedge of some garden shrub – conifers, privet or lonicera – it can be embroidered and at the same time recharged by introducing a few native plants here and there along its length. (See page 137 for planting a native hedgerow.) My own gappy hedge, consisting largely of elderberry, is gradually being thickened with little seedlings of hawthorn and holly found growing in the garden from seed obviously dispersed by birds. Alternatively, introduce climbers: the trumpet honeysuckle, which produces attractive berries and handsome foliage, vinelike Virginia creeper or, so long as the soil is not acid, *Clematis virginiana* or *C. viorna*. One of the handsomest of American vines is cross vine, *Bignonia capreolata*, which turns a deep bronzy purple in winter. Where it is practical, the hedge can support larger climbers: wild roses or blackberries for instance.

Enhancing the site

Artificial mounds and banks, apart from adding interest to a flat site, offer good shelter. Even a meter's height will provide a suprising amount of protection and, well planted, can become an attractive feature. In my own garden, which is very exposed and flat, occasional mounds and banks have been made here and there to give shelter from the cold north and east, the latter because certain early-flowering plants need shielding from the morning sun following frosts (a precaution not so vital where native plants rather than slightly tender exotics are concerned). A bank gives plants a deep root-hold, which means that tall plants as well as shorter, close-carpeting kinds can be grown on it. Plants can 'borrow' height this way. A meter high bank, for instance, will 'lift' a plant considerably, giving it greater importance in the landscape. Thickly planted with shrubs, some

evergreen, a bank makes an effective windbreak.

For the gardener who is growing native plants, a long mound running east-west offers two useful sites. One is in full sun and the other in shade. If such a bank can also be situated where it can give shelter, the benefits are manifold. The north face need not offer any problems. There are many plants for such a site: woodfern, Christmas fern and polypody will keep it green all winter, hepatica and bloodroot will pattern it with flowers in spring, while a great number of little flowering plants which enjoy cool, shady conditions, such as creeping jenny, rue anemone, celandine and cuckoo flower, will carpet a north-facing bank and produce blooms in spring and summer.

Sometimes, where there is the space and the setting, the bank can be cut away to make a little

ABOVE *Both natural and artificial banks can be clothed attractively whether they lie in sun or shade. Where the shade and the root soil are both deep, some of the moisture-loving plants, such as the tall purple* Lythrum *seen here, will grow luxuriantly and will mingle with shade-loving kinds. Where there exists plenty of cover, a bank offers a good home for fauna as well as flora.*

cliff, a background for certain plants to grow at its foot, or in little bays cut into its face. When planting a bank, whether it is steep or not, always begin at the top and work toward the bottom.

More plants can be grown on a terraced slope than on one which is simply steep and they can be grown much more attractively. Many will spill over prettily to the lower levels while some will grow in the crevices of whatever materials are used to support the terraces. These can be rock, peat blocks which are ideal for acid soils, tree trunks or boughs and turves. All of these have been used at some time or another in my own garden. Freshly dug turves are turned upside down so that the grass part is buried and set in place, first in a row, straight or curving, and then one over the other in the same way as bricks are laid. Soil is then brought level with the root portion of the turf and the terrace planted as soon as possible. The grass gradually rots but the turves stay intact for a long period, long enough for roots of other plants to grow into them and to hold. (See also page 125 for the peat block method of supporting a terrace.)

A very steep slope can be covered with spreading plants, rather than be closely planted. The exotic *Cotoneaster horizontalis* set at the foot will lean close to the surface as it grows upward. This plant also bears blossom attractive to bees, berries for birds, dense foliage and useful nesting sites.

The creeping willow, *Salix repens*, can be planted at the top of a slope and will gradually extend its prostrate stems over the summit and will cascade down the slope, meeting and merging with plants from below. Other climbing or carpeting plants can also be used to the same effect (see pages 38-40).

ABOVE *The cuckoo flower,* Cardamine pratensis, *is a plant of damp meadows yet it often grows in great drifts of color alongside rivers and creeks.*

LEFT *Columbines, cranesbills and sweet cicely provide a succession of flowers among the diverse leaves which cover this bank so attractively. Perennial plants ensure that the display is continual and those flowers which seed freely such as the columbine, ensure that the mixture is constantly rejuvenated. Some plants, and these are examples, accept almost any aspect – shady, semishady or sunny.*

Paths in the wild garden

Paths once established are difficult to eradicate and therefore the gardener is advised to proceed with caution before deciding the course a path should take. Walk around your plot to get a feel as to where your proposed paths should be set. It may take months, even the four seasons to decide upon the position, the nature and indeed the role of the path.

Frequently, once a path has been planned it is best to use the materials at hand. A simple natural panning of the surface may suffice, as in a woodland, where the fallen leaves are trodden and flattened. Suggestions for more permanent paths suitable for the wild garden are on page 128.

There are few gardens which do not yield a crop of stones, uncovered as the gardener plants or cultivates the ground. These can be used as path foundations or surfaces, in the sure knowledge that the material is local and is likely to be in harmony with the setting. Shingle and other small loose stones and gravel make admirable surfaces. Although some of these may look new and even garish when first applied, they soon settle down.

A sunken path can add to the charm and interest of a wild garden. It could become a little dell, enchanting when passing through a rock or alpine area. In a woodland garden one can make a path which runs below the general level of the ground in much the same manner as an old woodland track, its soft border mulched naturally by annual leaf fall. Sides of sunken paths, well drained and warm, provide ideal conditions for certain flowering and leafy plants and ferns.

Where possible, the path should wind in such a way as to direct one's steps to places or plants of interest, or to points where the garden or the surrounding landscape can be seen from an advantageous or unfamiliar angle. Paths that lead to some hidden, secluded or unexpected feature of great interest give the garden charm and an element of mystery.

For those who are making a meadow or orchard flower garden, one of the simplest of all paths is a passage made by a lawn mower, its width being the same or double that of the swathe cut by the machine. This kind of path is also practical because it is so much more pleasant to walk in short grass after heavy rain or dews than to try to pass through long grass. Such a path, sometimes called a 'ride', needs to be mown fairly regularly.

One way of softening paved paths is to allow certain plants to grow between the stones. Low-growing and creeping plants are best, although once the gardener no longer keeps these paved areas immaculately weed-free, a surprising range of self-sown plants will appear. To crowd out any

BELOW Grass, ferns and ground cover plants growing at the edge of a woodland path will help define its shape and direction. If these are trailing or creeping kinds, they will need cutting back from time to time so that they do not cover the surface. It is wise to keep paths narrow. Foot traffic is often then sufficient to keep the surface clear without the need to hoe it clean or to use chemical weedkillers. Plants growing on a path can make it slippery.

unwanted weeds, sow seeds of your own choosing between the cracks of larger stones. Where they are smaller, remove an occasional pavement stone, plant that area and allow the plant to establish its own colony. Several varieties of thyme are ideal for this purpose and have the advantage of smelling sweetly when trodden upon. Shaded paths can be planted with wood avens and bugle.

Guard against making a path too wide, at least in the early stages of creating the garden. This is particularly important when a path runs through a woodland or bushy area. If kept narrow enough, foot traffic alone should keep the path clean.

Beware, too, of raised paths, even an inch or two above the level of the surrounding ground. These can prove hazardous to the very young and the elderly. The same applies to shady paths covered with moss which can prove extremely slippery.

A MEANDERING PATH

Points of interest in a garden can be emphasized by a winding path. From the terrace before the house, a gravel path runs between a low hedge **1** and a border of herbs **2**, before entering a small coppice **3**. The path then opens out for a sitting area by the pond **4**, and then continues past a meadow area **5**. It leads back to the house as short cut grass, passing a border planned to attract butterflies **6**.

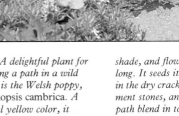

ABOVE *A delightful plant for bordering a path in a wild garden is the Welsh poppy, Meconopsis cambrica. A cheerful yellow color, it grows well in either sun or shade, and flowers all summer long. It seeds itself freely, even in the dry cracks between pavement stones, and helps the path blend in to the informal setting of the wild garden.*

SOIL TYPES

Those who are hoping to create a wild garden need to understand that much of the advice given for dealing with soils in traditional gardening practice is not of great value or consequence to them. Sometimes, a little soil alteration may result in being able to grow a great number of species and so may be justified, but on the whole, since wild gardening is also intended in the main to be trouble-free gardening, the principle should be to go along with whatever soil exists rather than try to change it.

In the landmass of Europe, a limestone subsoil predominates and where this occurs it influences the soils which lie upon it and, therefore, the wild flora and the kinds of cultivated plants that can most easily be grown. In North America only certain (mainly ericaceous) plants where bog, moor or heath conditions prevail and those that grow in areas of high rainfall in the east are calcifuges. Most woodland plants prefer a soil near neutral.

Acid soils

Acid soils are not all of the same type. Some may be peaty, others so rich in decayed organic materials that they are almost so. Some may be sandy, some clayey and heavy. Some may be very dry or liable to become so under certain circumstances, some moist and even boggy. Sometimes a part of a cultivated garden which has been generously and continuously mulched with organic manures and composts may have become acid. Simple soil testing (see page 122) will reveal this condition.

Acid soils offer the gardener the opportunity to grow a wonderful range of native plants, for many of the rarest and most beautiful subjects grow on this type of soil, although some need particular habitats prepared for them. On very acid soil, a plot could be made to support a miniature heath (see pages 78-85). Acid soil can also support a special kind of woodland, the plants of which are quite unlike those found in woods on limy soils.

Alkaline soils

One of the difficulties faced by gardeners in parts of England is encouraging plants to grow on chalk. Certainly it offers problems but one should keep in mind that some of the most treasured European wildflowers do grow on chalk and that chalk is a form of limestone. The latter has an abundance of

BELOW *Garden rhododenrons confirm that soil is acid here. The lovely little* Phlox divaricata, *from the north-east, has creeping rhizomatous roots which aid it in carpeting the ground, a characteristic of many plants favoring acid soils.*

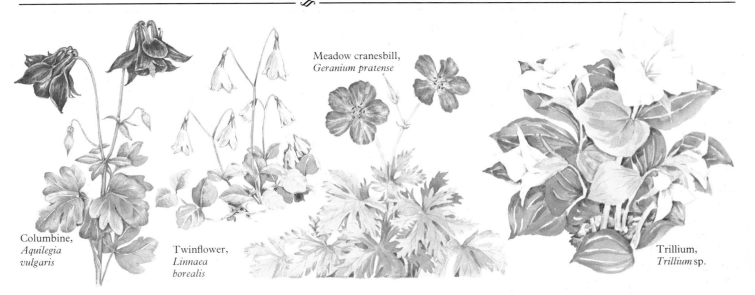

Meadow cranesbill,
Geranium pratense

Columbine,
*Aquilegia
vulgaris*

Twinflower,
*Linnaea
borealis*

Trillium,
Trillium sp.

inorganic material within it, while chalk is either lacking or very poor in other content. However, although gardens on chalk have a very shallow top-soil, they can support a variety of plants.

In the wild, on a base of limestone rock, plant material accumulates over a period of many years, producing a layer of acid humus. Despite the high alkalinity and if the layer is deep enough, some calcifuges will grow, the crowberry, *Empetrum nigrum*, for example. This natural phenomenon can be simulated in rock gardens where the gardener wishes to grow many diverse species of similar habit but differing soil requirements.

Neutral or mixed soils

Where gardens exist on neutral soil, that is one which is neither acid nor alkaline, often many species of plants preferring both soil types will flourish. Some plants are very adaptable, for example, in my own garden, herb robert grows freely in every part of the garden – in alkaline un-cultivated ground, in well-fed borders alongside cultivars, in the well-manured vegetable patch and on the acid peat mound.

When calcifuges are to be grown on neutral soil they will grow better with a little assistance, and there is no contradiction in importing extra peat to increase the soil's acidity.

Woodland soils

The soil beneath trees and shrubs is bound to be influenced by the spent leaves which fall upon it. If this soil is of poor quality, that can be an advantage so long as the plants are given some help at planting time (see pages 134-5). Where trees have been standing for a long period, as in a natural wood, the leaf layer may be very deep and each year's layer will be in a different condition from the one above or below. The state and even the rate of decomposition varies according to the type of trees contributing to the leaf layer.

Woodland plants are adapted to grow in this loose, leafy litter. Many of them (for example the wood anemone) have creeping stems or rhizomes, which can not only store up food but work their way through the litter grasping what small particles of leaf soil they can find for sustenance, thus spreading the plant further and further afield.

Where the gardener hopes to introduce some woodland or woodland plants, it is necessary to establish woodland soil. Import leafmold for planting and mix with good soil compost.

ABOVE *Although a remarkable number of plants will grow quite happily on ordinary or neutral soil in the garden, in the wild they tend to appear only on specific types. For instance, the four wildflowers shown here all have different tastes, the meadow cranesbill preferring clay, the lovely twinflower the acid soils of pinewoods, the large-flowered trillium, or wake-robin, a well-drained, humusy woodland soil, and the columbine, lime. By identi-fying the wild flora around you (or the garden plants in the neighborhood), it should be possible to gain a general idea of your local soil.*

WHAT TO GROW

New wild gardeners would be wise to realize that a bluebell-carpeted woodland, or a spacious heath garden, or a waterfall and babbling creek plus their attendant plants are not transformations that can be achieved instantly – at least, not without the expenditure of a considerable fortune. Even if the necessary time and labor were expended, and the appropriate plants carefully installed, the picture would hardly look natural, let alone wild, for several seasons however much care was taken over random planting and natural curves. Nature works relatively slowly. The changes in our own garden have been gradual, but the gardener can hurry nature along.

In the wild, plants form colonies naturally, often growing in such numbers that they make drifts of color and areas of different textures, perhaps among grass or in the shade beneath trees. Where one or two plants of the same species already exist in a garden, it is often worth propagating more to add to the group. Where the gardener hopes to establish a colony of plants from scratch, they have a better chance of survival if all the plants available are grouped fairly thickly in one patch; when you distribute individual plants widely over a larger area, the colony is likely to become invaded by a stronger, unwanted species (see page 44). Do not zone the plants too thickly, however; allow one species to merge into another at the edge of the group – even if the neighbor is grass. Left to go their own way, plants will usually do this, but you have to give new plants you are introducing a fighting chance.

Don't hesitate to plant thickly. In the wild most plants jostle each other. Often in many gardens one finds that the ground tends to become closely covered in spring when a great variety of little flowering bulbous plants colonize the sites under or between shrubs and trees and then once these have faded becomes bare for the rest of the year. These early flowering plants seldom object to other kinds growing above them. Their flowers will push their way up through the foliage of such plants as partridge-berry, wintergreen, creeping jenny or biennial seedlings such as mullein which bloom much later on. They also have the effect of masking any untidy phase in those which have bloomed earlier.

If the gardener wishes to grow established garden plants among the wild ones, they will mingle better if the garden plants are species rather than varieties or cultivars. Most varieties are a part of man's work, although some do occur in nature. All species are wild plants somewhere. Usually species mingle with species attractively, even when their countries of origin are far apart. It is fortunate, for those who admire diversity in plants, that the species from one type of terrain in

RIGHT *The thicker the plants are allowed to grow, the more quickly the wild garden takes shape. Some, like the yellow Welsh poppies at the center, and many umbellifers such as the fennel in the foreground, will prove ubiquitous, gradually moving to other places about the garden. Usually where they choose to grow they look most at home.*

BELOW *To create a wild look in some part of the garden, allow some of the 'weeds' to grow unchecked. It helps conserve many forms of wildlife if the grass grows long right up against shrubs and trees.*

one country will, so long as the climate suits, usually grow quite well in the appropriate soil of another. This means that a plant species from North America, such as dog's tooth violet, is likely to settle down in northern Europe, and, happily, migration of plants in the opposite direction is also possible. Some species are extremely adaptable, such as those of many of the poppy family, and all those plants that have 'escaped' into the wild.

If you hope to sow seed of native species, it is possible to find many of them simply by going carefully through a good seedsman's lists and looking for species rather than varieties. For instance, among the larkspurs in one leading firm's list of 'garden plants', you can find *Delphinium cardinale*, the rare scarlet larkspur. By searching under other flower names you will find more native species. However, certain firms (see page 168) now concentrate on supplying wildflower seed only, and the number of species listed grows every year.

At the time of writing it is illegal in the United States to pick or collect any plant on public reserves or parkland, and the Endangered Species Act prohibits interstate shipment of any endangered plant or animal. Regretably even this limited amount of legislation is difficult to enforce and commercial collectors are still plundering the countryside to provide material for speciality gardens. Plant collectors and lumbermen have thus nearly wiped out the epiphytic orchids and bromeliads in the tropical rainforest. Even sadder is the fact that this phenomena of overzealous collectors is world wide. Therefore since the gardener may not dig up many wild plants and since seed identification can be difficult (there are nearly 400 species), it is best to buy 'safe' seed from merchants.

Trees and shrubs

It is possible to buy fairly mature trees and shrubs. Even just three or four, set well apart, will give both shelter and cohesion to smaller specimens planted between them. Evergreens are good furnishers.

Choose plants which produce significant blossom to attract bees and other insects, followed by

berries or other kinds of fruits such as mountain ash, *Sorbus americana*, wild cherry, *Prunus serotina* and hawthorn, *Crataegus viridis*. The neat *Amelanchier canadensis*, the shadbush, known in Britain as the snowy mespilus, prettily colored in autumn, produces little fruits much appreciated by blackbirds.

Of a lesser height than any of these, plant wild plums for the first blossom, hazel and pussy willow for early catkins and a wild or species rose to add to the variety of blossom and fruit.

We found that it was well worth planting some trees as seedlings, and 25 years later these are now some of the tallest specimens in the locality. Trees and shrubs planted as more mature specimens

ABOVE *On acid soils, where rhododendron species and varieties provide color mass, native shrubs and trees planted among and below them will both soften their effect and provide more suitable plants for the conservation of wildlife. Deciduous species will cast the dappled shade enjoyed by many herbaceous flowering plants and ferns in summer and, before their leaves develop in the spring, will allow in the daylight essential for spring flowers.*

LEFT *The handsome, hardy, European spurge,* Euphorbia wulfenii *(also known as* E. veneta*), visually dominates a great many other plants, most of which, like the spurge, will furnish this garden space for most of the year. Corydalis, ivy in variety, cotoneaster and several different conifers mingle closely with one another. On the wall is growing the Kenilworth ivy, a creeping toadflax from Europe which is naturalized in warmer parts of the US.*

ABOVE *Often found naturalized in old dry fields, mullein,* Verbascum thapsus, *grows to 2m/6ft 6in. There are many beautiful species and varieties.*

seemed to stay fairly static for a year or two, after which they began to race away.

Creating close-knit communities

The secret of creating a permanent impression is to plant closely, to cover every inch of ground, which, after all, is what wild plants do. Use grass to act as a stand in, if needed, while other plants are being collected.

In one of my own fairly shaded borders topped by a giant walnut and shorter hawthorns, liquidambar, buddleia and buckthorn, sweet scented woodruff is allowed to spread where it will, sharing the ground as it emerges in the early spring with daffodils and other bulb plants, followed by bien-

nial, self-seeding forget-me-nots and the much taller sweet rocket, and then later by foxgloves and the autumn colchicums.

In other places I rely on woodspurge which so readily fills any empty spaces. In the area below three old lilac trees this plant merges agreeably with a low-growing, winter-flowering evergreen, the lovely *Mahonia aquifolium.* This is an excellent under tree plant thriving where most others fail. One quality which endears it to me is that its thickly clustered, honey-scented yellow blooms are there ready for the first foraging bees, butterflies and others. For guidance on other species to plant below and between trees, see the chapter on woodland gardens, pages 68-77.

37

Ground cover and carpeting plants

If the soil and site suits them, so many plants will spread over the ground covering it attractively and at the same time keeping other plants at bay. Bugle, a fast-growing perennial with blue flowers in early summer, throws out creeping growths and soon covers a wide area. It is a good plant for sites in deep, moist shade, although it will also furnish the ground at the fringes of trees and shrub groups. On light, calcareous soils it is frequently associated with the yellow archangel, *Lamium galeobdolon*, otherwise known as the yellow dead nettle, a charming and endearing plant which will soon make itself at home in the wild garden.

An unusual little violet with deep purple leaves as well as flowers, *Viola labradorica*, which likes a reasonably damp and shady spot will quickly colonize itself. In my own garden it has even left the shade and settles down among the rose bushes in what should be a formal bed.

Periwinkles, the lesser *Vinca minor* and the greater *V. major*, form ideal ground cover even for large areas and shady banks. They provide a good dense cover for wildlife also. These two have produced many varieties which differ in leaf and flower color from the types.

A species which birds sow in my garden is the woody nightshade or bittersweet, *Solanum dulcamara*. Although this plant is described as a climber it also trails and creeps over the ground attractively, covering the soil with trails of angular leafy stems bearing clusters of purple flowers followed by bright red shining berries, which are poisonous.

It is worth remembering that other climbers, such as honeysuckle and wild clematis, can be used to trail over and carpet the ground.

Self-propagating plants

Most annual and biennial plants will, once established, and so long as they are not deadheaded, set seed and reproduce themselves freely. In filling the space around the parent plant, the seedlings will grow to create an attractive ground cover – although this might threaten neighboring plants. If so,

restrict the new growth early. My own method is to decide how much space can be spared for a single species, take out the weaker seedlings and then to leave the new plants alone, and not, as one would do for a traditional garden, thin them out. This propensity of some plants for self-seeding can be very helpful to the new gardener who must begin with only a few specimens, for, where the parent plants are initially spaced a good distance apart, by dropping their seed the following autumn, the spaces in between will be filled by the next year.

In my own garden, red campion insists on growing among cultivars in a mixed border. It does look good there, but, since it is a woodland plant, it follows that I should transfer some seedlings to where bluebells and other field layer species grow. In another place the little St John's wort, *Hypericum perforatum* (syn. *H. vulgare*), grows so freely

ABOVE *Few plants offer more flowers to the square inch than the carpeting and mat-forming thymes. They are very versatile and spread freely, reveling in light, well-drained soil and sunshine. They can be used to top a wall, cover rocks, fill cracks between pavements, carpet floor between heathers, soften gravel, and even be used for a pungent-scented lawn. The creeping thyme,* Thymus drucei, *has produced a great many varieties with white, rose, crimson, mauve and purple flowers.*

that it has led me to search for other hypericums, both native and exotic. One of these, the berry-bearing tutsan, *H. androsaemum*, favored by birds, now freely seeds itself in many places.

Several native species will seed freely between pavement stones or along paths, such as the welsh poppy, herb robert, speedwell, sweet marjoram, forget-me-not and violets.

Not all plants depend upon seed to multiply. Some have creeping rootstocks. The lily-of-the-valley, for instance, makes its way across a piece of ground by way of a thick underground stem which produces two new leaves each year a little further from the point of origin. Such stems are known as rhizomes. Rhizomatous plants include creeping wintergreen, herb paris, Solomon's seal and wood anemone.

Others employ quite different methods. The rare yellow star of Bethlehem, *Gagea sylvatica*, can reproduce itself vegetatively by means of tiny

ABOVE *The red campion,* Lychnis diorca, *growing with flag irises here, has long been accepted as a garden plant, especially in its double form. In the wild it also favors mixed company, often mingling with bluebells and purple orchids. It makes itself very much at home in gardens in wooded areas. There, and in the wild, it frequently crosses with the white campion,* L. alba, *to produce a hybrid known as* L. x dubia, *with pink flowers. The white campion also produces a double form which, like that of the red, does not come true from seed.*

RIGHT *Low-growing plants can be encouraged, or allowed to increase, so that they carpet the ground. A most attractive effect is created if several different types are grown. Gradually each little colony will contrast and complement the other, often merging prettily, a tendency demonstrated by this pretty little phlox,* Phlox stolonifera, *which as its specific name explains, has its own method of propagation.*

bulbils which it produces in the axils of its leaves. These can be sown like seed, for when they fall to the soil plants are produced from them.

Besides seeding freely, blackberries reproduce themselves by stolons. When the tip of an arching stem touches the soil it will make and take root. This explains how a bramble bush, if allowed, will in time become a great mass of growth, simply because the outer curving branches root into the soil and so spread the plant. These rooted branches can be detached from the parent plant and used as individuals and transplanted elsewhere.

Climbers

In the wild, climbing plants use trees as support, most species growing happily one with another. In order to make the most of every bit of space, and to populate the plot with as many plant species as possible, one may profitably follow the same theme in the wild garden. In the garden, however, the plant associations can be by design rather than by accident.

The wild honeysuckle, which is very attractive to some hummingbirds, is frequently as much in evidence in wild hedgerows as it is in woods. It is a good plant to choose for clothing deciduous trees or to soften a formal hedge made perhaps of a single species, but it also looks good in holly. Wild roses and hops are also good choices for clothing hedges, and the yellow-leaved variety of hop looks most handsome when seen against dark leaves – try growing it against a purple-leaved hazel.

Clematis vitalba, traveller's joy, is an excellent climber for limestone soils, provided it is given a little initial help. Its long, fairly weak stems become entwined one around the other, gradually thickening and toughening. If either this clematis or any one of the sturdy species of clematis are to be grown against a tree, be sure to select a tall, sturdy specimen as host for small trees and shrubs may soon become smothered. Given height, clematis really can climb, even to a height of 15m/50ft – they will live for 50 years, too. These plants may need help in their early days for they do not climb

by using their tendrils or by twining their stems around a support, but by curling their leaf stems quite tightly around whatever they might happen to meet – even stems or leaves of their own plant. The weight of stem on stem will often pull the plant mass to the ground. Try fixing a cylinder of wire netting, 1m/3ft high, close around the base of the tree or subject being climbed, to encourage the stems to grow upward. There are a few exotic species which could be used in partial shade, such as the violet-blue Chinese *C. macropetala* and *C. tangutica*, with flowers a pale or deep yellow color, and the fragrant mediterranean *C. flammula*.

The two kinds of bryony both have handsome leaves, the black bryony's being heart-shaped and highly glossed, as are its berries. These are particularly beautiful, changing from green through an analogous color range to bright red, their clusters thickly studding the twining stems like enameled beads.

Other creepers that I love to grow are the many grape vines, such as Virginia creeper and its near relatives, the leaves of which assume such beautiful hues in the fall. All combine especially well with the Russian vine, *Polygonum baldschuanicum*, so that

ABOVE *The lovely English dog rose is very variable and has produced other forms with flowers richer in hue, larger in size, even stronger in scent than the type. These and other single-petaled rose species, including climbers, fit beautifully into many wild gardens. Most also provide handsome fruits, the rose hips, which are not only decorative in themselves but rich enough in flesh and seed to attract many wild creatures.*

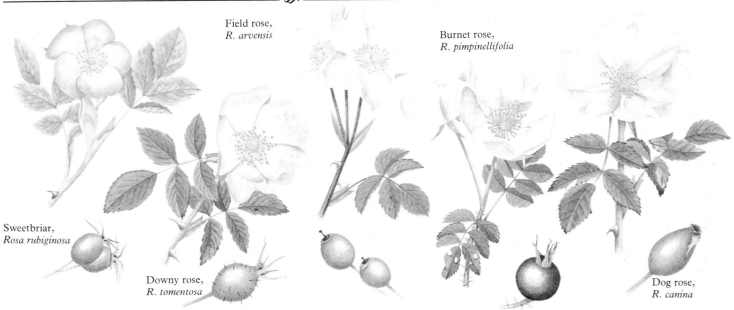

Field rose,
R. arvensis

Burnet rose,
R. pimpinellifolia

Sweetbriar,
Rosa rubiginosa

Downy rose,
R. tomentosa

Dog rose,
R. canina

foamy white flowers contrast with flaming foliage. Any of these can be used to drape a tall tree. Consider them also for a fence so that for a while at least it resembles a living leafy structure rather than a static artefact.

Roses

Fortunately, rose species abound in the wild in the northern hemisphere; in Britain alone there are a dozen or so species, many of which have produced varieties. The lovely dog rose, *Rosa canina*, with its exquisitely formed buds, once so very common in hedgerows, is a must for a wild garden. However, it is very variable, with blooms colored from rose to white. Some plants found growing in the wild produce blooms much deeper in color or a fragrance much stronger than their neighbors'.

Where one species of wild rose grows, it is likely that some of the other rose species would thrive. All of them are to be valued not only for their flowers but for their hips (or heps), which can be very showy. The hips of *Rosa villosa*, the apple rose, are round and rich in color; the blooms are a deep rose pink. The pretty little cream white field rose, *R. arvensis*, has small red hips and

purple stems. This species will grow in shade. The burnet rose, *R. pimpinellifolia*, grows near the sea, while the sweet briar, *R. rubiginosa*, which prefers calcareous soils, has deliciously scented leaves and lovely pink blooms, followed by round hips. The downy rose, *R. tomentosa,* will grow on limestone.

Most people want roses in a garden, and roses of one type or another appear to be tolerant enough to grow almost anywhere. However, not all rose varieties, for example hybrid teas or floribundas, would be acceptable in a wild garden. On the other hand, a species rose (single not double petaled), even an exotic, is likely to look quite at home. A plant of *Rosa rugosa*, originally from Japan and China, is in one of my own wild patches. Twenty years old, it is now several feet in diameter and grows happily enough nestled close to a frame of native shrubs and trees.

Obviously, where a traditional garden is being converted to a wild garden, and rose varieties or hybrids already exist, compromises will have to be made. One ploy is simply to leave them unpruned, treating them as shrub roses. However this is inadvisable with modern varieties, which will soon become a hideous mass of dead or half-dead wood.

WILD ROSES
The beautiful Rosa canina can be successfully grown in ordinary soil and can adapt itself to slight variations. The other species shown here are more specific in their soil requirements. R. tomentosa *and* R. rubiginosa *are found growing on limestone soils;* R. pimpinellifolia *on dunes and sandy heaths, while the trailing* R. arvensis *prefers the humus-rich soil of shady wood margins and hedgerows.*

Planting for shade

Shade is mostly an asset in a wild garden although some trees form such a dense canopy of foliage that they block out daylight from the ground below sufficiently to allow only a few species of plants, mostly early-flowering kinds, to grow freely. A greater diversity of plants, such as columbines, foxgloves and lilies, can be grown on the margins or at the limits of shade.

Deciduous trees cast the densest shade in summer, some, beech for instance, much more than others. Under such a canopy, it may be necessary to concentrate on planting those species that reach their peak in autumn when the leaves are thinning or in spring before they open. Many of these are bulbous types, the classic example being the bluebell.

Where a border of lower growing plants is to be made at the edge of a wood or near a tree or trees and shrubs, the outer edge of the border can be made to follow the line of shadow cast at midday. This ensures that all the plants in the border will be shaded for some time each day. Also, if a mown path through a meadow adjoining trees is made to follow this line of midday shadow it will appear much more inviting during the sunniest and hottest periods of the day.

A deep canopy of leaves may keep the ground below fairly dry, but plants growing near the edges of the trees' spread may be subjected to heavy drip during rainy periods. Not all plants tolerate this. One reason why the exotic hosta or plantain lily was so often to be seen in romantic gardens is because it is very tolerant of drip.

Planting for color

Color in a wild garden may be more subdued than that of, say, park bedding designs, and certainly the flowering period of individuals will not be so long as that of the seedsmen's hybrid annuals. Even so, color displays can be planned. One way is to allow some plants to occupy a large area of ground and so create sizeable drifts of color; there is more on this subject in the chapter on meadow gardens, pages 56-67. It is also possible to plan little patches of seasonal color so that one species follows another in bloom.

Having enjoyed through the winter the red and green of holly, the swathes of red bryony berries in the hedgerow, the orange berry-filled seed pods of the gladden iris, and the ever-present rosy hues of winter-flowering heathers, I look forward to the first aconites planted in little patches here and there, the little wild daffodils now colonizing a bank and grass, the bluebells and cuckoo flowers

BELOW *A wild garden can harbor plants that are endangered or threatened in the wild, whether they be trilliums from the Appalachians, primulas from the Himalayas or rare Japanese orchids. An example here is the spreading bell flower,* Campanulata patula, *found wild in only a few localities in England and Wales and in isolated spots in continental Europe.*

under the copper beech, the germander speedwell in the pavement and the red campion in the border. But the year really begins with snowdrops. They spread everywhere, but in my garden in one place they are part of a plan to give contrast of color, form and texture. They cover the ground below a dogwood, *Cornus sanguinea*, a species that has dark red stems which in spring, while they are still bare, become a brighter hue. Rising up from a carpet of white flowers with a thicket of silver-white honesty seed stems in the background, this plant is seen to great advantage. Willows also have good colored barks, conspicuous in winter.

Another dogwood, *Cornus mas*, flowers in early spring and presents a mass of tiny yellow flowers. Beneath it grows a carpet of primroses and violets. See also fine foliage, page 94.

For those who enjoy really flamboyant color in plants, none perhaps can excel the acid-loving rhododendron or eucryphias in splendor. However, few individual flowers are more gorgeous than peonies, easily grown plants that prefer soil with lime content and are tolerant of either sun or shade. One, *Paeonia mascula*, has become naturalized on Steepholme, a little island in the Bristol Channel where it was brought by monks for medicinal use in the Middle Ages. Other members of the same family are equally tolerant. In my own garden a seedling of the beautiful yellow-flowered *Paeonia lutea* is now a quarter of a century old and some 2m/6ft 6in high and as broad.

On the west coast the South American *Fuchsia magellanica* has naturalized itself to the delight of visitors and hummingbirds. In the south east another naturalized exotic is *Clerodendrum indicum*, the 'Okeefenokee swamp firecracker flower'.

Statuesque plants

Few of my wild garden plants give as much pleasure as the foxgloves, most of which by pure accident are of the white variety, plants so sophisticated in appearance that to call them 'wild' seems impertinent. Beginning with just half a dozen plants, the garden now holds several colonies of

them, for they seed freely. A large foxglove may produce a million seeds of which only a minute quantity grows into plants. Tall spicate shapes of this kind – monkshood and mullein are two others – bring a more stately quality to a wild landscape, especially if they are set in showy groups rather than just one or two plants spaced about the place. If possible, grow them with a plant with flowers in a contrasting form, angelica for instance. In some ways sweet cicely is preferable to angelica, which can be choosy about soils and positions, preferring a moderately damp situation.

Plant shapes are important in a landscape, especially in a small garden. The thistle, which has both beauty and architectural value, can be used to good effect. The towering cotton thistle, *Onopordon acanthium*, with its woolly-covered leaves and stems, is a handsome addition to any garden.

LEFT *A variety of leaf shapes add beauty, one reason why the exotic hostas are so popular. Foxgloves contrast well, with their distinctive leaves and stately flowers.*

ABOVE *Sweet cicely,* Myrrhis odorata, *grows to 1.5m/5ft high. Its leaves smell like licorice.*

CREATING A NATURAL GARDEN

From time to time, especially when they are not in competition with other plants, some species grow too exuberantly and will need to be subject to some measure of control (see page 138). An isolated country gardener can be fairly uninhibited in his or her choice of plants, but even here it may be necessary to consider farmer neighbors who may not particularly relish a plot within their area where plants such as dandelions and thistles are allowed to seed unchecked. In such cases some balance should obviously be sought. Problems arise mainly where one species of plant is allowed to dominate, but where the plant population is very mixed, troubles of this kind are not so likely to arise.

Many plants, for example, germander speedwell, soapwort, white deadnettle and toadflax, can be kept under control by cutting away the seed stems before they become mature and forking up the roots or smothering them by using the newspaper method (see page 139). Some perennials, too, will need to be controlled, such as creeping bellflower, named from its underground creeping runners, and also celandines which crowd out other species.

Sometimes, seed wanders and plants are found growing in quite a different part of the garden from that originally intended. This can be a nuisance. Often a wild plant appearing spontaneously in this way among cultivars in a border will look enchanting while it is young and in its early stages of flowering. But, in the rich soil of the border, the plant begins to grow so fast that it becomes gross and will smother the plants around it if left alone. It is best pulled out before it becomes too dominant, but after it has been allowed to make a decorative contribution.

Wild plants and self-maintenance

In an ordinary well-tended garden, herbaceous plants are spaced well apart and not jostled by neighbors, and their faded stems are removed at the end of the year. This means that they have no support for their new growth, and they have to be staked or supported in some way; thus twigs, canes or metal frames are used to encourage the shoots to grow upright.

By contrast, plants in the wild retain their spent stems unless the area has been grazed or mown. Sometimes the stems of one plant will help support plants of another species. The young growth pushes up through other vegetation, often using it as a means of keeping its frail stems upright, and holding flowers aloft in the sunshine and in the flight path of insects. In meadows, particularly, the support plants are grasses. When a grass plant invades a cultivated flower border and is removed, the result is often a floppy unattractive flowering plant which had up to that time used the grass as a natural support. So what is the wild gardener to do? He can either tidy stray grasses and then stake plants to provide support, or let the plants go their own way. Thus a climbing plant, a vetch for instance, will use a neighboring plant for support. Some plants will flop and sprawl, and why should this matter? Plants that sprawl on the ground also cover it. And a sprawling plant will disperse its seed more widely than a plant that has its stems growing neatly and vertically. In the early stages of plant colonization this is obviously important. Do not be concerned, either, if one species seems to collapse into another. Usually the plants sort this out on their own and what has been the situation one year is not necessarily the same the next.

Pruning and clipping

For appearance's sake, many groomed gardens are dependent upon the blade in some form or another: mown grass, clipped hedges, flowering plants deadheaded or cut back after flowering; shrubs and trees annually pruned. Often overpruned. But, admiring the countryside in spring and seeing the wealth of blossom of, say, hawthorn in England or dogwood in North America, one is tempted to

RIGHT *English bluebells grow readily in grass. Because stalks and foliage should be allowed to die down naturally, the grass which has grown unmown since autumn should not be cut again until after midsummer. Usually the uncut grasses, in flower by that time, are attractive enough, but where the gardener would prefer more color, other later-flowering plants can be grown to follow the bluebells.*

ask, who prunes them? There is no answer, yet no well-tended garden plant can really surpass them in abundance of blossom.

Plants left alone still flower and fruit, but in their own time and in their own way. In some seasons they will be better than others and this is to be expected.

The owner of a wild garden, therefore, need not be overconcerned with the niceties of pruning. Those wild plants which flower should not be deadheaded for it is planned that they should produce seed. Hedges that house birds and other animals should not be too frequently cut – once a year should do. See also page 138.

Toward an ecological balance

Sometimes the number of seedlings which appear on what was assumed to be a cleared site can be alarming. Yet if the gardener is not familiar with the plants and so long as he or she can bear to do so, once again it is prudent first to identify species that have appeared rather than to set about destroying them. (Apart from anything else they are likely to be a good guide to the type of soil and its condition, see pages 122-123). By selecting the more attractive plants common to your garden, you will be speeding the process of arriving at a good ecological balance for your neighborhood, as well as helping the species you have deliberately introduced from outside to increase their numbers.

Since the garden itself is so obviously an interference with the natural pattern of plant ecology, we cannot really hope to achieve a perfect natural balance but it should be possible to help more than we do at present. Take, for instance, the simple and widespread practice of spraying aphids to 'clean' plants. Because not only aphids but also insects that naturally prey on aphids are likely to be present on a plant, we are liable to spray these predators or their larvae at the same time as we destroy the aphids. This is so whether we use modern chemical sprays or the old fashioned soap sud solution. Insecticides and other pesticides are deadly not only for the target animal, say a wasp,

but for the other insects that wander into the treated area, and this may include interesting solitary moths that add to the rich spectrum of insect life typical of a well-planned garden.

It may take a bit of courage to stop using these 'garden aids', but after the initial onslaught, say by aphids on your unsprayed roses, there is generally an increase in aphid predators such as certain syrphids, ladybugs and lacewings, and in birds such as wood warblers which soon clear up the flower buds to redress the balance.

It is understandable that a gardener should be prejudiced against those insects which unpleasantly smother parts of a plant and sap its strength, as aphids do, or which, like so many grubs or caterpillars, consume most of its foliage, leaving it tattered and unlovely. Yet how often in normal seasons do we see a truly wild plant quite so devastated? The only reason for this surely must be that there exist more predators in the wild.

One hopes for a 'natural' method which could be used in all kinds of gardens, but so far the biological control of plant pests is effective only under certain controlled conditions. See also page 140.

ABOVE *Even a few simple means will help gradually to restore the ecological balance in a garden. Although a pond may be present, one or more bird baths placed about, kept clean and regularly filled, will attract many species of birds, for they also provide drinking water. Once inside the garden, and so long as plants are not sprayed with insecticides, they will stay and search for food, usually to return again and again. Some will seek nesting sites.*

LEFT *Confined and sheltered gardens sometimes offer a refuge to the less endearing forms of wildlife. Aphids, for instance, will settle on many kinds of plants. Roses are particularly attractive to them. The insects form unpleasantly thick masses on young shoots, sucking the sweet sap, weakening and sometimes even killing them. Fortunately, the aphids provide rich food for nestling birds. The parent birds collect the pests diligently, eventually diminishing their numbers.*

AN ENVIRONMENT FOR WILDLIFE

Whether you like it or not, and unless you still use pesticides, your garden already serves as an important refuge for wildlife of all kinds. Most people would include here birds, bees and butterflies but would discount nocturnal and dawn feeders as well as the multitude of understone inhabitants which all make up the surprisingly complex mix of animals that reside in or are visitors to the garden.

To be conscious of the role your garden plays in attracting wildlife, try and look at it as a series of distinct, interlocking habitats. For example, the lawn, often short-cropped and sterile looking, could soon be turned into an open clearing cum-meadow area alive with grasshoppers. A hedge is a kind of miniature thicket and, of course, if you are fortunate enough to have mature bushes and trees, you have a ready-made coppice or wood on your doorstep. To these you could add a series of micro-habitats: a wall, for example, functions in a similar way to a rocky outcrop and the numerous crevices are soon colonized by plants and insects as well as nesting birds.

Also helpful to wildlife are those plants that grow in such a way that they form a snug 'house'. One reason why it is not a good idea to tidy plants in autumn is because, combined with their own faded stems, leaves which have blown against them and grass or climbers with which they may have become intertwined, they offer good, warm, even windproof cover. One of these is the blackberry or bramble of which they are so many species, subspecies and varieties growing wild that here they will be considered as just one kind of plant. The fortunate fact, especially for those who live far from the immediate countryside, is that the host of insects which visit wild brambles do not refuse the cultivated kinds.

In gardens where space does not allow the plant over the years to produce the great natural dome of a mature bramble, it should be possible to grow the 'canes' trained against a flat framework of supports and wires situated perhaps at the side of a path or at the end of a plot. Grown this way the plant can be kept under control.

Even a trained plant such as this should attract a great diversity of insect life which visits the plant during many stages of its life, seeking leaves, shoots, blossom and fruits, fresh or decaying. So far as butterflies are concerned, wood nymph, ringlet, eyed-brown and the beautiful white admiral are four that visit the flowers for nectar, while the striped hairstreaks will lay their eggs upon the leaves. Red-spotted purples and hackberry butterflies will feed on its ripe or overripe fruit.

Raspberries also attract a great variety of creatures. Beautiful jade-green spiders are almost always to be found on them. Where there is sufficient space, a stand of raspberries would be well worth growing as food for birds.

Your compost pile, if maintained properly, doubles up as a manure pile and rich bed of leaf litter. It is especially rich in decomposers – mites,

LEFT Sedum spectabile, *a hardy succulent perennial from China, blooms at the end of summer when it attracts many different species of butterflies. The grass,* Festuca ovina glauca, *is a variety of sheep's fescue often used as an edging plant in formal gardens, and offering seed and cover in wild ones.*

RIGHT *Water in a garden attracts all forms of wildlife. Leafy cover at the margins ensures protection for vulnerable creatures, such as tiny frogs, leaving the water for the first time. Newly emerged dragon and damsel flies can climb the tall leaves growing above water level as they prepare for their first flight.*

fungi and bacteria, and also worms and insect larvae which are sought after by birds, such as the mockingbird and the Carolina wren, and small animals to keep them alive during very cold weather.

Feeding and reproduction take up a large part in the life of any animal, be it an insect or mammal. Your garden should therefore have as many food plants as possible and at the same time provide a sanctuary in the way of trees, shrubs and climbers. These will provide shelter for overwintering insects, nest and roost sites for birds and protective cover for small mammals such as voles.

The emphasis of any garden should be on variety and, with wildlife in mind, the more nooks and crannies you can provide, the more chance you have of attracting a greater variety of animal life. At the same time you should establish or improve nest sites for birds by putting up bird houses, well out of reach of cats. If you have a thick hedge, you can improve it by planting climbers until you get that wild tangled effect which will attract birds to nest in the deepest recesses.

Multipurpose plants and food webs

Many common plants are useful in that they fulfil several functions for wildlife. Take monarch butterflies and milkweeds, for example. Any patch of open ground in eastern North America is likely to reveal several species of milkweed growing on it. In dry sandy soil one sees the flamboyant orange butterfly weed *Asclepias tuberosa*; in moister soil occurs the rose or mauve swamp milkweed, *A. incarnata*. The flowers of both these species are pollinated by large butterflies and are accordingly aggregated into large flat, terminal clusters for ease of landing. In contrast, the flowers of *A. syriaca*, pollinated mainly by bees and flies, are disposed in smaller spherical clusters.

One species of large butterfly, the orange and black monarch, not only gains sustenance from the flowers as an adult but also lays its eggs on the milkweed plant. The yellow and black caterpillars eat the leaves of the plant and even pupate on it. Many species of milkweed contain a poisonous alkaloid in their milky sacs which, ingested by the caterpillar, renders not only it but also the adult that descends from it poisonous and thus extremely unpalatable to birds and other predators. The destinies of the milkweed and the monarch butterflies are thus intertwined, the butterfly receiving food and protection against enemies from a plant from whom it does little more than inadvertently transfer the occasional pollen grain from flower to flower.

With butterflies and moths in mind

Those who bemoan the fact that no butterflies ever visit their gardens, and a surprising number of people do so, are usually not aware that in spite of the garden being well furnished with blooms, there is nothing in particular to entice the insects or prompt them to linger. The first point to remember is that butterflies live in two distinct phases, the caterpillar and the adult. Each requires different foods, namely nectar-rich flowers for the adult butterflies and a particular kind of foliage for the larval stages. From the gardener's point of view, it is extremely rewarding to grow the flowers, and to see, year after year, a buildup in the number of visiting butterflies. For the caterpillars, first learn which are the best plants to grow for which species of insect, and what particular species might be induced to establish itself in your area.

Sometimes you may accidentally introduce a plant with butterfly eggs on it into the garden. This happened when some mullein plants taken from a friend's garden were found to be covered with the caterpillars of the mullein moth; fortunately, although the plants were initially ravaged, enough grew to set seed.

A sunny flower filled border

A good start in the creation of any wild garden is a border of plants attractive to both bees and butterflies. Most gardens will already have a sunny flower border and it takes relatively little effort to modify this for wildlife, so that it serves as a rich source of nectar from spring through until late autumn.

BUTTERFLY AND BEE BORDER
Because of the nectar they produce, some flowers attract a great number of insects. For short-lived species such as butterflies, nectar is a source of energy rather than food. Other insects seek pollen. A garden furnished with such flowers will be well-populated.

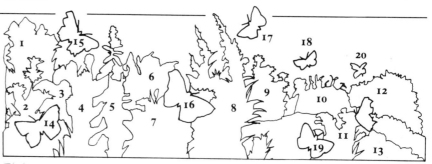

1 Canada goldenrod, *Solidago canadensis*
2 New England aster, *Aster novae-angliae*
3 Yarrow, *Achillea millefolium*
4 Teasel, *Dipsacus sylvestris*
5 Foxglove, *Digitalis purpurea*
6 Comfrey, *Symphytium officinale*
7 Batchelor's button, *Centaurea cyanus*
8 Fireweed, *Epilobium angustifolium*
9 Black-eyed susan, *Rudbeckia hirta*
10 Virginia cowslip, *Mertensia virginica*
11 Cuckoo flower, *Cardamine pratensis*
12 Sage, *Salvia officinalis*
13 Lesser celandine, *Ranunculus ficaria*
14 Tortoiseshell butterfly
15 Comma butterfly
16 Red admiral butterfly
17 Fritillary butterfly
18 Blue butterfly
19 Orange-tip butterfly
20 Bumblebee

Your border, although designed primarily to attract bees and butterflies, will also lure many other insects. Among these, syrphids will be most noticeable, darting about from flower to flower. These insects are not only interesting to look at, often banded yellow and black, but they should be encouraged because many of their larvae feed voraciously on aphids. Because they have only short feeding mouthparts they are particularly attracted to flat, open flowers, especially those of the daisy family. The larvae develop in a number of sites including rotten wood, so if possible it is a good idea to leave one or two felled logs in situ to aid your syrphid population; however, the larvae of a few species of syrphids can do damage to bulbs.

Bushes, shrubs and nettles

Many shrubs and bushes are rich in nectar, some much more than our native plants. Among the favourites are the early summer small-flowered *Buddleia alternifolia*, and the pale mauve and white forms of *B. davidii*. Their flowers act like magnets to butterflies. On a sunny day they become crowded with coppers and fritillaries. Bumblebees and swallowtail butterflies also lap up the rich nectar source. Some moths will visit the flowers at night. Sadly, the lovely deep-colored cultivars are not so effective. If more than one buddleia is planted, a longer period of flower can be obtained by cutting only one back; the uncut one will still flower first. Since these plants self-seed freely and are now escapees in both town and country, all the better reason to incorporate them into wild gardens.

Escallonia virgata, one of the hardiest of this genus, from Chile and other parts of South America, is also a great favorite in my own garden where a few bushes have been allowed to grow wild. On a fine summer's day, a plant in blossom can be thick with many different species of butterflies and bees, all sipping in harmony among the pale pink flowers.

The nettle is in vogue again, not for its fibers that were once woven into a cloth nor for its shoots

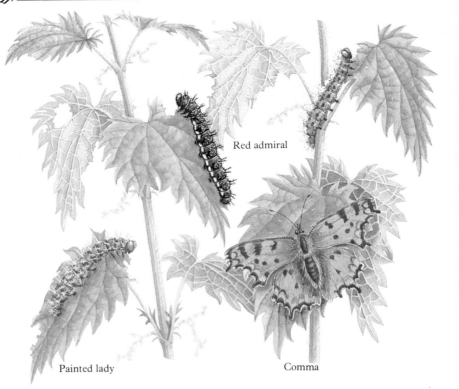

Red admiral

Painted lady   Comma

eaten by countryfolk, but because the caterpillars of five attractive butterflies, the red admiral, the satyr anglewing (*Polygonia satyrus*), the comma (*Polygonia comma*), the question mark (*Polygonia interrogationis*) and Milbert's tortoiseshell (*Aglais milberti*) all feed on nettle leaves. Many people judge this plant as unsightly and I suggest therefore, that if you have a small garden and you want to experiment with nettle culture, that you relegate your nettle patch to the end of the garden, bearing in mind that butterflies will only use young nettle growth in full sunshine. The eggs of these butterflies are laid in the spring and the caterpillars should have left by the end of June, to pupate away from the nettle plant. If the nettles are cut down to just above the ground, new growth will attract a second generation of small butterflies. Nettles can become rampant and will need to be pulled out or cut back regularly. See page 139 on management of them.

ABOVE *Stinging nettles are food plants of the caterpillars of some of our most beautiful butterflies. The painted lady will sometimes take them as an alternative to the preferred spear thistle, but for others they are the essential source of sustenance. Cut the plants down in midsummer so that they produce young shoots ready to receive the eggs of the late broods of these insects. This practice also prevents the nettles from making quantities of seed.*

PLANTING SUCCESSFUL WILD GARDENS

A CHOICE OF RURAL SETTINGS

Whether you are adapting a traditional garden – or perhaps starting a new one – or whether you want to make a special garden feature to show off wild plants, you will find many ideas for developing the potential of your garden, whatever its scale, terrain and soil type, in the chapters that follow. Here, wild plants can be seen and enjoyed on their own, or in carefully thought out groupings of native and naturalized, or native and exotic.

Any lawn can be translated into a meadow garden, with old-fashioned wildflowers in a sequence of blooms for most months of the year. Where an orchard exists, the gardener has the perfect site for a meadow garden and the late summer – early autumn routine of the second grass cut will ensure that the area is mown and convenient for fruit harvesting.

It might be that the house stands on a wooded plot or, particularly if the house is on a new site, on one that was once wooded. In this case, the soil could already be right for the gardener to exploit the situation and create a picturesque wildwood. This can be underplanted with shrubs and an attractive carpet of varied plants.

On land which adjoins heathland, where the soil will be acid, it is possible to create a heath garden in which the many members of the heather family, the taller shrubs and trees as well as the shorter, ground-covering heaths, would provide color and interest every day of the year, for most are evergreens. They include some of the rarer wild plants, such as the trailing bear-berry, the glossy-leaved cowberry, or if the site is moist enough, the cranberry or *Chamaedaphne calyculata*. If more variety is desired, then there are many other native plants which will grow along with the ericaceous kinds. Silver birch, in particular, looks delightful rising up from the colored heather carpet.

An attractive green garden can be made using different species of hardy ferns, distinctive grasses and green-flowered plants such as hellebores, spurges and others. There are many suitable native species and, here, wild-ginger species can play a useful role, either as ground covers or as climbers. Such a garden offers year-round interest, and might be particularly suitable for an enclosed courtyard or very shaded plot.

A green garden could merge with, or be part of, a wild herb garden. Handsome angelica, tansy and mints will furnish the shadier, moister places, with sun-lovers such as fennel, marjoram and thymes attracting butterflies.

Water gardens offer great scope to the imaginative gardener, for there are so many lovely native aquatic plants, which are more versatile than exotic floating water lilies. Where a pond is not a practical option, perhaps because young children use the garden, most of these waterloving species could be grown in a small artificial marshy area.

The characteristics of a rocky or very stony site can be easily exploited by making a scree, alpine or gravel garden since most of the essentials, such as sharp drainage, already exist. Where the soil is sandy, plants need to be chosen carefully if they are to thrive. There are many suitable attractive species, both native and exotic, particularly Australian species which should do well. In frost-free areas a 'desert' garden with succulents such as *Mesembryanthemum edule*, the Hottentot fig, which is naturalized in California, and even cacti is not beyond the bounds of possibility.

RIGHT *A weedy lawn left unmown so that existing plants and grasses can mature and flower will become a meadow garden. Other plants can be added to those already present as time goes by. Any part of the lawn which for some reason needs to be kept* more closely mown can be flower-decked in springtime. Daisies, cowslips, self-heal and other plants which form rosettes pressed down on the grass are able to withstand summer mowing without irreparable damage and so live to flower another year.*

WILDFLOWER LAWNS AND MEADOWS

Few features of the landscape are as beautiful as a 'flowery mead'. Until a few decades ago, such meadows full of flowers were a common sight in the countryside. Daisy-spangled in spring, the well-cropped grass then rapidly became covered with a rich carpet of ragworts or dandelions once the cattle or sheep were moved off. Buttercups followed in early summer, quickly succeeded by the oxeye daisies, sorrel, clover and sweet vernal grass, that together brought such a sweet fragrance to the swathes of hay cut in midsummer.

Nowadays, sadly, such floristically rich grasslands can usually be found only on slopes too steep to cultivate or in isolated corners of the countryside which modern agriculture, with its fertilizers and herbicides, has failed to reach. Perhaps more unfortunately, the loss of this attractive habitat, with its great variety of nectar-producing flowers, has contributed to a decline in the butterfly population, and the loss of some species.

Wildflower meadows can, however, be recreated quite easily on a much smaller scale in gardens everywhere, even in the center of a town. Today, there are a number of seedsmen ready to supply a range of suitable seed mixtures of native meadow grasses and wildflowers.

The area set aside for wildflowers and meadow grasses need not be flat: it could be a boundary bank, or a bank sloping down to or away from a more formal lawn, or any steep ground as long as it is accessible and not too large for hand-scything.

Not everyone has precisely the same understanding of the term 'flowery mead' or wildflower meadow. For me, there are three types of wildflower lawn or meadow. The simplest is an area of existing lawn where the broad-leaved plants (weeds to the purist lawnkeeper) have been encouraged to reproduce and a few wildflowers have been introduced. I find these lawns more attractive than the best-kept velvety sward. If well managed, they can resemble the pretty front lawns you see in Switzerland and Austria – themselves derived from the Alpine flower meadows. There, the myriad hues of speedwells, field daisies, cowslips, primulas, cuckoo flowers and self-heal jostle in uncut grass in the spring sunshine.

For the more romantic, and for those with a strong interest in conservation, a spring-flowering meadow lawn or a small-scale summer meadow might be created on virgin ground using specially selected mixtures of wildflowers and grasses.

Although there is nothing to prevent you from creating a wildflower meadow which will flower throughout the year, you will find the meadow easier to maintain if you divide the proposed area into two sections: one for spring flowers, some of

RIGHT *The poorer the soil, the more colorful the meadow flowers. Species such as the yellow loosestrife and foxgloves growing close to the trees have a richer soil and deeper shade and so grow in a different environment.*

BELOW *Annual cornflowers and poppies, typical flora of a preherbicide wheatfield, are mainly represented here by their garden varieties, such as Shirley poppy in the foreground. Left to seed themselves they will in time revert to the species.*

which grow from bulbs so that the grass must be left uncut until midsummer, and one for summer flowers, where the grass is cut early in the year and then left until late summer. I have done this in my own garden where the area beneath a large copper beech holds a spring-flowering meadow lawn which comes into bloom before the beech leaves form a dense canopy. Beyond them, stretching down the garden, the summer meadow flowers grow among the feathery plumes of the grasses.

To some, the term 'wildflower meadow' conjures up an image of drifts of scarlet poppies, blue cornflowers, yellow corn marigolds and, perhaps, purple-pink corn cockle. These are really inhabitants of the preherbicide wheatfield, amongst the annual cultivated crop of oats, wheat or barley. If you want to create a small patch of old-fashioned wheatfield flowers, it should be kept away from the wildflower meadow for these annual species require quite different cultivation.

Bear in mind, though, when planning a wildflower meadow, that most species of meadow flowers do best on poor soil. Rich soils are to be avoided as they promote the growth of vigorous grasses like the perennial rye-grass which tends to dominate other species of wild grass and smother the very flowers you hope to encourage.

Some people go to great lengths to create patches of poor soil on which to sow their wildflower meadow, removing existing turf and the good soil immediately beneath before sowing with a wildflower mixture. If your garden soil is generally too rich to favor a wildflower meadow, I suggest you put the area down to grass using a fine grass seed mixture, but then leave it largely unweeded, apart from removing by hand any invasive perennials like plantain, docks and thistles. In a couple of years' time, provided the grass is not fertilized and the cuttings are religiously removed when it is mowed, the soil will gradually become poorer and some of the more interesting wildflower species can be introduced. In the meantime, you can try introducing some less fussy species – knotweeds, black medick, oxeye daisy, knapweeds, columbines and white clover, for example.

Adapting a formal lawn

If you are toying with the idea of making an informal flower lawn out of part of your existing lawn, and you are in no hurry, then you might consider the approach I took in my own garden. I simply let the grass in a small area at the end of the garden grow, completely untended, for one year, to see which plants would flower. I eliminated some which grew too abundantly – dandelions appeared in great profusion – and in doing so made space for species I wished to introduce. I dug out each unwanted plant, carefully removing all the root (dandelions have deep root systems), to prevent it reappearing, and replaced it with a new plant.

The first rule, if you are trying to encourage wildflowers to grow in an existing lawn, is to stop using any weedkillers or fertilizers. Broad-leaved plants such as daisies, cat's ear, speedwell, white

MEADOW FLOWERS THROUGH THE YEAR
You could make a calendar of meadow flowers, for there is one or another in bloom for most months of the year. In mild winters, there will be a few daisies and dandelions which, like many others, spread their leaves tightly against the ground, thus claiming their living space and preventing grass from closing in and smothering them. Others each have characteristic ways of pushing their way through the lengthening grass so that their flowers are in the sunlight and fully visible to pollinating insects.

1 Field daisy, *Bellis perennis*
2 Dandelion, *Taraxacum officinale*
3 Germander speedwell, *Veronica chamaedrys*
4 Meadow buttercup, *Ranunculus acris*
5 Cuckoo flower, *Cardamine pratensis*
6 Cowslip, *Primula veris*
7 Lesser trefoil, *Trifolium dubium*
8 Common cat's ear, *Hypochaeris radicata*
9 Oxeye daisy, *Leucanthemum vulgare*
10 Field scabious, *Knautia arvensis*
11 Birdsfoot trefoil, *Lotus corniculatus*

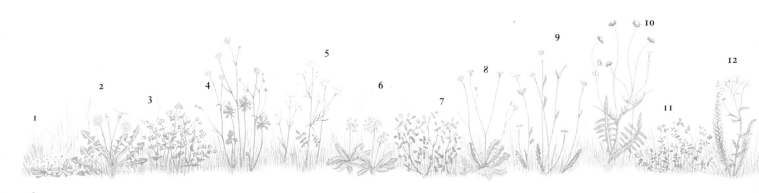

RIGHT *Lawn weeds allowed to grow naturally may be considered anti-social in the suburbs, perhaps, but they are heavenly in the country. Dandelions* en masse *provide pleasure for people and food for wildlife. Bees will find pollen and nectar in abundance from blossom above and meadow flowers below. Later, gold-finches and other birds will enliven the scene as they feed from dandelion seeds.*

12 Yarrow, *Achillea millefolium*
13 Self-heal, *Prunella vulgaris*
14 Pyramidal orchid, *Anacamptis pyramidalis*
15 Meadow cranesbill, *Geranium pratense*
16 Lady's bedstraw, *Galium verum*
17 Common centaury, *Centaurium erythraea*
18 Common mallow, *Malva sylvestris*
19 Common restharrow, *Ononis repens*
20 Feverfew, *Chrysanthemum parthenium*
21 Field gentian, *Gentianella campestris*
22 Greater knapweed, *Centaurea scabiosa*
23 Dyer's greenweed, *Genista tinctoria*
24 Meadow saffron, *Colchicum autumnale*

A MEADOW GARDEN IN SUMMER

A wild meadow garden is divided into different zones for management and color. Paths can be defined simply, by close-mowing the grass. Low-growing lawn plants flower in the more regularly mown area near the house, though this area is left unmown for several weeks from midsummer to give all the species a chance to bloom. Herbs in pots and nectar-rich flowers grow on the sunnier side, though the hedgerow of close-growing shrubs (hornbeam, holly and wild privet) is scented with honeysuckle. Beneath the oak, the fading leaves of bulbs in the spring-flowering area indicate that the time has come when the grass here may be mown.

At the junction of the paths is a miniature 'wheat-field' where poppies and other 'weeds of cultivation' grow, providing a blaze of color. Beyond, in the summer meadow, are knapweed, yarrow, fritillaries, hawkbit and other members of the dandelion family, together with apple and plum trees and a crab apple. Tucked away, at the end to the left, is an area of very rough grass and nettles which also conceals the compost pile.

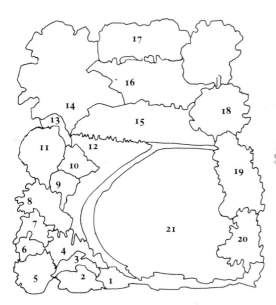

1 Thymes, *Thymus* sp.
2 Marjoram, *Origanum* sp.
3 Sage, *Salvia* sp.
4 Rosemary, *Rosemarinus officinalis*
5 Lavender, *Lavandula* sp.
6 Michaelmas daisy, *Aster novi-belgii*
7 Black-eyed susan, *Rudbeckia hirta*
8 Rose, *Rosa* sp.
9 *Alchemilla* sp.
10 Periwinkle, *Vinca minor*
11 White lilac, *Syringa vulgaris*
12 Spring bulb area
13 Old man's beard, *Clematis vitalba*
14 Oak, *Quercus* sp.
15 Wheatfield border: poppies, *Papaver rhoeas*, and cornflowers, *Centaurea cyanus*
16 Summer meadow: fritillaries, *Fritillaria meleagris*; knapweed, *Centaures nigra*; yarrow, *Achillea millefolium*; cat's ear, *Hypochaeris radicata*
17 Fruit trees
18 English hawthorn, *Crataegus* sp.
19 Hedgerow with honeysuckle, *Lonicera periclymenum*
20 *Clematis montana*
21 Flowering informal lawn: daisies, *Bellis perennis*; speedwell, *Veronica chamaedrys*; dandelions, *Taraxacum officinale*

clover, self-heal and birdsfoot trefoil can be encouraged by mowing the grass only every fourteen days or so throughout one growing season, with the mower blades raised to leave the grass height at 8cm/3in. In early summer, stop mowing for four to five weeks, to allow the flowers to bloom and set seed. In the autumn, spring-flowering bulbs could be introduced into the lawn, planted in groups and drifts, to provide welcome early color for next year.

Whether you want to have a spring display of flowers, or a succession of flowers through the summer and into autumn, you will need to introduce new species. One, or a combination of, the following methods can be tried.

If you wish to sow seed, you must first rip away the surface of the grass with a steel rake or spiked harrow. Remove any debris and sow the chosen seed mixture in autumn (see page 134).

You can introduce small pot-grown plants directly into the turf, if your budget allows and the area is not too large. Plant them in groups, having first removed pot-sized patches of turf, which can be done most successfully using a bulb-planter (see page 133). Again, it is best to plant in autumn to prevent the plants being smothered by more vigorous grasses. But, if you are prepared to keep them well-watered, you can plant at any time.

If you or a friend already have a well-established meadow area, you could transplant small chunks of turf from it into an existing lawn to diversify the plants. This has also been done experimentally on bare soil using turf from an area about to be quarried, arranging the turves in a spaced checkerboard pattern, and sowing a meadow grass mixture around them.

ABOVE RIGHT *The 'Alpine meadow' comes in many forms depending upon the terrain and the indigenous flora. Not all are to be found on mountains. Here a natural hillside, where flowers are allowed to grow anywhere, is just one delightful example.*

RIGHT *Unweeded lawns in spring will produce an alpine meadow of a different pattern, with field daisies, speedwell, dandelions and others which will flower each year, even if the grass is regularly cut in summer – so long as it is not treated with weedkiller.*

LEFT *The garden at Great Dixter is one of the most famous of English gardens and its present owner, Christopher Lloyd, one of the century's great gardeners. A beautiful and unusual feature through which the house is reached is the meadow garden. Here among the grass, a rich flora from spring to autumn includes narcissi, orchids, fritillaries, oxeye daisies, colchicums and autumn crocuses.*

BELOW *A meadow mixture can become richer and richer, not only because of species continually introduced by the gardener but also by those seeds and spores brought in by insects, birds, animals and wind. Often some plants, for example orchids, do not appear until others, such as fungi, are also present. Gardeners lucky enough to have old grassland nearby may have many pleasant surprises in store.*

Creating a new wildflower meadow

If you decide to make a wildflower meadow on fresh ground, there are several ways of tackling it. Don't forget, however, that the soil should be poor for best results. It is probably cheapest to create a fairly large wildflower meadow area from seed, but for a smaller area you might consider a mixed sowing and planting approach (see below, and page 134).

Whichever method you adopt, it is essential to clear the ground completely, getting rid of all invasive perennial weeds, like couch grass, docks, nettles and ragwort. You can either dig the site over with a fork, removing all perennial weeds, including the roots, by hand or, for a larger site, you could spray with a herbicide such as glyphosate and then use a rotary cultivator to turn the soil. Before sowing or planting, the soil should be broken up and free-draining. It can then be raked over to a firm and fine tilth, as you would for a lawn.

Autumn is the best time of the year to sow a new meadow as there will be adequate moisture in the soil. Also, the cold winter months will help to break the dormancy pattern of some of the seeds, ensuring that a larger number will germinate than if sown in spring (see also pages 130-131).

If you are using a packeted mixture of grass and wildflower seed (or seed that you have collected yourself), mix it with several times its volume of damp sand, so that it is distributed more evenly during sowing. The grass and wildflower mixture is normally sown sparsely, using about 4 grammes per square meter ($\frac{1}{6}$ oz per square yard). I would recommend broadcasting the seed by hand, but if you are sowing a large area you could use a hand operated lawn fertilizer spreader to do the job. Again, first mix the seed with sand. After sowing, the seed should be raked in or, on a small plot, lightly covered with soil and trodden in.

An alternative method for small areas is to sow the grasses only and introduce the wildflowers as plants. You can start by sowing the seed of the meadow grasses in round patches over the proposed site. The following spring, when any patches of bare soil are visible, you can introduce the wildflowers which you have raised in nursery beds (see page 131).

Using seeded hay

Hayfield mixtures from species-rich meadows can be purchased from some seed merchants. This will consist of a mixture of chaff and seed, and the quantity to sow depends on how clean the seed and chaff mixture is. It is important to follow the seed merchant's recommendations. Another method, used with good results in Holland and Sweden, is to use the hay itself, from species-rich meadows. If the hay is loose-baled when still green, most of the seed will remain attached to the seed heads. The hay is spread loosely over the surface of the proposed meadow area in autumn, and left to decompose. Seed from the hay will then germinate the following spring. The quantity of seed from one

bale of species-rich hay can vary from around 150-200g/5-7oz – enough for sowing an area 30m/198ft square.

Choice of flower and grass seed

If you buy packeted wildflower meadow seed mixture, it will normally contain up to 20 species of wildflowers and up to half a dozen different grasses. Specialist firms produce seeds suitable for different soil types and drainage conditions, and it is important to follow the advice in their catalogs and buy seed to suit your own conditions (see also charts pages 142-145). Some distinguish between spring- and summer-flowering species. Most grasses are very adaptable and will grow anywhere, although some species do best in certain soil conditions. You may find that the number of species of grass in the bought mixture is not as great, nor the grasses as attractive, as hoped for. Generally, the mixture can easily be augmented by sowing seed of any pretty grasses found growing wild in your locality. But beware – some grasses can be a nuisance. Tall, aggressive grasses like tall fescue, *Festuca arundinacea*, orchard grass, *Dactylis glo-*

ABOVE *Unclean seed is one reason why wheatfields produced such colorful flowers; the seeds came in with the grain. Another reason: because cereals are an annual crop, soil is disturbed before sowing and after harvesting, thus inhibiting the growth of perennials which would ultimately smother the annual flowers. Nowadays, clean seed and herbicides combine to prohibit the growth of annual flowers, like poppies, on farms.*

merata and Timothy grass, *Phleum pratense*, should be avoided, as should all agricultural cultivars of rye grass, *Lolium perenne*. The worst of these, like fescue, are robust and clump-forming. Once established, nothing can gain a foothold where this grass grows. Before adding wild grass seeds to your meadow, it would be wise to check first with a conservation body that they are suitable for your soil conditions and local climate.

Many people who have kept formal lawns are unfamiliar with flowering grasses and you may find it worthwhile to let a small area of a formal lawn go uncut for a season, just to see the appearance of the mature grasses. You may be surprised how lovely some of the grass 'flowers' are, and how much the plumes vary in length, shape, texture and hue. You might also consider incorporating some of the more exotic grasses in your meadow mixture. Once these grasses have become established, they should seed themselves and spread, flowering year after year (see also pages 90-93).

Wheatfield border

Should you decide to establish an old-fashioned wheatfield flower border to your meadow area, you should adopt the same soil preparation methods as you would for sowing the wildflower meadow. After sowing, you must periodically remove any dominating perennials that find their way there, to prevent the annuals being smothered by them. Provided you leave the area uncut until after the seed heads have ripened, the flowers will reseed themselves. For a longer flowering period the following year, remove some of the seed heads after harvesting in late summer and store the seed (see page 129) for sowing the following spring in seed flats or seed beds. Flowers sown in spring will bloom later than those produced from seeds falling to the ground *in situ* in autumn. For rarer species of wheatfield flowers, it is probably best to raise the seed in seed beds or seed flats to ensure germination. Some specialists offer a collection of colorful wheatfield flowers – poppies, cornflowers, pheasant's eye (*Adonis annua*), and corn cockle – all of

which are now rarely seen in modern arable fields.

It would be worthwhile including some of the lovely annual grasses, both native and exotic, such as quaking grass and hare's tails (see pages 150-151). Some of the farm cereal crops, like wheat, oats and barley, can be mixed with annual wheatfield flowers and the grasses mentioned above. Although not wild plants, the seed of the cereal crop will be appreciated by wildlife. The natural sowing time is again autumn.

Nurse crops

Many wild grasses grow slowly and may take a while to get established. Slow-growing forms are usually preferable because they are easier to manage, but for aesthetic reasons you may wish to put in a fast-growing 'nurse' crop which will germinate quickly and then die back, allowing the permanent species for the meadow to replace it. The best kind of nurse crop is an annual grass – one that germinates readily, grows quickly and vigorously, and disappears after a few years. Grains such as wheat, barley, oats or rye fit the bill and in addition are much cheaper in quantity than most other sorts of seed. Since cereal grains need tilled

ABOVE *The practice of planting bulbs in grass in gardens has long been known as 'naturalizing' them. Certainly they can look attractive when grown this way, but where the grass around them is kept closely mown, hardly natural. Where the grass is not only allowd to grow but is also filled with little flowers the garden varieties take on a much less sophisticated appearance.*

land for germination in this country, it is not necessary to prevent the nurse crop from seeding, as it will not persist long after the first year. The sowing rate for the nurse crop is still experimental but 30kg a hectare has been used for commercial operations, and less might be used successfully. (Packets containing just 500g/17.5oz are available, and are cheap compared with wildflower seed.) They are worth using when a quick, cheap cover is required and have been used successfully by various conservation bodies when establishing flower meadows.

Managing the wildflower meadow

Grass cutting is a tiresome chore and you may think, if you are trying to create a really wild corner of your garden, that you can escape it altogether. If you gave the plot over to nature and left the grass uncut or ungrazed year after year, the ground would simply revert naturally to scrubland, as the seedlings of shrubs and trees tend to dominate most other species.

It is not possible to lay down hard-and-fast rules for cutting a meadow since much will depend on the nutrients in and moisture content of your soil, as well as on the species of grasses and wildflowers that it contains. There will also be considerable seasonal differences. General guidelines can be given for the three types of lawn or meadow that I have previously identified: the informal flower lawn, the spring-flowering meadow lawn and the summer-flowering meadow.

Mowing an informal flower lawn has already

LEFT Primrose paths are legendary, but daisy paths may be easier for some gardeners to establish. One of the most cherished of all flowers (and Chaucer's favorite), it is also the most persecuted by lawn enthusiasts. It has a role to play in wild gardens not least because it blooms so early in the year and stays so late into the season.

BELOW A spring meadow can be in flower from the early months of the year with the first bulbs, and continue flowering to midsummer with oxeye daisies, violets, cat's ear, self-heal and cuckoo flowers. Around or a little later than midsummer (depending on the season and appearance of the flowers) mow the meadow and remove the hay. Either keep mown at 10cm/4in, or leave for a second crop.

MOWING REGIMES
1 Spring meadow

Midspring to summer — Midsummer — Later summer and autumn

2 Summer meadow

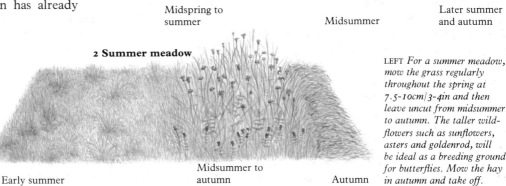

Early summer — Midsummer to autumn — Autumn

LEFT For a summer meadow, mow the grass regularly throughout the spring at 7.5-10cm/3-4in and then leave uncut from midsummer to autumn. The taller wildflowers such as sunflowers, asters and goldenrod, will be ideal as a breeding ground for butterflies. Mow the hay in autumn and take off.

been discussed (see page 61). For a spring meadow, where you are concentrating on a spring show of flowers, leave the grass uncut until midsummer – haymaking time. Cut it once then and leave it uncut until autumn.

For a summer meadow – and summer flowers come in greater diversity than spring ones, and attract more insects – I would cut the grass regularly in the early months of the year and then not cut it again until the summer flowers are over in late summer or even autumn. Some species will flower twice, and you may need to give it a second

cut in late autumn. Alternatively, leave it until early the following spring, and cut when the weather is not frosty or too wet.

Meadow grass, and even informal lawn grass, should never be cut really short. The only area to be so treated would be a path leading through it. The grass should be cut about as short as it would be if grazed and you can either use a hand scythe to do the job, or a lawn mower with the blades set to 8cm/3in. At this level, the broad-leaved plants will not be ruthlessly destroyed and light and air will still reach them.

BELOW *Few flowers are as endearing as oxeye daisies or marguerites – to give but two of its many popular names, evidence that it was once much more familiar than it is today. Shallow-rooted, it will thrive on the poorest of soil.*

Although all long grass mowings should be removed from the meadow to prevent fertility from building up, you will find the work less arduous if you allow them to lie and dry out on the ground for a few days. It makes them much lighter to handle.

Never let grass cuttings rot on the meadow. If they are left lying on broad-leaved plants they will damage or kill them and if they are allowed to stay *in situ* and enrich the soil, it will be less welcoming to meadow species.

Although infrequent mowing or scything sounds easy compared with managing a lawn, and even if you use a lawn mower to do the work, collecting up the grass cuttings is laborious. For a large area, however, it might be worth hiring or borrowing a small garden tractor and also using it to cart the cuttings away on a trailer. Since, in this case, the quantity of mown hay will be too great to compost, you may well find friends with animals who would be glad of it.

Wildlife in the meadow

Summer's meadow flowers come in a much greater diversity and attract more kinds of insects to their nectar than do those of spring. The most attractive include skullcap, thistle, sunflower, coneflower and evening primrose. The seeds of most of these are attractive to birds, especially those of the evening primrose, on which goldfinches feed during winter. Insects continue to visit the meadow until cold slows down their activities, and the long grasses afford a safe place for the pupae of moths and butterflies to hibernate.

A grassy area grown for butterflies as well as for its flowers should be rough cut twice a year, once at midsummer, when the first flush of flowers is over, and again at the very end of summer, to tidy up. But even then, leave some long grasses, round shrubs at the edges of the meadow area, for instance. By this method, the caterpillars are left undisturbed to pupate and hibernate. Always allow cut grass to lie for a few days before raking it up so that any caterpillars, larvae and other creatures have time to find a new refuge on the living

Salad burnet, *Poterium sanguisorba*

Oxeye daisy, *Chrysanthemum leucanthemum*

Marjoram, *Origanum vulgare*

Red clover, *Trifolium pratense*

Dwarf thistle, *Cirsium acaule*

grass left standing in the meadow or elsewhere.

Among the many butterflies and moths that use grasses as larval foodplants, the browns are most common, especially the wood nymph which lays its eggs on various species of meadow grass. Another easily enticed grassland butterfly, the eastern tailed blue will breed on clover, trefoil and other legumes.

Now that the grass grows long, one of my great joys is to stand on the mown path and look around, to try to identify the ever increasing numbers of butterflies, moths and other insects which come to the graceful grasses and winsome flowers alike. I also hope to glimpse one of the small mammals that find a retreat there, such as bank-voles and pygmy shrews.

ABOVE *Bees collect both pollen and nectar for honey, but butterflies and moths and other insects come to the flowers simply to sip. Each tiny floret of clover, daisies and thistles holds a minute store of sweetness. Marjoram which like some thistles blooms late in summer attracts late brood butterflies. Salad burnet attracts pollen beetles and syrphids, although it holds no nectar.*

WOODED GARDENS

Few wild places are as enchanting as a little wood, but if you have only a very small garden you may have to remain content with a small tree or two and an assortment of shrubs. However, if your plot is large enough, and certainly if it was once part of a wood and vestiges of woodland remain, you might feel inclined to create your own wooded area. It is no great problem to use an existing shrub border, a few trees or even one great tree, an orchard or the remains of one, even a mixed hedge-row, as a basis for this type of garden and to build on that, bringing in other trees, shrubs, climbers and smaller plants to complement those which already exist and to help build an ecologically viable plant community. Some of the native fruits could be grown; wild cherry and wild plum (the latter a neater, smaller tree than the former), as well as crab apple, shad bush and mountain ash, all of which will attract wildlife and fill the scene with special seasonal beauty in spring and autumn. With these can be grown a number of exotics, for instance the European bird cherry or the Caucasian medlar (a near relative of the shad bush). This will increase the profitability of the plot and will at the same time add to its content and interest. Fruit blossom, lovely to look at and often among the first flowering, is a great attraction to early-foraging insects.

If you want to plant a proper woodland from scratch, you must be prepared for it to take time – a couple of decades rather than a couple of years. Where no large trees already exist, you should not rush ahead and plant them, but concentrate on the underwood first. On the outer edges of your area, plant young specimens of light-seeking shrubs, and shade-tolerant species within. Once these have had at least a couple of years to become established, start introducing trees. This method has the advantage that the wood can be planned gradually, and by following the sequence that occurs in the wild, will give a much better long-term result.

Where you want a clear way, shrubs can be cut back to ground level or 'coppiced' (see page 138). The ground can be carpeted with woodland plants while you decide what trees you want and where best to position them. In this way, the mature woodland profile can be built up, and you can be sure that it will soon attract a variety of wildlife.

It is good practice to use leaf litter and chopped bark as mulches for your new woodland plants (see page 124), as these naturally organic materials not

RIGHT *Layers of fallen leaves gradually decompose to produce leaf soil, rich in humus, well-drained yet moisture-retentive, an ideal rooting medium for many lovely plants.*

BELOW *A glade is enchanting when carpeted with flowers, such as these bluets or quaker ladies, which are free-seeding annuals.*

only help to sustain the vitality of the soil, but also help support many forms of life – beetles, woodlice, chafers – which find shelter and food beneath. In a similar spirit, already established trees should be provided with bird houses.

If there are fallen trees or branches to be cleared, take some pieces of them into your new woodland area and leave them to rot there. Rotting wood, with its considerable population of insects, fungi, mosses and lichens, also has an important role to play. Even one or two logs, taken perhaps from your fuel store will help. In my own garden I grow ferns around them which helps to keep the soil moist.

The woodland profile

Every wooded country, indeed each geologically different area, has its own type of woodland, often with four layers of plants (though one or other of the lower layers may be barely present in certain woodland types). The traditional oakwood is a good example of this four-tiered structure.

At ground level are the mosses and liverworts which will be more in evidence where the soil is shaded and damp. Above these are the herbaceous plants growing in what botanists call the 'field layer'. The third layer consists of shrubs together with the climbing plants, and finally, often covering all with a dense leafy canopy, grow the trees. Though interdependent, each layer has its own part to play and contributes to the whole woodland scene. If the gardener follows this pattern, the result is sure to be pleasing. The floor of the wooden garden becomes prettily covered with a diversity of earth-based foliage and flowering plants, from which rise up climbers, some weaving through the stems of other shrubs to the top of the trees, some, like virginia creeper, creeping first over the floor until a tree trunk is reached, others cascading to the ground, forming screens.

Oaks are native to or naturalized in many countries throughout the world. Some species are deciduous, some evergreen. Most will grow well in a deep, loamy soil; some species are not lime-tolerant. There are many native oaks suitable for

the wild garden. In the east, white, black and red oaks are common in the uplands and pin oak in wetter areas. White oak is common in pine barrens and is tolerant of extremely acid soils. On the slopes of the Alleghenies and into the midwest, one finds two lime-tolerant species, the mossy-cup oak and the yellow or Muehlenberg oak, more abundant. From Virginia south, the huge, spreading evergreen live oak is a feature of every landscape. The dry hills of California, too, are covered with oaks, many of them evergreen, like the coast and canyon live oaks. Thus there are oaks suitable for every region and every soil type and aspect.

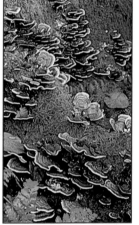

BELOW *Handsome bracket fungi and lush emerald green mosses grow upon and attractively mask a mass of rotting wood which in turn sustains a considerable population of lesser wildlife.*

LEFT *Scentless but beautiful, the dog or wood violet, a plant of the open woodland, favors sloping land and banks, flowers and seeds freely and clothes the ground with pretty heart-shaped leaves.*

There is no need for an oak to dominate a small garden at the expense of many other plants. This tree is considered to be one of the best 'mother' trees. Its roots go down quite deep, thus presenting little, if any, competition to the near-surface rooting plants which grow readily in its shade. This applies to shrubs and field layer plants alike. Those who have oaks in their gardens can grow a wide range of plants in the deep humus that forms beneath them.

Of the early-flowering plants, the hepaticas and bloodroots are first. Roundleaf hepatica, *H. triloba*, grows in acid soil; sharpleaf hepatica, *H. acutiloba*, occurs only in neutral or alkaline areas. Bloodroot is very adaptable, growing in a variety of soil types and aspects. Its lovely flowers are unfortunately short-lived, but those of the 'double' form, with many petals, last much longer. Rue-anemone, smooth and downy yellow violets and the many species of blue and white violets follow soon after the hepaticas. Trout lily or dog's tooth violet (*Erythronium*) are lovely plants of the lily family which come in many colours. There are several species from the West Coast that are especially attractive. Any of the several species of trillium will grow along with these. Try also exotic woodlanders like primrose, the rarer oxlip, *Primula elatior*, herb paris, moschatel, *Adoxa moschatellina*, and wood forget-me-not, *Myosotis sylvatica*. Sheets of bluebells, woodruff and windflowers might be used to complete the garden picture.

The birch tree probably offers the wild gardener a greater scope than many others because of its adaptability. Two birches native to North America, white or canoe birch, *Betula papyrifera*, and gray or old-field birch, *B. populifolia*, have handsome white bark, and the latter will grow in sterile barren soils. On wet ground grow the river birch, *B. nigra*. The seeds of all these species are valuable food for winter finches. Many beautiful species can be readily grown, such as *B. jacquemontii* and *B. platyphylla*. Their elegance can be truly appreciated if the trees are well-spaced.

The black alder, *Alnus glutinosa*, one of the last to lose its leaves in autumn, belongs to the same family as the birch. Although it will grow quite well in drier sites – I have a beauty in a coppice being created in my own garden – it is most often seen in moist places, even by the waterside. It is the dominant tree in damp woods where it is associated with ash and birch. The gray alder, *A. incana*, is a useful tree for growing on very difficult soils, and is used in land reclamation schemes.

Trees for the smaller garden

While a garden may be large enough to contain a little woodland, it may not be really large enough to give space to the true forest trees. Though not

ABOVE *Many species of woodland flowering plants can be grown in the soft, dappled shade cast by shrubs and small trees. Where the leaf canopy is formed by large trees and is likely to become very dense in summer, creating deep shade, those kinds of plants which flower in spring before the trees are in full leaf or in autumn when the leaves begin to fall are best grown.*

very large when first planted, the day will come when they reach great proportions. In this case it is more prudent to select smaller trees or the larger understorey shrubs, those which seem to hover between being a bush or a tree, such as hazel, horn-beam and dogwood. (I have hazel trees in my woodland and hazel shrubs in my hedgerow.)

If these little trees play the role of the top storey, there are still many other shrubs that can be grown as attractive and useful understorey plants. There is also a bonus. Since the foliage canopy of these smaller trees is unlikely to be as dense as that of the larger trees, the field layer can be extremely varied and at times truly colorful, much more so than in a densely canopied wood. I suggest that the more varied the canopy trees, the better so as to provide different zones of light and deeper shade.

There is no reason why natives and exotics should not be mixed if this is what the gardener would prefer. I have visited many attractive small woodlands where exotic species of maples, mag-nolias, pieris, arbutus, Turkey oak, dogwood, rhododendrons and others are seen to mingle rather attractively with an assortment of native trees. These often shelter a correspondingly mixed undergrowth of shade-tolerant plants.

ABOVE *The oxlip,* Primula elatior, *is like a giant cowslip, but like the primrose is found in woody areas and not in meadows. All these species grow well in woodland gardens.*

LEFT *A beautiful woodland plant, and one that illustrates also the close connection between plants of eastern Asia and eastern North America is* Iris cristata, *the crested dwarf iris of the south-east. A member of the group called crested or Evansia irises, its nearest relatives grow around the Great Lakes of Canada, in the Himalayas and in eastern China and Japan.*

A WOODLAND GARDEN

A woodland garden in which the trees are neat, small species mingling with the shrubs, and with native climbers on the boundary fence, will together produce blossom, fruits and foliage necessary to many different forms of wildlife. In this garden, a curving path leads to a pond in a clearing, and crosses it by means of a timber bridge. Rustic seats overlook the pond, close by a wild cherry, so that people can sit and watch the water and pond life. The path continues toward a hideout in the guise of a summerhouse draped with honeysuckle. Going back toward the house, now treading in grass, you pass alongside a woodland border where many different kinds of woodland and wood edge flowering plants carpet the ground, beneath as well as between the trees: violets, *Viola* sp.; primroses, *Primula vulgaris*; star-of-bethlehem, *Ornithogalum umbellatum*; wood anemone, *Anemone nemorosa*; periwinkle, *Vinca major*; wood forget-me-not, *Myosotis sylvatica*; foxglove, *Digitalis purpurea*; greater celandine, *Chelidonium majus*; lily-of-the-valley, *Convallaria majalis*.

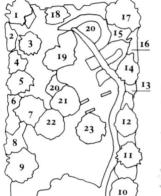

1 Whitebeam, *Sorbus aria*
2 Bramble, *Rubus* sp.
3 English holly, *Ilex aquifolium*
4 Blackthorn, *Prunus spinosa*
5 English hawthorn, *Crataegus oxycanthus*
6 Guelder rose, *Viburnum opulus*
7 Field maple, *Acer campestre*
8 Hazel, *Corylus avellana*
9 Wayfaring tree, *Viburnum lantana*
10 Wild service tree, *Sorbus torminalis*
11 Common privet, *Ligustrum vulgaris*
12 Hornbeam, *Carpinus betulus*
13 Black bryony, *Tamus communis*
14 Silver birch, *Betula pendula*
15 Alder buckthorn, *Frangula alnus*
16 Old man's beard, *Clematis vitalba*
17 Small-leaved linden, *Tilia cordata*
18 European elder, *Sambucus nigra*
19 Downy birch, *Betula pubescens*
20 Shrub dogwood, *Cornus sanguinea*
21 Mountain ash, *Sorbus aucuparia*
22 Crab apple, *Malus pumila*
23 Black cherry, *Prunus avium*

My own little wood, still very much in its early stages, is of necessity influenced by those trees which already existed, and those planted when the garden was first made, when a wild garden was not a part of the plan. There are the original Turkey oak, copper beech, small-leaved lime, 'Aurora', variety poplar, apple, plum, quince and eucalyptus spread about. Now, among these older trees, others are gradually being established. Most of them are raised from those seedlings (known as 'volunteers' by farmers) which appear, usually unwanted, about the garden. When they are a few inches high, the plants are lifted and transplanted in the wood area. Meanwhile, I raise others from seed I have collected or from cuttings, or I buy saplings from nurseries (see pages 129-132). It might seem, when one looks at the tiny plant which has come from, say a cotoneaster or pine seed, that it will take years for it to grow to a good size, but it is both surprising and reassuring to know that, once these little plants have reached two or three years, they will quickly catch up with and overtake older bought in nursery stock. Examples of some useful plants for the woodland garden that can be obtained in this way are alder, aspen, field maple, blackthorn, wayfaring tree, pine, willow, hazel, English holly, guelder rose and shrub dogwood.

One can buy a whole range of tree seedlings, usually 2-year old, from nurseries. Where understorey plants or garden boundary plants are needed, these trees and shrubs can be grown into one another as they do in the wild. In this way they can provide a useful screen or windbreak for those other, perhaps choicer, plants in your wood area.

Shrubs and climbers

The shrub layer of a wood contains the plants with which we become most familiar, for they are near at hand, growing more or less at our level. These we can touch and in turn they touch us as we pass by. They need careful choosing because they are the plants which add so much to the character of a woodland interior. We are likely to be more aware

of them than we are of the trees which create the canopy above them. Fortunately, there are many shrubs both native and exotic which readily accept woodland conditions and which will grow either in the deepest shade at its heart or in the lighter shade at its margins, or maybe in clearings within.

One of the simplest ways of furnishing a woodland is to allow some dominant shrub to grow. Hazel comes to mind because it so often occurs in a wildwood. It will grow on any loamy soil, and a varied field layer will grow quite luxuriantly beneath it.

However, most gardeners prefer to collect and grow a wider range of plants than a single species.

ABOVE *Where a traditional-style garden ends in a wooded area, existing garden plants mingled with the wild ones help to merge the two areas. If the plants sprawl informally, even flamboyant kinds such as yellow alyssum – when in flower, softly gray in leaf alone – will suit the scene. It helps to interplant them with some of the old-fashioned garden plants that are really native species, such as forget-me-nots.*

European elder,
Sambucus nigra

Black cherry,
Prunus avium

English holly,
Ilex aquifolium

Snowberry,
Symphoricarpos rivularis

Mountain ash, *Sorbus aucuparia*

Where there is a certain amount of moisture or where the shade is really deep, as it can be on some northfacing margins, the guelder rose will thrive.

Here also can be grown the various buckthorns, arrow-wood and mapleleaf viburnums, and perhaps the best native shrub for dense shade, the rosebay, *Rhododendron maximum*. Box, especially the arborescent varieties, thrives in shade where it is hardy, as do tutsan (*Hypericum androsaemum*), *Mahonia aquifolium,* the commoner privet and yew and most species of holly. One of the best shrubs for shade is the Japanese five-leaved aralia, *Acanthopanax sieboldianus,* a large shrub with arching, spiny branches and handsome foliage.

Some of the plants designated as small trees can also be grown as shrubs under woodland conditions. Good examples are the pussy willow or the sumacs, sallow, *Salix caprea* and the field maple, *Acer campestre*. In any case, where any of these small trees are planted as shrubs, they can be kept under control if they threaten to grow too large, by being cut back from time to time (see page 138).

Climbers can play an important part in a wooded area. Since these are fairly fast-growing, they can be used to furnish existing trees quickly to give them a more informal and sylvan look. It is better if the support tree has had two or three years to become established. (See also pages 38-39.)

ABOVE *Holly, elder, cherry, mountain ash and snowberry, five fruiting trees or shrubs which brighten the woodland scene. Some fruits are taken by birds as soon as they are ripe, others not until the weather is harsh. Holly berries feed thrushes and snowberry is a favorite food of game birds and of bees, for this plant like all the others serves wildlife and the gardener in more ways than one. All have blossom which supports bees or other insects and also brings beauty to the garden.*

Although it is classified as a climbing shrub, cross-vine will cover the floor of a wood, especially in heavy shade where other plants are less likely to grow. Remember that the deeper the green and the tougher the texture of a leaf, the more it can tolerate shade. This applies to all kinds of plants.

Evergreens

There is more variety in evergreens than is at first apparent, sufficient to provide the gardener with a diversity if this is wanted. Rhododendron, juniper, yew, holly and ivy in particular have all produced great numbers of varieties. Some of these are extraordinary and differ considerably from the type in their habit and appearance: prostrate junipers, for example, columnar yews, bushlike ivies or hollies with untoothed leaves like a camellia. A cultivar of English holly, 'Ferox', has leaves smothered in prickles like a hedgehog, while a cultivar of American holly, 'Villanova', has fruits of clear yellow rather than scarlet. All this difference in leaf size, shape and color, variegation, habit, color of fruit, and so on, provides an assortment of specimens from which the gardener can choose to suit his or her specific needs or desires, so it is best to visit a shrub nursery or an arboretum to see what is available before deciding to remain with the type only.

The presence of conifers in a garden is desirable, since many of them, the pines for example, provide splendid windbreaks, while those thickly clothed with foliage provide cover for nesting birds. Most conifers give shade but do not tolerate it. Hemlocks, *Tsuga*, arbor-vitaes, *Thuja* and false-cypress, *Chamaecyparis*, all tolerate some shade.

Hedgerows and woodland edges

Very old hedgerows, which contain a diverse collection of species, are thought to be remnants of ancient wildwood. As the land was cleared for farming, a line of trees and shrubs was left to mark boundaries or for shelter. Once laid, a good thick hedgerow would soon be formed. The microclimate of a hedge is therefore not dissimilar from conditions in a wood – there exists shade, humidity and shelter for both plants and creatures.

If you wish to make a wild hedge, plant it fairly thickly (see page 137). Local hedgerows should guide you to the species most suitable to grow, but most native species will do well on ordinary soil. One of the joys of my local hedgerows is the field maple, the leaves of which persist long after others have fallen. Grow this with hawthorns, black-haw viburnum, wild roses, holly, privet and the wild plum. I grow blackthorn, also, in spite of its suckers, because I love to see the first blossom in the hedge. I remove the suckers with a 'lopper', pushing this down into the soil to sever the root.

Where space does not permit a wooded area or coppice in the garden, an existing border could be widened and given a woodland appearance. It can be planted as though it were the edge of a wood. If the border is near a hedge, the woodland effect will be easier to create, especially if the hedge is of mixed species. If you stake one main stem of each hedge species so that it grows above the hedge top, it will not be long before you have a series of little trees – hawthorn, oak, willow and holly among them, perhaps.

ABOVE *Fireweed*, Epilobium angustifolium, *is a tall perennial found commonly in woods and on heaths and wasteground.*

BELOW *Common in woods of the north temperate zone,* wood sorrel, Oxalis acetosella, *has a creeping root and so will soon spread and carpet an area of shady, moist woodland garden.*

On the fringes of the woodland border or hedge-row, grow ferns, campion, spurge, wild geraniums, willow herb, foxgloves, mullein and honesty. According to soil conditions, the pretty field roses and other climbers can grow.

Where the soil at the wood edge is moist but not wet, yellow deadnettle, yellow loosestrife and its low-growing relative creeping jenny, purple loosestrife, monkshood and tansy can be grown.

Where the soil becomes dry, stony, or gravelly, the bloody crane's bill, various St John's worts, mulleins, yarrow, black-eyed Susans and low species such as *Aster spectabilis* can be encouraged to grow.

On acid soils, woodland edge plants such as bilberry and other low shrubs of this family, fetter bush and heathers can form a mixed community into which ferns, woodsage and other Labiates could be introduced, many of them wild herbs.

In some gardens it may be the woodland edge which is most on view, in which case the gardener will wish to make it look as attractive and as inviting as possible. Remember that a densely foliated plant will set off one which is more delicately structured, a spreading plant can be grouped against or at the foot of a thin or columnar one.

A woodland border can solve a problem for those gardeners who regret that so much of their plot is in shade. Perhaps a neighboring tree is so large that it creates a leafy barrier to the sun along part of the garden boundary, or perhaps a high wall projects a harsh shield against sunlight, at least for much of the year. However, plant a woodland edge and the high tree presents a ready-made sylvan backcloth. The high wall, once creeper covered, would seem less aggressive, and the foliage it carried would merge with shade-loving shrubs, which, in turn could frame a field layer, as bright and interesting as mine is.

LEFT *A thicket of ivy offers a secluded nesting site for the wren. Holes or cracks and crevices in banks, walls and woodpiles and dense bushes are other favored places.*

RIGHT *A border can resemble a wood margin for, given the same conditions of leafy soil and shade for some part of the day, the same kinds of plants can be grown. Those of the field layer include many with handsome foliage which in turn give shade to smaller plants below.*

HEATHS AND HEATH GARDENS

The heather family, the Ericaceae, consists of some 1500 plant species that thrive in peaty, acid or slightly neutral conditions. While many people associate heathers with cool northern hillsides, the greatest number of species occur naturally on the windswept tablelands of South Africa, and indeed most heather species do best in exposed gardens with a mild yet blustery climate.

Heather gardens in which an overlapping patchwork of different heather species is created have long been popular. However, they can look very contrived and formal which is not the effect you should aim for in creating a wild heather garden. Most ericaceous plants are low-lying, slow-growing shrubs and are therefore seen to advantage in a contoured landscape, discreetly clothing a slope, and forming soft, cushioned areas between rocks.

Contours, which create a more attractive landscape, can be created by growing plants of different habit and height. One can begin at the lowest level and, if there should be a depression in the land, this can be exploited. Grassy paths or open spaces can be made with the grass kept short, or creeping plants can be used as ground covers. Thymes grow well on the same types of soil, and a creeping thyme lawn can be a most attractive and colorful feature, and extend the season of floral hues.

Apart from heathers, there is a wide range of ericaceous plants available for planting, such as cranberry and other berry-bearing bushes as well as the more natural-looking azaleas and smaller rhododendron species. There are also a host of nonericaceous companion plants that do well in acid conditions and that will fit well into a heathland scheme, for example, many of the brooms, and conifers, such as junipers, which make a good vertical contrast to the prostrate heather forms.

Many members of the Ericaceae are evergreen in habit, although green is by no means the predominating color, for the fading stems of blossom and the young tips of the foliage create a perpetual variety of hue. When evergreen heathers are mixed with deciduous species, such as bilberry, a rich harmony of color is created.

Calluna vulgaris, sometimes known as 'ling', is the common Eurasian heather, which flowers from late summer on moors and marginal woodland banks. Heather is naturalized in eastern Canada and the US but is not common anywhere except on some islands in New England. There is only one species in the genus, but this is extremely variable in habit and flower color. The true heaths, *Erica*, are abundant in South Africa. Spring heath, *E. herbacea (carnea)* is the most adaptable.

Heath gardens

Most heaths grow best in a peaty acid soil and it is therefore best to dig plenty of moist peat into your bed and spread a further layer of peat onto the newly dug surface so that this can be worked around the roots. Although it is possible to create artificial peat beds when gardening on an alkaline soil, in the long term this is not worthwhile as a substance called iron sequestrate must be applied to prevent a yellowing (chlorosis) of the leaves, a problem that gets more acute with the years.

There are certain attractive cushion-forming plants among the peaflower family, Papilionaceae, for example, which can be used to give the impression of little hillocks. (See plants for dry heaths, below.) Rising above these, taller shrubs and trees will add both interest and beauty to the landscape.

If there are to be heaths planted below the trees and shrubs, try to get them in at the same time. This will avoid disturbing any growing roots at a later date. This means also that all the plants can be cared for in their early days and both can quickly adjust to each other while they are still young. It is often much more helpful and less damaging if a deep mulch of peat or compost is first spread and the young plants rooted in this.

Plants on this type of soil tend to dry out

ABOVE *Ling*, Calluna vulgaris, *occupies extensive areas of moorland near the sea on some islands of New England like Nantucket. Like the nearly related heaths or ericas, it is a favorite bee plant.*

RIGHT *A slope on acid soil is an ideal site for a heath garden. Apart from anything else, each plant is so well displayed, whether it sprawls on the ground or grows upright among a mass of others. Birch trees harmonize beautifully with these evergreen plants, in winter their silver barks providing a soft, glistening contrast of color and texture. Some heaths such as the Irish heath,* Erica mediterranea, *become really bushy, growing as tall as 1.5m/5ft or more.*

speedily if they are not kept watered until they are obviously established and capable of looking after themselves. It is advisable for as long as two years after planting and especially at times of drought to keep a close eye on the new inhabitants to make sure that the soil in which they are growing is sufficiently moist.

Young heaths appear to do best when they are planted close together, so where only a few plants are available it is helpful to fill small areas and then extend these as more plants are obtained.

If there is an elevated area in the garden, it could be made into a rock garden or a rock hill. If it is associated with a pond or perhaps a water course, this would suit acid soil areas very well, as the presence of water helps to dispel any dry, arid impression which can sometimes haunt a heath in summer. Those ericas and other species which tolerate a hotter, drier situation could be grown on little plateaux made for them on the mound.

Color harmonies

In some cases, on acid soils, there may exist little woodlands or coppices in which rhododendrons dominate. Aged and mature plants often grow to be quite large. In mountains from New England to Alabama, the rosebay, *Rhododendron maximum*, grows very thickly and so forms dense thickets in which game can hide and on which deer can browse in the dead of winter. In the garden, thickets of rhododendron may be too dense in their style of growth for those who wish to see a more varied landscape and may need to be thinned.

Popularly known as azaleas, but really rhododendrons, there are some deciduous American species which lend themselves attractively to the wild heath garden. They color the landscape in late spring and early summer with blossom and with colored foliage in the autumn. The lovely brilliant orange flame azalea, *Rhododendron calendulaceum* (syn. *Azalea calendulacea*), and the fragrant western azalea, *R. occidentale,* and the Pinxter flower or pink azalea, *R. periclymenoides,* are examples. A Japanese species, *R. japonicum* (known

to many gardeners as *Azalea mollis*), is a great favorite for informal gardeners.

Rhododendrons grow best under thinly planted trees such as oaks, where the light dappled shade protects the blossoms from intense sunshine so that they are not too quickly spent. They look delightful on the edge or in a clearing of a wood.

Heaths for milder aspects

Many gardeners with neutral or limy soil make successful cultivated heath gardens mainly because there are two species, *Erica herbacea (carnea)*, a native of the limestone Alps, and *E. mediterranea,* the Irish heath, native to Galway and south-west Europe, which are actually tolerant of a very little lime in the soil. Both of these species, like *Calluna*, have given rise to many commercially raised varieties. The Irish heath grows to 3m/10ft in time, and flowers early.

E. vagans, the Cornish heath, native also to south-west Europe, flowers right through the summer until early winter, but it is less hardy than the Irish heath and so should be grown only in climates where the winter is mild. It is a straggling shrub, 1m/3ft in height, with thick bushy racemes of small pale purple-pink flowers. Its cultivated

ABOVE *Abundant on heaths, European gorse, furze and broom with their conspicuous yellow, pealike flowers are often found complementing the rosy-purples of heath and ling. Gorse,* Ulex europaeus, *is the species shown here, and, where more yellow is favored, nurseries sell varieties of different species of ericas which have vividly-colored foliage. When purple-flowering varieties are also grown, together they make a brilliant patch of color.*

forms have flowers of deeper and clearer colors.

Taking its name from an Irish saint, *Daboecia cantabrica*, St Dabeoc's Heath, looks a little like an outsize heather. It differs from the true ericas in that its corolla falls from the stem, while those of ericas remain, turning to many lovely russet hues – particularly striking when wet with rain or mist. This heath flowers through the summer months and is a striking plant when in bloom. There is a variety *D. alba* as well as *D.c.* 'Bicolor' which has three-color forms on the same individual – some flowers are purple, some white, some purple and white! Like the Cornish heath, this species is apt to become damaged in severe winters although it does seem to have good restorative powers. Any damaged part should be cut away once all danger of frost is passed.

Ericaceae for wet conditions

Those species which need constant moisture, such as the bog heather or cross-leaved heath, *Erica tetralix,* can be grown most successfully by the water's edge, although no heath will thrive in a completely waterlogged situation. If there is no natural water, arrangements should be made for plants of this species to be watered in some way.

A HEATH GARDEN

Heath colors can be naturally soft or vividly vibrant. Therefore many of the green-leaved species have produced varieties with bright flowers and foliage. Some flower through summer until late into autumn: *Erica vagens* 'Mrs Maxwell' **1**, and the bell heather, *E. cinerea* **2**, its variety *E.c.* 'Alba minor' **3** and *E. mackaiana* **4**. Ling, *Calluna vulgaris*, flowers similarly: *C.v.* 'Golden King' **5** and *C.v.* 'Silver Queen' **6**. Purple thymes **7** carpet the ground. Behind are *C.v.* 'H.E. Beale' **8** and *C.v.* 'Peter Sparkes' **9**. Others are Scotch broom, *Cytisus scoparius* **10**, *Hebe* **11** and *Juniperus horizontalis* **12**. On the right are cowberry, *Vaccinium vitis-idaea* **13** and its relative bilberry, *V. myrtillus* **14**. Between the strawberry tree, *Arbutus unedo* **15,** and the birch, *Betula* sp. **16** is St Dabeoc's heath, *Daeboecia cantabrica* **17**, and gorse, *Ulex europaeus* **18**.

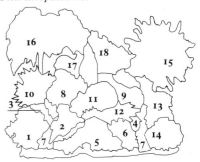

The soil can be kept in the right condition by the use of a trickle irrigation system, which can be bought and operated as necessary.

This heath forms a spreading plant, anything up to 50cm/20in high, with downy young shoots and rose-pink flowers from summer until late autumn. It has many lovely varieties in cultivation, all of which greatly resent dry soil, a fact which is not often appreciated by those who buy on impulse from garden centers. More straggly than the cross-leaved heath, the Dorset heath, *Erica ciliaris,* has larger, deeper colored flowers from midsummer onward. It is also a procumbent shrub, rarely exceeding 30cm/12in in height.

Described as an attractive carpeting plant in heath and woodland gardens, the cowberry, *Vaccinium vitis-idaea,* one of the Ericaceae, has obviously earned the approval of traditional gardeners. The variety *minus* grows wild in sub-arctic regions of Canada or at high elevations further south. It is a dainty evergreen creeping shrub with tough leathery-green leaves with paler undersides. Its flowers, which bloom from late spring, are very pale pink and bell-shaped. They are followed by small, edible red fruits. Similar plants forming small bushes include the whortle-berry, *V. myrtillus,* and the cranberries, *V. macrocarpon* and *V. oxycoccus,* all of which need ground moisture and humidity. Here also can be grown the evergreen marsh andromeda, *Andromeda polifolia,* from Eurasia as well as northern North America. *A. glaucophylla* found wild only in eastern Canada and the US is similar but more attractive.

Among these moisture-loving acid soil plants is the aromatic *Ledum palustre,* a plant of the northern lands of America, Europe and Asia, with terminally clustered and wide open flowers so unlike the general bell shape of most of the members of the Ericaceae. It is a broad, thick-set evergreen bush, 1m/3ft high with dark green leaves which are rusty-colored and tomentose on the undersides. The flowers are creamy white. It has been cultivated in our gardens for many years and is popularly known as Labrador tea.

Other plants for moist and wet acid sites

The beautiful bog asphodel, *Narthecium ossifragum,* which produces orange-yellow lily flowers in midsummer, many on one stem, is a creeping perennial some 15cm/6in high. Actually, this species will grow in ordinary soil in moist beds and borders, as well as in the margins of a bog or pond. The very rare *N. americanum* has smaller flowers and narrower leaves.

For those who seek wild rarities, there is the lovely creeping harebell or ivy-leaved bell flower, *Wahlenbergia hederacea* (sometimes known as *Campanula hederacea*). It needs a peaty site and

ABOVE *Where the shade is never dense, the margin of a wood on acid soil provides an ideal area for an assortment of shrubs such as the yellow-flowered gorse, cistus and rhododendron. All can be attractively mingled with heath, ling and other erica-ceous plants. Where space permits, these plants can gradually spread outward to make a heath border in which the taller species can give way to those which grow closer to the ground.*

should be kept moist in dry weather. Gardeners recommend that it is best established by sowing seed on living sphagnum moss.

Another uncommon plant, of damp mountain sides in west Europe, rather than the damp woodland edge, is the petty whin, *Genista anglica,* a dainty 60cm/24in high little 'broom'.

Plants of dry heath
Bell heather, *Erica cinerea,* also called purple heather or fine-leaved heath, often forms wide stretches of drier heathland and makes for an attractive ground-cover shrub, up to 60cm/24in

high, for a dry heathland display. The flowers are a dark crimson-purple and appear from summer through until late autumn.

The bilberry, or whortleberry, associates well with heather and is worth growing for its lovely autumn hues. One of the delightful features of heath gardens is that you can expect such fine colors in both autumn and winter.

Other *Vaccinium* species which look good with the above are the various low bush blueberries such as *V. angustifolium,* with edible fruits for human and animal life. The pine barrens that stretch down much of our eastern coast are home of many very

ABOVE *A house which seems to have grown up from its garden, an effect enhanced by the thick cover of ivy varieties which clothe its walls. The heaths which reach right up to it, covering large areas with free-flowering evergreen plants, need little further attention once they have become established. Such a garden becomes both labor- and wildlife-saving since it provides so much undisturbed cover. There are many other shrubs which can be planted among the heaths.*

beautiful ericaceous plants. Sand-myrtle, *Leio-phyllum buxifolium,* is a small white-flowered ever-green like a refined ledum. A much taller, more statuesque species is the mountain-laurel, *Kalmia latifolia,* with the impact of a rhododendron.

In the hottest, sunniest areas of the pine barrens the ground is carpeted with bearberry, *Arcto-staphylos uva-ursi.* Through the mats of bearberry foliage poke shoots of many interesting non-ericaceous plants: *Aster gracilis* and *A. spectabilis,* with beautiful lavender daisy flowers in autumn, and the upright goldenrods, *Solidago stricta* and *S. erecta.* Among shrubs we find inkberry holly, *Ilex glabra,* with evergreen leaves and black fruits, the red chokeberry, *Aronia arbutifolia,* and the wax-

yielding bayberry, *Myrica pensylvanica.*

There are many choice, low-growing ericaceous native shrubs. In acid soil beneath pines or in dry beech woods are found the pipsissewas, small stoloniferous shrublets with beautiful, evergreen leaves and large, waxy white or blue-pink flowers. Wintergreen, *Gaultheria procumbens,* trailing arbu-tus, *Epigaea repens,* and other dwarf heaths grow well in shade or partial sun. A member of the related diapensia family is Oconee bells, *Shortia galacifolia,* which thrives in shade and acid soil.

Of the smaller flowers, the violets are especially attractive, and seed freely once established. Fore-most among these is the gorgeous birdsfoot violet. Other violets for acid heaths are *V. brittoniana,*

BELOW *Spring-flowering bulbous plants, such as these daffodils, can look attractive planted among heaths. However, one of the great qualities of the latter is that they cover the ground with color throughout the year for the plants are seldom just plain green. Their flowering shoots provide color for months on end, becoming tinted as the buds begin to form and gradually taking on a deeper hue as the flowers mature. Most of these persist and fade to warm russet colors which may continue until the new shoots arrive.*

ABOVE *Less hardy than some species, in mild climates the Cornish heath,* Erica vagans, *flowers from midsummer to late autumn. It has produced several varieties, different in color and appearance from the type.*

the coast violet, and the arrow-leaved *V. sagittata*.

Often associated with pine barren violets are wild lupine, *Lupinus perennis,* and savory-leaved aster, *Aster linariifolius*. The lupine blooms with birdsfoot violet and to see clumps of the two in flower together along roadsides is to see one of the most effective natural combinations imaginable.

Plants for rocky outcrops
Where stone is combined with acid soil conditions it should be possible to grow the bearberry, *Arctostaphylos uva-ursi,* a dwarf, trailing, shining evergreen shrub.

Rock, carefully positioned, can help to create the atmosphere of a moor or heath. One or two large pieces placed with care are often much more effective than many small pieces assembled in a rock garden or dotted about. Used in unison with a tree, or group of trees, a piece of rock can look most dramatic. Sometimes, by grouping two rocks, it may be possible to give the impression that the tree is growing from a cleft in the single rock. The same ploy can be used on a smaller scale on a rock hill when smaller, perhaps prostrate shrubs including heathers and some conifers can be used. (See also Rock gardens, pages 114-120.)

FERN AND FOLIAGE GARDENS

A northfacing border, or sometimes the north side of a wide border, or a tree-shaded path might appear to pose a problem when planting a garden. Yet, this is often an ideal site for an all-green garden of ferns and grasses. And there are many other kinds of plants, both native and exotic, that have handsome foliage that can be pleasantly mingled with them.

Ferns and grasses growing together create a pleasing harmony of green shapes and textures which are often overlaid with other hues according to the season or to the variegation of a variety of species. They are delightful subjects for bordering woodland walks, and for fringing woodland and shrub borders, or for furnishing shady or partly shaded places.

Where only part of a garden is used for wild species, ferns and grasses can be planted to fill it in summer while, in early spring with these two not yet really active, smaller plants such as primroses, violets and celandines could be planted to carpet the ground between the green plants. When the flowering plants are fading and no longer decorative, the growing grass and ferns will mask them.

Ferns and grasses add a light touch to some of the denser plants such as holly, ivy and other evergreens (including rhododendrons), whether they are grouped immediately below and around them or in the spaces in between. Ferns of different species, with various heights and forms, will look most attractive, and tall ferns will add their charm where trees and shrubs cast a dappled shade.

ABOVE *The handsome leaves of* Lysichitum americanum, *called western skunk cabbage, follow its giant yellow arumlike flowers. It is a fine plant for the waterside or for damp places where (to the right) the royal ferns,* Osmunda regalis, *also flourish. Both plants furnish the scene for many months, the fern gradually assuming lovely russet hues as the year end approaches. In the background is* Cedrus atlantica.

RIGHT *The large-leaved ivy beyond the arch and the variegated box to the left are just two examples of varieties of two evergreen common plants which have many diverse forms. Both provide splendid cover for many forms of wildlife. The little Kenilworth ivy growing in the wall and the yellow-flowered* Corydalis *are two species which seed freely. Foliage in the foreground is of* Bergenia *from Asia, some species of which are hardy.*

Ferns

One of the most useful qualities of ferns is that they will grow well where most flowering plants fail, and although most require moisture, some will flourish in dry situations. In dense shade, even in that cast by overhanging tree branches which drip heavily in rainy weather, you can grow a fern garden or simply plant one or more species in groups. Most of the buckler fern genus, *Dryopteris,* which has a world-wide distribution of a great number of species, are suitable. One of the most familiar is the handsome marginal woodfern, *Dryopteris marginalis,* which survives even in dusty town gardens.

Given shelter, it will remain almost evergreen and prove a handsome tenant to border and woodland alike. The exception for deep shade is *D. fragrans.* This is one of those ferns which will grow in sunny, dry and even exposed places.

Among the most ancient of plants on earth, ferns grow wild all over the world and there are thought to be some 10,000 species. Obviously not all are hardy in the northern hemisphere. Some of the fern families are very large. The polypody, the largest, has some 170 genera and possibly as many as 7,250 species distributed over all parts of the world. In many fern species, the young fronds are

A COURTYARD FERN GARDEN

In a corner of a tiny paved town garden, water is more than an ornamental feature. Most importantly, it cleans and humidifies the air around, thus generating the ideal micro-climate for growing ferns and other moisture-loving plants. Gardens of this nature are so often shaded by neighboring buildings. Fortunately many foliage plants will accept the shade. The darker the green of their leaves, the more tolerant of it they will be. If, on the other hand, the yard is sunny, then take advantage of all shade, even that which at some time of the day is cast by tall, leafy plants such as the royal and lady ferns and Solomon's seal. As they grow, they can protect the carpeting species.

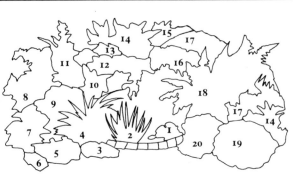

1 Scented water lily, *Nymphaea odorata* 'minor'
2 Sweet flag, *Acorus calamus*
3 Creeping jenny, *Lysimachia nummularia*
4 Pendulous sedge, *Carex pendula*
5 Violets, *Viola* sp.
6 Thymes, *Thymus* sp.
7 Bog arum, *Calla palustris*
8 Lady fern, *Athyrium filix-femina*
9 Male fern, *Dryopteris filix-mas*
10 Parsley fern, *Cryptogramma crispa*
11 Solomon's seal, *Polygonatum multiflorum*
12 Ivy, *Hedera helix*
13 Maidenhair spleenwort, *Asplenium trichomanes*
14 Hart's tongue fern, *Phyllitis scolopendrium*
15 Kenilworth ivy, *Cymbalaria muralis*
16 Common polypody, *Polypodium vulgare*
17 Starry saxifrage, *Saxifraga stellaris*
18 Royal fern, *Osmunda regalis*
19 Common quaking grass, *Briza media*
20 London pride, *Saxifraga × urbicum*

LEFT *A large tree in a garden can be complemented by many kinds of smaller plants which will accept its shade and shelter. They will thrive so long as the gardener ensures that the soil in which their roots grow is kept continually recharged with mulches of leaf soil or other organic moisture-retaining material. Ferns are especially suitable for this environment, and can be interplanted with other plants of contrasting shapes and textures.*

tinted with attractive hues of copper or bronze, and even pink or magenta. Often the coloration may be more marked in a variety than in the type, and the shapes and characters of the fronds may differ also.

Nowadays it is wrong, and illegal in some countries, to uproot ferns from the wild, but many are to be found in nurserymen's lists. If you are unfamiliar with fern species but would like to start a fern garden, why not begin with four of the easiest species, the lady, Christmas, spinulose and silvery spleenwort ferns? The most majestic ferns are Ostrich fern, *Mattencia struthiopteris,* and members of the genus *Osmundia* such as the lovely royal and cinnamon ferns (*O. regalis* and *O. cinnamomea*), all of which are deciduous, except in mild winters or in very sheltered gardens. True evergreens are the ferns of the *Polystichum* genus, and these prefer a slightly acid soil and must be kept moist at the roots at all times. See page 135 for cultivation of ferns.

Gravel areas often unexpectedly harbor some of the ferns we find growing wild on walls, and these ferns do not generally need shade or much moisture. For instance the pretty, yet tough, maidenhair spleenwort, *Asplenium trichomanes,* is to be found growing wild in very exposed situations. (I am growing this species on the ground in well-drained soil between pavement stones.) Wall rue, *A. ruta-muraria,* will also grow on flat, stony, well-drained alkaline soils. Even the handsome, much taller lady fern is sometimes to be found growing there, although it is mainly known to luxuriate in woods and on shady banks, even near water, on lime-rich soils. This fern has deeply divided fronds, some 45-90cm/18-38in long, and it is very variable. An attractive collection of lady fern varieties could perhaps be made.

Ferns which grow wild on walls can also be grown in rock gardens and, so long as they are covered by a shallow layer of soil, compost or leaf-mold, on stony banks, or even on piles of rubble. (It might be one way of camouflaging the latter.) Two species suitable for this purpose are *Ceterach officinarum* and *Asplenium adiantum-nigrum*. Other

LEFT *The handsome male fern,* Dryopteris filix-mas, *will thrive almost anywhere. Like many native fern species it, too, has produced a great number of forms treasured by fern lovers. These differ, often greatly, in shape or size from the type. Although classed as deciduous, in a sheltered place or mild season it will remain almost ever-green. It can be grown informally, or in a border with other kinds of ferns and plants.*

species are the bladder fern, *Cystopteris fragilis,* the common polypody, *Polypodium vulgare,* and the lovely hart's tongue, *Phyllitis scolopendrium.* This last species has many interesting varieties.

The hart's tongue will grow well in borders and in crevices on the level, but bear in mind that these are ferns that will wilt badly if they are in a too dry situation. They are much more handsome when they are grown in shade than when they are sub-jected to sun and drought. In my own garden some have appeared quite spontaneously on a north-facing hedge bank where they grow among the lush grass and hedgerow plants.

Should you wish to decorate an old wall, you can top it with the common polypody. Either make spaces, or find existing crevices, to fill with leaf-mold and plant young ferns. These have the best chance of survival. This little polypody, which grows on trees, is one of Europe's few epiphytic plants, but it also grows on rock faces, old walls and sometimes roofs, especially if these have become mossy. It can be planted on an old tree stump, and

will withstand drought. It grows a little differently from most of the other ferns and it is rhizomatous. When divided and transplanted, the rhizomes should not be completely covered by the soil, but, like flag irises, should be half in and half out, with the root portion anchored and the top part open to the air.

The polypody appears to prefer to stay apart from other ferns and to colonize its particular site. Give it a little area to itself so that its rhizomes can spread without competition. Division of plants can take place at any time of year.

Ornamental grasses

Those who hope to create a wild garden that is also a sanctuary for wildlife should find some space for

RIGHT **1** *The hart's tongue fern,* Phyllitis scolopendrium. **2** *The deer fern,* Blechnum spicant. **3** *The male fern,* Dryopteris filix-mas. **4** *The lady fern,* Athyrium filix-fermina.

I

2

3

4

grasses – as assorted a mixture of species as possible. Apart from the fact that almost all of them are decorative in some way, they offer cover and even nesting places to many creatures. Some species are host plants to both moths and butterflies (see also chapter on wildflower meadows, pages 56-67). One reason why it is helpful to retain some long grass throughout the winter is so that hibernating pupae are safe. Grass seed is highly nutritious and forms an important part of the diet of many birds and some mammals.

Borders of different tall grasses can be full of interest and beauty, but some of the loveliest effects come from those with long, arching stems that rise and lean out from a dense green cover.

One native grass which gives great pleasure for many months in my own garden is the tall, drooping woodland brome, *Bromus ramosus.*

Often to be found growing with it is the slender false or wood brome, *Brachypodium sylvaticum.* However, not all bromus grasses (many of which are meadow grasses) are welcome in gardens or on farmland. Others, mainly natives of the Mediterranean region, have become naturalized in places, such as *Bromus briziformis* which, cultivated, is used dried (and sometimes dyed) in flower arrangements.

The giant fescue, *Festuca gigantea,* is also found growing with bromus. The tall fescue, *F. arundinacea,* is another handsome species with varieties that appear to have become adapted to different types of soils and habitats. This species can reach

LEFT *Green plants are wonderfully restful and, in their way, reassuring. Most are furnished with living leaves at all times of the year, a solace for those who may be townlocked for days, even weeks on end. Varieties of plants such as variegated flag, grasses and ivy, flourish in this little paved yard and mingle with spurges and the handsome* Euphorbia wulfenii.

1.5m/5ft, and those who want to grow it for height should take seed only from really tall specimens.

The wood or reed fescue, *F. altissima,* grows in woods, shady places and on watersides. It has wide, flat leaf blades which distinguish it from other fescue species.

The wood millet *Milium effusum,* an evergreen perennial, can grow to 1.2m/4ft and has ribbon-like leaves up to 30cm/12in long. Gardeners may be more familiar with the variety *M.e.* 'Aureum', known to some as Bowles' golden grass.

Grasses to plant in drifts

On the very edge of a dense beech wood near my home, a misty drift of the wood melick, *Melica uniflora,* covers a steep bank where the light from above shines through the frail, arching stems. When it is not growing high on a wooded bank, it is seen at its prettiest reaching out from a shaded hedgerow or over a stream. It grows well on light or heavy soils. (*M.u.* 'Variegata', striped green and cream, as well as an albino form which has white spikelets, are often grown in gardens.)

For those who favor golden grasses, there is a golden-leaved form of timothy, *Phleum pratense* 'Aureum', also known as golden timothy. It is a good plant for informal positions in sunny or slightly shaded sites.

Presumably an escape from packets of seed fed to both cage and wild birds, the annual canary grass, *Phalaris canariensis,* a native of Mediterranean regions, is often to be found growing wild, mainly on wasteland. Another annual, *P. minor,* a species with a longer flower head, sometimes also appears in the wild. A much more vigorous species is the tall perennial often to be found growing wild near water, the reed canary grass, *P. arundinacea,* with its most handsome purple panicles. It has a variegated variety, *P. a. picta,* known as gardener's garters, which has long been cultivated in gardens

SOME FLOWERING GRASSES
1 Upright brome, *Bromus erectus*
2 Madrid brome, *Bromus madritensis*
3 Reed sweet grass, *Glyceria maxima variegata*
4 Hare's tail, *Lagurus ovatus*
5 Giant fescue, *Festuca gigantea*

1   2   3   4   5

where it grows well in ordinary soil and in sun or shade.

Possibly the most endearing of all grasses are the quaking grasses, of which three species are naturalized in the United States. The lesser or small *Briza minor,* which is a native of the Mediterranean regions and so prefers a sunny situation, is now a common escape from gardens. It can also be grown in a meadow garden. The large quaking grass, *B. maxima,* is a good plant for dry banks. *B. media,* the common quaking or totter grass (to give it but two of its trivial names) is perennial, found on calcareous soils, but will grow in ordinary heavy or light soils and in dry or moist situations. The quivering pendulous shining spikelets are purple. *B. media* has two varieties, one with greener, one with yellower spikelets.

A native species resembling *Briza* is the sea oats, *Uniola paniculata,* found on the sea shore from Virginia to Texas. Where it is hardy, it is a most desirable ornament to the garden, especially in dry, sandy soils. Its showy panicles can be cut and dyed for use in dried arrangements.

Often to be seen in traditional gardens, where it is used as an edging plant or grown in clumps among flowering plants in borders, is the strangely named Yorkshire fog, *Holcus lanatus,* also known as velvet grass.

The lovely *Hierochloe odorata* was used to make baskets by the Indians of North America, where it is called sweet or vanilla grass. Native also to Europe, it was used as a strewing herb placed at church doorways, and thus earned the name holy grass. It is scented like coumarin. The tall manna

6 Tall fescue, *Festuca arundinacea*
7 Quaking grass, *Briza media*
8 Wood mellick, *Melica uniflora*
9 Wood millet, *Milium effusum*
10 Velvet grass, *Holcus lanatus*

6   7   8   9   10

grasses, *Glyceria striata* and *G. grandis,* have graceful panicles and large seeds which attract waterfowl. Both grow on streambanks and in ditches and swampy places.

Sedges and rushes

The rushes and sedges may also play an important useful and decorative part in the wild garden. There are in all nearly one thousand species, most though not all of which prefer wet, acid soils.

The fluffy cotton grasses, *Eriophorum,* members of the Cyperaceae, like the sedges, and not true grasses, are found in peat bogs yet will grow in ordinary soil as well as on the margins of ponds.

Sow the seed where the plants are to grow. *E. angustifolium* is a most beautiful species found throughout North America and Eurasia. Its heads of drooping white flowers from a distance look like enormous snowdrops.

A few of the sedges and rushes are cultivated in gardens. Certainly the best known is Fraser's or flowering sedge, *Carex (Cymophyllus) fraseri,* which grows in mountain woods from Pennsylvania to South Carolina. The conspicuous white anthers and bracts of its flower heads render it among the showiest of all sedges in flower.

In woodland gardens on damp, heavy soils, the pretty wood sedge, *Carex sylvatica,* will bring variety into the field layer. For wet, peaty soils try *C. rostrata,* the beaked or bottle sedge with its yellow-hued fruits.

Some of the genera will grow in dry situations and on limestone soils, for example the commonly found glaucous sedge, *Carex flacca,* the spring sedge, *C. caryophyllea,* and the dwarf sedge, *C. humilis.* These are just a few of those species attractive and interesting enough for the garden.

A group of aquatic or partly aquatic sedges are called club rushes or bulrushes; they are statuesque water plants with bright green stems topped by clusters of chocolate-brown spikelets. Most need expanses of water to do well. Among the few used in traditional gardens is the variety of *Scirpus tabernaemontani* called 'Zebrinus', which has stems

banded green and white. Another is the cosmopolitan *S. cernuus,* an evergreen species just under 30cm/12in high, which is often grown as an edging in greenhouses. It is not hardy in the north.

Three-square or chair-maker's rush, *S. Americanus,* is a widespread species found throughout the US and southern Canada, and it also occurs in Eurasia and South America. Its tall (up to 1.5m/5ft high) triangular culms are extremely decorative but need a great deal of space. The true bulrushes should not be confused with the totally unrelated cat-tails (*Typha*), which often grow with them.

Fine foliage

Most of the exotic foliage plants, such as hostas, ligularias and rodgersias, which are grown in traditional gardens, happen to be Asian endemics. Many plants from other areas, however, are also worth growing for foliage. The cuckoo pints, *Arum italicum* and *A. maculatum,* have leaves which are handsomely sagittate. These are variable plants, some with plain apple-green leaves, others prettily spotted. In one, *A. italicum,* the leaves begin to appear in autumn, others in spring. They linger on into summer growing in thick groups while the young spikes of berries take the place of the arum flowers. They then die down.

The palmate leaves of the early flowering stinking hellebore, *Helleborus foetidus* (it really does not smell very unpleasant) are produced generously as are the thick clusters of green flowers. Together they give the plant a handsome mien. *Helleborus viridis,* the green hellebore, is equally handsome in or out of flower.

The gladdon, *Iris foetidissima,* has long, bold, deep green, spearlike leaves which stay evergreen all winter, a welcome touch. Although the flowers are drab, the plant produces pods of bright orange berries which add considerably to its decorative value in the dark days.

In woods and partial shade, the long leaf-laden stems of Solomon's seal, *Polygonatum multiflorum,* contrast well with shorter neighboring plants, the leaves outliving the flowers, from which sometimes

ABOVE *Cuckoo pint, also called lords and ladies,* Arum maculatum, *is found in woods and hedgerows in Britain. It has a spike of bright orange berries, much loved by birds.*

little black berries are produced. The leaves turn a golden yellow in the fall.

Daphne laureola, the spurge laurel, is an attractive little evergreen characteristic of beechwoods. It bears clusters of green, slightly scented flowers in early spring. The mezereon, *D. mezereum,* is rarely found wild nowadays but is often to be seen in cottage gardens where its scented flowers in early spring bring as much pleasure to the gardener as its red-purple berries bring to the birds.

The spurges or euphorbias are among the loveliest of all plants for the wild garden. The caper spurge, *Euphorbia lathyrus,* with gray-green leaves and stems, which often grows to 1m/3ft, has the presence of a shrub. It is an annual, although sometimes it behaves as a biennial.

All the foregoing can mingle with related native species, such as the native Solomon's seals, *P. commutatum* and *P. biflorum,* Solomon's plume, *Smilacina racemosa,* Jack-in-the-pulpit, and the wild-gingers, *Asarum canadense* and its evergreen relatives *A. shuttleworthii* and *A. virginicum.*

BELOW *Most foliage plants are adaptable to different areas of a wild garden. The lush, exotic hosta or plantain lily, growing here in grass in the moist, humid atmosphere on the fringes of a water garden, will flourish under trees. The graceful Solomon's seal nearby, a woodland plant, will accept the slighter, dappled shade of shrubs instead of an overhead canopy of foliage.*

THE HERB GARDEN

Through the centuries, herbs have been of great service to mankind, not only for cooking but as medicines, dyes, perfumes, salves and potpourris. I would urge those people about to create a wild garden to find space for as many species as possible for, practical uses apart, they are beautiful, fragrant and often irresistible to insect and bird life.

Most of the cultivated herbs belong to either the mint (*Labiatae*) or the parsley (*Umbelliferae*) families and very many of these are indigenous to the Mediterranean region. Thus if one wishes to grow savories, marjorams, thymes and germanders well, one must emulate a Mediterranean landscape of sunlight, rocks and dry summers.

Those herbs that are not Mediterranean endemics are often found naturalized in the US. Most people, for example, have no idea that spearmint, *Mentha spicata,* and peppermint, *M. piperita,* are originally European, for these occur along nearly every brook or in every wet meadow in America. Other naturalized species for the herb garden are the enormous elcampane, *Inula helenium,* with yellow daisy flowers, catnip, *Nepeta cataria,* and common balm, *Melissa officinalis.* Among the umbellifers, naturalized plants are almost as varied. Queen Anne's lace, *Daucus carota,* is now one of the commonest roadside wildflowers in America. The daintier caraway, *Carum carvi,* is less common. Parsnip, fennel, dill, coriander and chervil are often found in cultivated places and in some areas are quite common.

There are of course many aromatic plants belonging to these two families which are native to the US: the pennyroyals, mountain mints (*Pycnanthemum*) and monardas, for example, and the nondo or Canada lovage, *Ligusticum canadense.* One should remember, however, that many poisonous plants occur in the *Umbelliferae,* most notably the hemlock.

One of the most attractive of native shrubs are the myricas, the fruits of which are among the most important foods for late-migrating tree swallows and myrtle warblers, and the leathery, aromatic leaves can be used in soups and casseroles.

It is not the purpose of this book to deal in depth with food from a wild herb garden, but there are times when a too generous crop of some plant or other might smother a species more cherished. If it is edible, then it is better eaten than thrown away!

Where to grow herbs in a wild garden

Traditionally, herbs are grown for convenience either in rows in the kitchen garden or in a herb plot or border near the house, a number of different species generally occupying the same plot. The gardener then tries to develop one type of soil to suit them all, although there is no horticultural reason for this measure. Growing wild, herbs will be found on many types of soil, and in sun or shade (whether dry or moist), or along the waterside. This means that most can happily be introduced into the less rigorous confines of the wild garden, and grow happily among other plants.

LEFT *A beautiful poppy with handsome glaucous leaves,* Papaver somniferum *has been described as 'a weed of cultivation'. An alien, it was probably first introduced in grain seed. The large, pot-shaped seed vessels contain thousands of black, oily seeds, provenance for wildlife.*

RIGHT *A display of sweet-scented herb leaves in a great variety of hue and texture. Many herb species – fennel, mint and marjoram, for instance – which are naturally green, produce golden, variegated, purple or bronze-leaved varieties. Most die down in winter but their seeding stems, a source of food for many creatures, should be left uncut until spring.*

In my own garden I have compromised, and have a long bank, on the site of an old hedge, which is entirely given up to herbs. The bank has been raised artificially, so that now, being much higher than the ground on either side and closely planted, it acts as a screen for the kitchen garden.

The bank itself offers several different habitats. It runs east to west, with one side in full sun, the other in full shade, and varying degrees of shelter and shade for species which occupy positions in between. Along its 20m/66ft length, the really dominant and would-be invasive species such as apple mint, tansy and soapwort have room to struggle among themselves for ascendancy, their contrasting foliage merging in a delightful harmony of woolly, shiny or lacy green. Between them and elsewhere, fennel, blue-flowered alkanet, marjoram, lemon balm and purslane increase in size and seed freely.

Among the umbellifers, a favorite is sweet cicely, *Myrrhis odorata,* a graceful and lovely plant for the wild garden, which tolerates most types of soil. The white umbels bloom in spring, followed by long seeds which can be eaten in salads when fresh, as can both leaves and roots.

The two burnets used as herbs grow side by side on the shaded slope of the bank. Salad or lesser burnet, *Poterium sanguisorba,* grows in dry, calcareous fields and has cucumber-flavored leaves. Great burnet, *Sanguisorba officinalis,* usually grows in damper fields and will grow on heavy clay.

Excellent for clothing a bank and for holding the soil secure is tansy, *Tanacetum vulgare,* which grows naturally on river banks, roadsides and in hedgerows. It has distinctive, fernlike foliage. The creeping rootstock enables it to cover ground quickly and effectively, so it may need restraining.

Various thymes have been planted at the foot of the bank, the carpeting species in sanded or shingled spaces between pavement stones on the sunny side, where trampling does not harm them.

Mediterranean sages, rosemary, hyssop and lavender keep firmly to their original planting sites, growing in girth as the years pass.

Certain annuals are left to fend for themselves: the gray-leaved poppy, *Papaver somniferum,* the seeds of which are eaten by humans and mice alike, and pot marigold, borage, feverfew and chervil.

The prostrate mint, pennyroyal, *Mentha pulegium,* is a perfect plant to cover ground or damp pavement where there is also sand, and those who have ditches, damp or marshy ground should find space for the water mint, *Mentha aquatica,* a handsome plant with a delightful, characteristic scent, which is why it was once popular as a strewing herb. As it was harvested, so it was kept under control, for it can be invasive like most other mints.

The cultivated angelica, *Angelica archangelica,* from central Europe, is cultivated for its edible leaf stalks. In a wild garden it does best in shade in deep, moist loam, and it is a fine plant to grow near a pond. The British species, *A. sylvestris,* is also a handsome plant for a moist spot, but should not be eaten.

Alexanders, *Smyrnium olusatrum,* can be eaten, its thick stems peeled and cooked and eaten like asparagus. It used to be cultivated as a salad before the introduction of celery.

LEFT *For those who wish to gather herbs frequently, a path is essential, but it need not be conspicuous. A straight-sided path can be softened by yet more herbs growing at its edges and between the pavements. Thyme flowers bloom for weeks on end, but even after they have faded they leave dense mats of little, tough, pungently scented leaves which bear the pressure of treading.*

ABOVE *Once an esteemed culinary and medicinal herb, tansy,* Tanacetum vulgare, *is often to be found growing luxuriantly on river banks. The fernlike leaves have a spicy, pungent scent.*

Rocky coasts in both Europe and North America are the home of Scotch lovage or sea parsley, *Ligusticum scoticum,* which gives a celerylike taste to soups. It grows in ordinary soil and, in my own experience, best where there is some humidity and where the roots can be kept fairly moist in dry weather.

The garden heliotrope, *Valeriana officinalis,* is a graceful plant with flowers ranging from white to deep rose, and is happy in damp woods, ditches and all moist alkaline or slightly acid ground.

The calamints, as their generic *Calamintha* ('beautiful mint') implies, are beautiful, with their scented leaves and little flowers, and generally are found on dry, grassy banks, especially on limestone soils. The lesser calamint, *Calamintha nepeta,* has

THE HERB BANK
Most cultivated and sweet herbs are English plants which for centuries have been grown alongside more treasured exotics. In a wild garden they look well grown on a bank, which can also form a lively and interesting boundary between one area and another, as well as providing a sunny and a more shaded site, sharply drained soil at the top and moister soil at ground level. The nectar-rich flowers of the herbs and later their seeds appeal to a variety of insects, birds and small mammals; butterflies, moths and bees are all frequent visitors. Unexpectedly perhaps, bees collect nectar also from the globular blooms of chives and rocambole.

1 Curry plant, *Helichrysum angustifolium*
2 Thymes, *Thymus* sp.
3 Good King Henry, *Chenopodium bonus-henricus*
4 Everlasting onions, *Allium perutile*
5 Welsh onion, *Allium fistulosum*
6 Clary sage, *Salvia sclarea*
7 Chives, *Allium schoenoprasum*
8 Red sage, *Salvia officinalis* 'Purpurascens'
9 Egyptian onion, *Allium cepa* 'Proliferum'
10 Lavender, *Lavandula* sp.
11 Wormwood, *Artemisia absinthium*
12 Angelica, *Angelica archangelica*
13 Fennel, *Foeniculum vulgare*
14 Rocambole, *Allium scordoprasum*

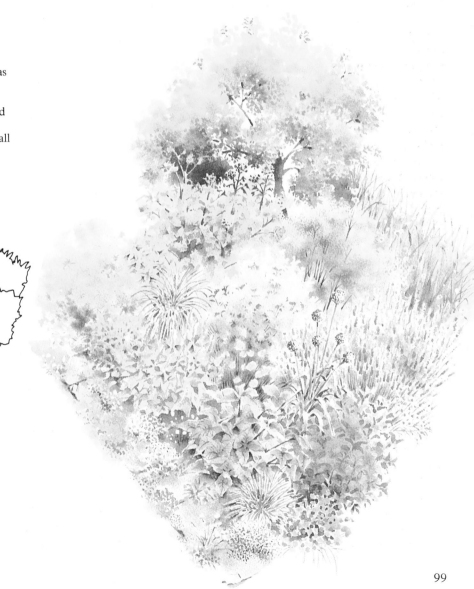

paler flowers on stalks. Said to be rare in Britain, it appeared from nowhere in my gravel drive. For a tall herb, grow the lovely wood calamint, *C. sylvatica,* with its large, lavender-colored flowers blotched with purple.

Another tall, handsome herb is mugwort, *Artemisia vulgaris,* seen growing luxuriantly on roadsides and wastelands. It has narrow leaves, green above and white-green below. The name comes from 'midge-plant', for it was once believed that it would keep away these irritating insects. Its relative, wormwood, *A. absinthium,* was widely used to repel fleas, being strewn upon the floor or dried and bagged and placed among clothes. A beautiful plant, more aromatic and bitter than mugwort, it also grows on wasteground, especially by the sea. Whiter and woollier than the others is the aromatic *A. maritima.*

Herbs for bees, butterflies and birds

Always find room for those herbs which are particularly attractive to wildlife. Your garden will be alive with bees and butterflies and, later in the year, birds greedy for the seeds.

All thymes will attract bees. The common wild thyme, *Thymus drucei,* native to Britain and Europe, which is found growing through the short grass on dry banks and heaths, is sometimes called mother of thyme. The larger wild thyme, *T. pulegioides,* which has larger leaves and creeping stems, can be distinguished by the extra whorls of little flowers below the main head. It grows wild on calcareous soils, and has produced a great number of variants. No thymes are native to the new world, but creeping thyme, *Thymus serphyllum,* is naturalized in old fields and barrens in North America.

Another interesting European bee plant is white horehound, *Marrubium vulgare.* Silvery and woolly, it grows best on poor soils. Even more popular, however, is the misty-leaved, bright blue-flowered borage, *Borago officinalis,* which makes really excellent honey. Found growing wild, it is a garden escape and, though ideal for a dry bank or other dry spot, it can be choosy.

LEFT *Wild angelica,* Angelica sylvestris, *is a native of Europe and is naturalized in the United States. Its close American relative is* A. venenosa. *Cultivated angelica,* A. archangelica, *has larger round umbels and cut, fernlike leaves. For centuries it has been and still is used in confectionery and medicine. All angelicas are handsome enough to be grown in any garden, wild or cultivated.*

BELOW *Naturalized in waste places, river banks and road-sides, comfrey,* Symphytum officinale, *with white, purple or rose-colored flowers, has long been a valued medicinal herb and was once used as a wound dressing. It is still used in cookery: the leaves, dipped in batter, fried and sugared, are delicious! The species has produced several varieties, all of which appear to be attractive to bees.*

A beekeeping acquaintance always grows common balm, *Melissa officinalis,* near her hives, a beekeeper's tradition since it is believed that bees find their way home by its smell. This herb makes up for its lack of beauty by its refreshing lemon scent and the delight the bees take in it. The bee balms, Oswego teas and horsemints, *Monarda,* are native to North America. Horsemint, *M. punctata,* is excellent for dry soil in sun. Its small cream colored flowers are subtended by showy white or lavender bracts. Showiest of all is the bee balm or Oswego tea, *M. didyma,* which has scarlet flowers that attract hummingbirds. It needs moisture-retentive soil and partial shade.

The mints flower in late summer, bringing a soft, lavender haze and attracting a great variety of insects. Many have been in cultivation for centuries and there should be a species to suit everyone.

The round-leaved mint, *Mentha rotundifolia,* is one of the best flavoring mints and appears to grow anywhere. Its leaves are indeed almost round, and gray and downy on the undersides. The lovely variegated form has a slightly different, very sweet fragrance, with leaves marked in white and pale cream, sometimes with the palest magenta tips.

The land at the end of my garden was once a wheatfield, and while cornmint, *Mentha arvensis,* a strongly fragrant weed, has largely vanished from the countryside, it does still grow here.

A favorite of butterflies is marjoram, *Origanum vulgare,* which grows happily in a sunny hedgebank and seeds itself freely in calcareous soil. The flowers will vary considerably in color, ranging from green white to a deep purple. The gold-leaved form 'Aureum' is as bright as any flower.

Chives, *Allium schoenoprasum,* are native to north central Asia like so many species in this genus. Their pretty purple flowers attract all sorts of insects. Among the relatively few American alliums are *A. canadense,* which has pale lavender flowers similar to those of chives, and the beautiful nodding onion, *A. cernuum,* the flowers of which vary from purple to pink to white. These species all need some sun. A woodland onion is *A. tricoccum.*

Fennel, *Foeniculum vulgare,* one of the food plants of the beautiful black swallowtail butterfly, is often to be found naturalized on wasteland, roadsides or sea cliffs, in the sun. A native of southern Europe, there are green and bronze-leaved forms which, grown together, can make a handsome group, often reaching 1.8m/6ft in height.

Many herbs proffer large quantities of seed, so do not hurry to tidy plants, cutting them down once they have flowered. With the exotic lavender and marjoram growing near the house or in the butterfly border, you will be able to enjoy the antics of gold-finches, house finches and chickadees as they walk the stalks to collect the oil-rich seeds. Such species as fennel, sweet cicely, parsley and chervil will be visited time and time again during the lean months until only the skeleton ribs of the umbels remain silhouetted against the winter sky.

ABOVE AND TOP *The bright-yellow composite flower of* Hieracium *and the orange of pot marigold – the first a wild-flower, the second a garden-flower – prettily and naturally complement the vivid blue of the herb borage. Like its close relative comfrey, borage is a bee plant.*

WATER GARDENS

One of the most engaging areas in my own garden is around a tiny, fiberglass pond, installed in the days when I was seeking to show the readers of a women's magazine how quick and easy it could be to make a water garden. Since its introduction, my husband and I have spent many hours on a seat beside it. We watch the newts, some of them beautifully crested, identify the occasional visiting dragon or damsel fly, note that both wasps and bees stand on lily pads to drink; we introduced tadpoles, later to be met as tiny frogs as we worked in the borders. We admire the floating water lilies and the marsh marigolds and savor the musky scent of meadow sweet. From the house we often see magpies and crows waddling in or hopping away, shaking their wet feathers, hurrying to a place in the sun to dry. Our next project is to make a larger pond, for a greater number of native plants.

A pond can be designed so that it offers suitable areas for special plants, deep in places for some, shallow at the edges for others. It can be made to spill over to provide a habitat for marsh plants. It can be fringed with a great variety of plants, with a flower for most seasons, or it can be simply surrounded with grass and a little shore to step on.

Pond plant life is at its best where there is open light for at least eight hours a day. Some plants, water lilies for instance, should grow in full sun if they are to flower well. Pond creatures that prefer shade will take cover under the lilies' leaves. Floating leaves help to prevent the excessive growth of algae by cutting off much of the light supply to the lower depths of the water, thus creating an essential balance of light and shade.

Although a natural woodland pool may have great charm, it is best to make a pond well away from overhanging trees because shade and fallen leaves combine to produce stagnant water. An accumulation of leaves at the bottom of a pool will result in gases being given off that have a deleterious effect on fish and other wildlife.

Pond preparation

Begin making a pond (see page 127) in early spring to give time for it to be filled and for the water to become weathered and warm and plant-furnished before pondlife becomes seasonally active. Get the waterplants in place before introducing fish, so that the latter need not be unduly disturbed.

For a small pond, it is recommended that plants be grown in containers. The plants can then easily be lifted out, thinned and replanted. These containers can be wickerwork baskets, or crates made from 2.5cm/1in square slats of wood or from specially manufactured mesh plastic. Alternatively, four bricks can be stood on the pond bottom to form a shallow box and the cavity filled with soil. Heavy soil is required, the best mixture being half well-rotted cow manure and half soil. For poor soils, in place of the manure use a slow acting organic fertilizer, such as bonemeal, in the proportion of a tablespoon to a two-gallon bucket of soil. Pack the enriched soil into the lower half of the plant holder and place the ordinary soil on top.

Rather than fill slatted or perforated plastic crates directly with loose soil, line them with turves. These are grass squares on which the grass has been allowed to rot, but not so much that the turves disintegrate. Plant and gently lower the filled crates into the water.

Oxygenating plants

Vital to the life of a pond, oxygenating plants very quickly and efficiently replace lost and consumed oxygen in the water. Few could be called decorative. One of the most common is the Canadian pondweed, *Elodea canadensis*, which has blunt olive-green leaves that become tightly wrapped up during the winter months. *Elodea* can be invasive and is therefore best planted in a container and sunk into the water.

The water starworts, *Callitriche*, are useful tenants for a pond for, apart from being excellent

ABOVE *Native to most of the northern hemisphere, the water plantain,* Alisma plantago-aquatica, *growing wild beside ponds and ditches, was once highly valued as an antidote to rattlesnake bite.*

RIGHT *A water garden soon becomes an ideal environment for many little creatures, for where plants luxuriate there are secure hiding and breeding places. Some haunt the marginal plants, others stay close under floating leaves or in the safe mesh of waterweeds. When they leave the water as unlovely larvae, about to change into dragonflies and damselflies, they scale tall stems and hang there, jewel-like, until they are ready to take to the wing.*

oxygenators, their lush, interwoven growth holds many kinds of spawn safely and the young leaves are nibbled by fish.

There are also the tiny-flowered water milfoils, *Myriophyllum,* including the whorled and the spiked water milfoil. The alternate-flowered water milfoil, *Myriophyllum alterniflorum,* is found in lakes, slow streams and peaty water. One of the prettiest, a native and for long a favored water garden plant is the water violet, *Hottonia palustris,* which makes a deep mat of submerged stems and foliage, but holds its lilac, yellow-eyed flowers in whorls some 25cm/10in above the surface of the water. One of my own favorites, although it can be invasive, is the water crowfoot or water buttercup, *Ranunculus aquatilis,* with flowers like a white celandine. This species is very variable.

Water weeds also help provide cover for young fish, which frequently are consumed by their elders, and for tadpoles, which suffer from several different predators.

Where the pond has a mud bottom, oxygenators are simply planted by tying a cutting of a plant to a smooth stone or pebble and lowering it into the water at the deepest part of the pond. Add one cutting approximately to each 30 sq. cm/12 sq. in of water surface. Or, plant the cutting in a container.

Some species are extremely rampant. They grow fast and need to be kept under control. This is best done by drawing a rake through the mass of stems, a few inches below the surface of the water and then tugging out as much as possible from the base of the plants.

Sometimes, on the other hand, an oxygenator does not thrive. It is not possible to say why. Obviously so much depends on local conditions as well as the size and content of the pond. For this reason it is usual, initially, to introduce at least four or five different species.

Deep water aquatic plants

When water lilies are to be grown, they should be planted in containers standing on bricks or cinder blocks with at least 15cm/6in of water above the

rim of their containers. As the leaves begin to unfurl, the blocks should be removed at intervals so that the leaves float on the water's surface. Mature plants require a water depth of 30-45cm/ 12-18in above the rim. The white water lily, *Nymphaea odorata,* needs to grow in plenty of sunshine for the flowers to develop fully. The yellow water lily or brandy bottle, *Nuphar luteum,* and the smaller yellow-flowered *Nuphar pulimum* will tolerate some shade. Though unrelated to them, the charming fringed water lily, *Nymphoides peltata,* resembles a miniature yellow water lily. It is seen in pools and ditches throughout most of the US and tends to root well down into the mud.

ABOVE *A small garden or a part of a garden devoted to water will prove, after the initial effort, to be both labor saving and constantly full of interest. In addition to the handsome foliage of most aquatic plants, flower color can be vivid and continuous, beginning in spring with, for instance, marsh marigolds, then following in summer with flowering rush, water plantain, forget-me-nots and yellow loosestrife, and on to purple lythrum and russet seedheads in autumn.*

Some other, less showy floating-leaved rooted plants include the broad-leaved pondweed, *Potamogeton natans*, and the bur-reeds, *Sparganium* sp. Both plants appreciate a soft rich pond bottom.

The arrowhead, *Sagittaria latifolia,* is a common plant found in slow-flowing rivers. It actually sends up a series of three types of leaves: long, light green grass blades, followed by oval ones that lie flat on the surface, and later in the summer, arrow-shaped and emergent ones. This interesting plant appreciates clean water and appears to thrive with regular cutting back. Its leaves die down quickly after frost.

Those who have a large pond or slow stream may already be familiar with the vigorous reed sweet grass, *Glyceria maxima*, with tall stems bearing long branching panicles of spikelets. This particular species grows in deeper water than the other glyceria, as deep as 75cm/30in. Its roots will help prevent banks eroding at the waterside. A variegated form is also sometimes seen growing at garden pool sides.

Waterside or marginal plants

In gardening terms, aquatic, waterside or marginal as applied to water plants covers a range of species which in nature are found in quite different habitats. (The botanists' term is 'emergent' plants.) While some grow right down at the water's edge or even in the water itself, many others grow well above the water level, even high on top of the river bank. But even in this instance the plants benefit from the proximity of the water – the roots are constantly in contact with the moist soil, kept in this state by capillary action, and the plants also benefit from the high humidity.

In the garden, marginal plants can be slotted into different positions around your pond. Plant them either directly into the soil or in turves placed on specially installed shelves, or in containers placed on the shelves on the pond bottom and raised if necessary to provide just the right shallow depth of water. Bricks, upturned crates or flower pots will do for this purpose. Cover any sharp edges to

prevent any possible perforation of the pond lining.

For a pond edge, the water forget-me-not, *Myosotis scorpioides* (sometimes called *M. palustris*), about 30cm/12in tall, has the brightest of blue flowers from spring to autumn. Given the opportunity, the plant will also paddle in the pond. Try it also in a marsh garden. Again true blue are two veronicas, the water speedwell, *Veronica anagallis, aquatica,* a tall plant flowering through the summer, and the brooklime, *V. beccabunga*, not quite so tall. These two will grow also in marshy conditions. Flowering in midsummer is the yellow-flowered seedbox, *Ludwigia alternifolia*.

Sedges, tall and statuesque, and rushlike plants

ABOVE LEFT, RIGHT, *and* TOP
Most flowering waterside plants are free-flowering. The buttercup family (above right) is perhaps the brightest among the wild species. There are also several beautiful natives, mainly members of the balsam family, such as Impatiens capensis, *the orange balsam (above left). Another quite widespread species is the monkey flower,* Mimulus guttatus, *escaped from gardens (top). It can be seen growing wild by, even in, some rivers and canals, ditches and marshes.*

with their attractive, irregular umbels of mahogany in late summer add an exotic touch to any water garden.

The scarlet cardinal flower, *Lobelia cardinalis*, which is found in wet meadows and marshy places, has long been accepted by gardeners as a suitable plant for the edges of a wild pond. Sometimes known as marsh trefoil is the bogbean, *Menyanthes trifoliata*. Its leaves are rather like those of the broad bean plant which, like its pretty flowers, it holds well above the water. It grows well in soil at the very edge of a pond, flowering from late spring to midsummer.

One of the most attractive marginal plants in my own tiny pond is the great water plantain, *Alisma plantago-aquatica*, which will only flower well if the water is shallow. The loosely branching stems of

ABOVE *and* LEFT *Lush water-side grass offers a perfect environment for meadow flowers, and if it has not been heavily weeded or constantly mown, or in an area newly turved with meadow grass, you can expect to find a good range of native plants. In time, some species may appear as if by magic. Depending upon the nature of the soil, you may find wild orchids of some species or another – ladies dresses or one of the many fringed orchises. It is unwise ever to attempt to lift and transplant these parti-cular plants. They resent disturbance and may die.*

A WATER GARDEN

A water garden is a wonderful place to linger by. Here, a little jetty and stepping stones enable one almost to stand in the water, as it were, all the better to peer into its depths. There is one important point to note. The stones, whatever they are made of (here, brick pillars capped with wood) should only be used on a cement base. Where the pond lining is of some form of plastic, the base of the stones and the pressure on them would in time damage the lining and cause the pond to leak. But, whatever its construction, the pond can be fringed with many lovely plants. In the water, some are completely submerged, producing essential oxygen. Others, like the water lilies, grow long stems so that leaves and flowers can float on the surface in the sun. Some paddle their roots in the water, while others sit happily at the edge.

1 Water lily, *Nymphaea alba*
2 Arrowhead, *Sagittaria sagittifolia*
3 Sweet galingale, *Cyperus longus*
4 Great spearwort, *Ranunculus lingua*
5 Meadowsweet, *Filipendula ulmaria*
6 Flowering rush, *Butomus umbellatus*
7 Monkey flower, *Mimulus guttata*
8 Bogbean, *Menyanthes trifoliata*
9 Hemp agrimony, *Eupatorium cannabinum*
10 Crested woodfern, *Dryopteris cristata*
11 Royal fern, *Osmunda regalis*
12 *Hosta fortunei*
13 Marsh marigold, *Caltha Palustris*
14 Yellow flag, *Iris pseudacorus*
15 Western skunk cabbage, *Lysichitum americanum*
16 Ragged robin, *Lychnis flos-cuculi*
17 Purple loosestrife, *Lythrum salicaria*
18 Brooklime, *Veronica beccabunga*

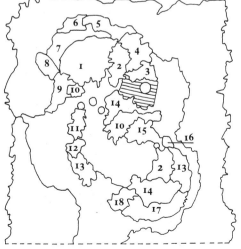

little rosy flowers grow up to 1m/3ft tall. A smaller, less common species is *A. lanceolatum*.

Another plant that is well worth growing since it has been described as one of the handsomest aquatic plants in cultivation is the sky-blue pickerel weed, *Pontaderia cordata*. It has lovely large, glossy green leaves and flowers through summer into autumn. It grows best in water 15-30cm/6-12in deep. It is so accommodating that it can be propagated by division at almost any season, a point to bear in mind when visiting a friend whose pond is generously furnished with this plant.

Marsh gardens

An artificial marsh area is made by much the same method as a natural one, which is to allow water to overspill constantly at some point. Only very little water is needed to keep such an area moist without it becoming waterlogged. Natural marsh areas are, in fact, well drained and aerated. Use trickle irrigation, and experiment until you think that the volume is sufficient. Too little water can result in drought, and the death of water-loving plants, and too much can lead to an overfull pond and the drowning of the same plants.

I had a neighbor who kept an entire water and marsh garden moist simply by putting a hose on an outside tap that had a faulty washer, which allowed a permanent drip. She planted the wet area with many kinds of water-loving exotics, dominant among which were the garden varieties of mimulus or musk. Species of this plant have become naturalized in Britain. Recently, in summer time, I saw a great drift of yellow *Mimulus guttatus*, the monkey flower from western North America, in marshy grass, following a little stream which saturated an area in a steep field.

The floral color in a marsh can be extended over many months. One of the earliest of our native water flowers to bloom, the marsh marigold, is followed a little later by the stately blue flag iris and its European counterpart with its bright yellow flowers. The cuckoo flower will grow well among these plants.

Many aquatics recommended for other sites will grow well in marshy ground. For instance, the purple loosestrife, with its tall spikes of purple flowers and the not quite so tall yellow loosestrife (which sometimes reminds me of an upright creeping jenny), which could grow at marsh edges. Meadowsweet will scent the air. From summer to autumn the great spearwort, an outsize buttercup some 1m/3ft tall, can contrast with one of the most beautiful of our wildflowers, the flowering rush, *Butomus umbellatus*, which blooms through most of the summer.

ABOVE *The graceful scirpus is the true bulrush, a term often used mistakenly for the handsome cat-tail, a much larger and more invasive plant suitable only for large ponds. There are many native species of* Scirpus, *most known more familiarly as club rushes, a reference to the shape of their inflorescences. They are easily grown, but in small ponds they need to be divided from time to time to restrain them.*

If the pond is made in a grassed area, the plants can be encouraged to merge into this in a natural manner. Grass does help to create a cool area around them, promoting essential humidity. It also provides safe cover for frogs and other little creatures which inhabit the pond area.

Some plants will gradually move into the grass as they seed, cuckoo flowers, marsh marigold, meadow rue, fleabane and meadowsweet for instance. Others such as fritillary and summer snowflake, bulbs of which can be bought, can be introduced further away from the pond.

Because marsh and many other water plants grow both damply and thickly, they offer good, shelter for a great many different invertebrates adapted to the lush amphibious conditions. For example, there are interesting marsh grasshoppers and spiders. Frogs and newts will breed in the pond, but outside the breeding season can be found hunting for insects in the marshy area. Grass snakes are attracted to marshy areas mainly for frogs, but of course the tangle of vegetation also houses mice and other prey, such as shrews and short-tailed voles.

ABOVE *The aquatic* Iris pseudocorus, *the* fleur de lys *of legend, one of the loveliest of our spring flowers, grows in wet fields and on marshy land as well as at the margins of rivers and ponds. It is known as the yellow flag ('flagge' is the Middle English for sword, an allusion to the plant's leaf shape) to distinguish it from the sweet flag,* Acorus calamus, *which is not an iris but a member of the arum family.*

Bog gardens

A true bog is carpeted with bogmoss or sphagnum. It supports a special community of plants, some of which, because the static natural bog water is acid, are of the heath family. These, and other plants growing there as they decayed and decomposed over the centuries, helped to form the peat layer on which the bog lies. Bog plants include the insectivorous sundews, cranberry, chamaedaphne, bog asphodel, marsh andromeda, orchid and the Labrador tea. There are also grasses, sedges and ferns which have become specially adapted.

In the early days of wild gardens where money was no object and the achievement of a 'natural' feature in a garden a case for pride, a great deal of effort was put into making a bog, often in association with a rock garden, so that rare and beautiful plants could be grown. The modern gardener is usually less ambitious, mixing bog, marsh and marginal water plants together to create an attractive wetland area.

A pond can be made to overflow, or alternatively made in much the same way as a pond but providing means for the water to soak gradually away so that the area is drained. An example would be an excavation some 45cm/15in deep, lined, the plastic being perforated here and there to allow the water to escape. A layer of drainage material, shingle, pebbles or stone, some 8cm/3in deep should lie on the base. The soils should be well mixed with peat. Success will then depend upon never allowing the soil to dry out, yet also never allowing it to become waterlogged.

Many of the so-called bog plants on sale are exotics and in my own view most of them look very out of place in a wild setting, but this is a matter for the gardener. There is a wide choice.

Of our native bog plants, many have been grown in gardens, the grass of Parnassus for instance, the bog asphodel, *Narthecium americanum,* recommended as 'suitable for naturalizing in boggy places' and the marsh helleborine, *Epipactis patustris.* Large-leaved plants suitable mainly for large gardens are Virginia chain fern, *Woodwardia virginica,* Cinnamon fern, *Osmundia cinnamomea,* and the lovely royal fern, *Osmunda regalis,* for contrast, as well as some of the smallest and most endearing of flowers, the little butterworts, sometimes because of their shape and color known as water violets. Surprisingly perhaps, these are insectivorous plants.

A wildlife oasis

A healthy pond should be able to support a great many creatures. Whether these should include fish to keep down the numbers of annoying insects such as mosquitoes, midges and gnats is a matter of

BELOW *One delightful way to establish a boundary, as well as to prepare one for a change from one part of the garden to another : a little canal separates the paved area near the house from the main garden. On its banks, on both sides, aquatic emergent or marginal plants, marsh marigold and mimulus among them, mingle with meadow oxeye daisies and globe flowers, which enjoy the cool of the lush grass.*

ABOVE *Once common growing in watery bogs, the beautiful bogbean,* Menyanthes trifoliata, *a member of the gentian family, takes its common name from its leaves' likeness to the vegetable plant.*

LEFT *If you are fortunate enough to have a small stream, its sides can be planted with pond-side plants and other water lovers. In this rather sophisticated version of a wild garden, exotic primulas have been planted among ferns.*

choice, for it is possible that these might perform their role just too effectively and eliminate other creatures we would like to see there. Although fish will prey on tadpoles, for instance, I have seen a goldfish attacked by the large dragonfly nymph. One way to ensure that as mixed a community as possible exists, is to see that there are shallow, weed-covered areas into which the smaller creatures can escape and hide. But bear in mind that in natural ponds all types do exist together.

Stocking a pond is a matter of trial and error. In my own pond, successive introductions of goldfish (aliens, incidentally) were lost to various unseen predators, and so now I just accept what nature sends – which I find exciting enough. However, for those who want to see fish in their pond, sun fish and bluegills are an excellent choice. Mill roach are also a possibility and suckers will help to keep the water clear by cleaning the debris off the pond bottom; some of the other creatures,

ABOVE *Enjoying acid, boggy conditions, the royal fern,* Osmunda regalis, *furnishes a waterside for most of the year. Above its green pinnate fronds, it produces panicles of furry, fertile pinnules. In autumn and winter these, with the dying fronds, become a beautiful warm russet. The fern is almost cosmopolitan in distribution.*

such as water snails, will also perform this task. But before deciding which fish to stock, seek advice from local fish experts who will know which species are most likely to be ecologically at home.

Once there are fish in the pond, you can expect occasionally to be visited by their predators, perhaps a heron. Take precautions depending on circumstances. For example, if birds do become too much of a nuisance, secure a fine nylon string around the pond's edges, just a few inches off the ground, which will prevent them from wading in.

Let the insect population in the pond build up for a month or two before installing fish so that there is food waiting for them. As a rough guide to stocking the pond, allow one fish to every square meter of water surface.

If it is hoped to attract frogs and toads to the pond to breed, and especially if the pond has been stocked with the spawn of either of these creatures, make sure that it is possible for the young to leave the water. It is easy enough for the adults to jump in or out but not so easy for the tiny creatures to get out if the edge of the pond lies several inches above the water. One method is to have a landing stone or stones lying just under the water in one place or at several points according to the size of the pond. This is best situated where there also exists some cover, between two marginal plants for instance.

It is fascinating to learn how well so many creatures are hidden and protected by the water plants. Sitting immobile, a frog is hardly visible in the shadow under leaves which reach out over the pond edge, while in the depths of the water it is often not until you lower a hand and stir the weeds that you can detect the life which abounds there.

RIGHT *One of the advantages of having water in your garden is the interesting wildlife it attracts, such as this beautiful damselfly. Both dragonflies and damselflies require water to breed. Their aquatic larva, known as a nymph, is extremely voracious and will feed on tadpoles as well as on small fishes.*

ABOVE *A 'jungle' in a town garden where water and water-loving plants dominate the scene. Such a place becomes an oasis for wildlife, both local and visiting. The paths leading to the water and the safe wooden slats that bridge it, mean that there are many vantage points to stand and quietly become a part of the scene. In late summer, purple valerian, loosestrife, tansy and rushes provide pleasing color.*

ROCK GARDENS

The natural effect of a wild rock garden can only be created with time and care, and it is not just a matter of introducing wild plants in between a random arrangement of rocks and stones. The natural features of a mountain landscape can be followed on a smaller scale, creating a series of ledges, overhangs and scree slopes. Alternatively, or incorporated into this design, one can have, on the level, a rock strewn area interspersed with shrubs, say junipers of different species. A stone pavement can add to the variety of rock garden planting with a whole range of different rock plants sprouting from between the crevices. For example, careful placement and alignment of the rocks is essential, which means that fissures and cracks should run in the same direction. Of the many crevice plants, species such as hens and chickens, *Sempervivum tectorum,* Kenilworth ivy, *Cymbalaria muralis,* and various sedums are useful plants to link the pieces of stone together.

Professional rock garden architects usually make the top of the rock garden flat, like a plateau, where dwarf shrubs such as tiny willows can be planted. Below this, according to the way the other stones are placed, there should be a series of plateaux, some in full sun, some in partial shade, some in full shade, depending upon their aspect and the shadow cast by the rock and stone.

At the lowest level the rock can continue outward, perhaps joining gravel, pavement, grass or a path. Most rock plants will grow equally well on the flat, but here especially is a place for true sun lovers, for instance, thymes and rock roses such as the hoary rock rose, *Helianthemum canum,* or the semispreading common rock rose, *H. nummularium* which has many attractive garden varieties.

There are many examples of wild groupings that can be copied at home. For example, often on a hillside on a rock outcrop growing in shallow soil, you can find sparse rabbit-grazed turf with rock roses and pussy-toes. This effect can be repeated in the garden with or without the grass and the rabbits. Another effective and easy cover is to plant some prostrate shrub, a juniper perhaps, so that it caps the rock, furnishing it softly. You can also create a rocky outcrop some distance away from the main rockery, and allow grass to grow almost to its base, and plant by it a prettily-shaped tree such as the dwarf birch, *Betula pumila.*

Where a rock garden already exists, sometimes all that is necessary to create a more natural blending is to alter some of the plants, replacing the hackneyed kinds such as aubretia and yellow alyssum with less flamboyant but still colorful wildflowers such as harebell or wild pink.

Scree

Those gardeners who are striving for a really natural effect might consider making a scree which slopes gently down from the higher levels of the rock garden, spreading out as the slope lessens at the bottom. This can be made of two parts rock chippings to one part loam and one part peat or leafmold, should be 30cm/12in deep and should

ABOVE *The rock rose,* Helianthemum nummularium, *often found on limestone formations in the wild, is the source of many gorgeous garden varieties. As its generic name implies, it is a sun lover.*

LEFT *Well-drained rock offers a home for many kinds of plants. Plateaux, crevices and clifflike areas of the rock face provide a favorite habitat for a diverse number of species. Most like a good, open, light soil and sunshine but some prefer a rock's shadow or the shady or partially shady site of the rock. Some will seed or can be grown in a gravel or screelike surface at ground level.*

RIGHT *The rocky slopes at the side of a steep, stepped path and its summit are overlain with acid soil in which some of the less familiar wild plants can be grown.*

A WILD ROCK GARDEN

So many gardeners enthuse about rock gardens. Specialist nurseries have made it possible for them to collect beautiful species whose natural habitats are in faraway places on mountain sides and among rocky terrains. But some of the lovely native plants have always been given a place among the exotics. It is possible to make a rock garden which holds indigenous plants only, even creating a conservation area of rare rock plants. Some species that are rare in the wild will grow with exuberance where the ground suits them – the rock-loving bitter root, for example.

The rock garden here creates a harmony of rock and stony or gravelly areas, and such plants. There is a dry scree 'stream' bed, bridged at one end below a scree 'pool', and opening out into a larger 'scree' pool at the other. (For those gardeners who would actually prefer to see water here, this could be made into an artificial water course with a pond – the plants would have to be modified to suit.) At the top of the garden is a gravel area – which could be sanded instead.

1 *Thymus* sp., maiden pinks, *Dianthus deltoides,* thrift, *Armeria maritima*
2 European golden elder, *Sambucus nigra* 'Aurea'
3 Shrubby cinquefoil, *Potentilla fructicosa*
4 London pride, *Saxifraga* × *urbicum*
5 Mezereon, *Daphne mezereum*
6 Burnet rose, *Rosa pimpinellifolia*
7 Rock cotoneaster, *Cotoneaster horizontalis*
8 English holly, *Ilex aquifolium*
9 *Erica* sp.
10 *Juniperus horizontalis*
11 Creeping willow, *Salix repens*
12 Birches, *Betula* sp.
13 French tamarisk, *Tamarix gallica*
14 Mountain avens, *Dryas octopetala*
15 Roseroot, *Sedum rosea,* houseleek, *Sempervivum tectorum, Thymus* sp.
16 Ling, *Calluna vulgaris*
17 Gorse, *Ulex europaeus*
18 Barrenwort, *Epimedium alpinum*
19 Purple saxifrage, *Saxifraga oppositifolia*
20 Roseroot, *Sedum rosea*
21 Spring cinquefoil, *Potentilla tabernaemontani*
22 Field maple, *Acer campestre*
23 *Thymus* sp., stonecrops, *Sedum acre, S. album*
24 Mountain pansy, *Viola lutea,* spring gentian, *Gentiana verna*
25 Chalk milkwort, *Polygala calcarea*; autumn crocus, *Crocus nudiflorus*

preferably be situated on the sunnier side of the rockery. To make it more authentic and provide ideal conditions for alpine plants, occasional rocks should be sunk in the scree to allow a cool root-run, because the small stones that make up the scree can get extremely hot.

Most screes seen in well-tended gardens are furnished with beautiful species, both native and exotic, such as the twinflower (in cool regions only) and pyxie moss for acid soils. Of the lime lovers, the spring gentian, *Gentiana verna*, the alpine catchfly, *Lychnis alpina*, and the chalk milkwort, *Polygala calcarea* are outstanding.

Limestone gardens

A new gardener can be forgiven for looking at a mass of bare stone in despair, incredulous perhaps that it could ever offer a home for such delicate-looking plants as so many rock plants appear to be. To visit a natural, flora-rich rock area is to appreciate more fully what it is that such plants ask of us. One such area, which remains for ever in the minds of those who know it, is that gaunt limestone pavement in Ireland's County Clare known as The Burren. There, within sight of the sea, there is an astounding collection of rock plants, many of which do not grow in the open but luxuriate low down in crevices between the giant rocks. One of the dominant plants there, and one of the alpine gardener's favorite, is the mountain avens, *Dryas octopetala*. Once it has taken its hold between the rocks, it grows in what one can only describe as carpets, with drapes of dark green leaves studded with yellow-centered flowers, which mature into beautiful fluffy seed heads.

In the crevices on a limestone rock garden, and so long as the root soil is well drained, you can grow *Alchemilla conjuncta*, which seeds freely; rose root, *Sedum rosea*, with its roots which when dried are rose-scented and both the Cheddar pink and its near relation cottage pink, *Dianthus plumarius,* the origin of the sweetly scented garden pink. Lower down, in a place where the roots will not dry out but where the site is open, the pasque flower,

ABOVE *Yellow rock roses brighten and contrast with the pinks, white and green hues of their companions. Grown this way most plants should seed freely, eventually filling fissures and holes in the rock with their own kind, which also will cascade or sprawl in the sunshine.*

Pulsatilla vulgaris, might be coaxed to start a colony.

Where a prostrate plant is required, encourage the alpine milk vetch, *Astragulus alpinus*, to sprawl. This is a plant which resents being moved and so should be grown from seed. In my own garden, the showy blue gromwell, *Lithospermum purpurocaeruleum*, covers the soil gloriously but often a little too enthusiastically and has to be controlled.

Certainly, running water enhances any rock garden site, the spray providing the moisture many alpines like, providing that there is free soil drainage. The saxifrages thrive in this situation and form dense mats, cushions or simple rosettes, depending on the species. Commonest are the starry saxifrage, *Saxifraga stellaris*; the yellow bog saxifrage, *S. hirculus*; the lesser bulbous saxifrage, *S. cernua*; and the yellow mountain saxifrage, *S. aizoides*, for instance. The kinds known as mossy saxifrages are attractive at all times. *S. caespitosa* is an extremely variable species which forms dense cushions studded with starry white flowers.

London pride, *Saxifraga × urbicum*, familiar to many people, grows best in the shade or partial shade, and changes personality in sunshine! The light, foamy flowers look well growing with ferns. Also, for the shady side of a rock garden is Eve's cushion or Dovedale moss, *S. hypnoides*, whose spreading cushions remain colorful long after flowering is past.

Many of the cushion phloxes such as *Phlox subulata*, *P. bifida* and the Rocky Mountain species do well on limestone in full sun. For shade, any of the wild corydalis and dicentra species thrive.

Plants for acid soils

Here, plants of the heather family, both ericas and the low-growing shrubs (see Heath and heath gardens, pages 78-85) can be used as rock plants. Most will cascade prettily over the edge of a rock and even grow out from a crevice so long as the roots are not likely to dry out. Being evergreen and often varied in color, and whether covered in new tips or old, or flowering stems, the plants are always decorative.

Where a soft gray carpet would look well, the native immortelle, pussy-toes, *Antennaria plantaginifolia*, demands only a light, well-drained soil and no competition from taller plants. It could be contrasted with partridge-berry, *Mitchella repens*.

One of my favorite rock plants comes from the seaside. I have happy memories of it draping cliffs in Devon and in Ireland. It is the little thrift or sea pink *Armeria maritima*, which, so it seems to me, is prepared to grow anywhere it is planted so long as the gardener is liberal with sand. Apart from its attractive mode of growth, neat green cushions of tiny grasslike leaves, its globular flowers which ornament the plant from June until August are especially attractive to bees. The species varies

greatly in the color of its flowers, you may find them pale pink in one place, bright magenta-rose in another. This is a plant which will grow as well between pavement stones as it does nestled down on the angles between a vertical and horizontal rock.

The enchanting harebell, *Campanula rotundifolia*, is most adaptable in any soil so long as the situation is not too shady. Southern harebell, *C. divaricata*, is taller and not so elegant, but will grow in fairly dense shade.

For a shady place, even under low-growing shrubs such as those that might top the rock, the naturalized barrenwort, *Epimedium alpinum*, will gradually fill the area, sending up new shoots from its creeping rhizomatous roots.

ABOVE *Herb robert, an annual geranium, becomes smothered with flowers through spring and summer. Seeding freely, it is an ideal plant for quickly covering an area of poor, stony soil.*

LEFT *The flat surface of a rock can quite quickly become naturally populated by plants. Often, in shade, mosses are the first to appear, sometimes thickly carpeting the stone. Seeds or fern spores falling or blown onto the moss germinate. Drifting soil and plant particles gradually and continually deposit enough humusy soil around the seedlings for them to become well-rooted even though the barren rock lies so near below.*

Gravel and stone gardens

Gravel can be used on its own with local stone. All the small stones collected from the soil where flower beds are made can be spread as a foundation for gravel. Some people like to lay gravel on a foundation of sand, 2-3cm/1in or so deep. In one little area my method was first to lay sand, then use whatever flat stones I had available (laying them quite closely), and finally I filled any spaces which were more than about an inch wide with gravel.

Once you have an area of gravel or laid stone, you soon discover that there are many wayside and wasteland plants which enjoy growing in a well-drained soil, sprawling in the sun on sun-warmed stones. There are, for instance, the bedstraws, those fragrant lacy ground covers of high summer (which, as we have seen, also attract some of the most handsome moths), the little pink lesser bind-weed which is sometimes seen sprawling along the edges of country roads, toadflax, yarrow, herb robert, hawkweeds, teasels, mullein and campions, to mention a few. Groundsel and hairy bitter cress may not be so welcome, but can be hand-weeded.

Gravel is usually bought by the cubic meter and 1 cubic meter is usually sufficient to cover an area up to 30 sq. m/320 sq. ft with a layer 2-3cm/1in deep. A deeper layer will last longer, but if much walked on, gravel will usually need resurfacing every two or three years.

Plants which are not readily associated with rock or stone sometimes appear among gravel. In a little shady corner in my own garden a colony of dog violets has become established. The seed must have been brought in leafmold used as a mulch around some ferns growing in a nearby border. From a single specimen, the plants now cover an area of about 3m/10ft square. Elsewhere, unexpectedly and uncharacteristically, sweet violet and creeping jenny, both self-sown, thrive in gravel, in sun.

Broom does better on gravel and sand than elsewhere and thymes will grow well on shingle. Like the rock roses, thymes tolerate some treading.

The little pinks seem to fit in wherever they can be given gritty, well drained soil and sunshine. The

ABOVE *Well-drained and consequently comparatively warm, a gravel garden can hold a rich mixture of plants. The provision of low-carpeting plants ensures that the stones are well-covered.*

LEFT *There are some 40 species of* Sempervivum *native to Eurasia and North Africa; many are treasured garden plants. In cultivation they hybridize readily.*

sweetly scented Cheddar pink, and the maiden pink, *Dianthus deltoides,* will furnish stones with neat gray-green leaf tufts at such times as they are not in flower. Trailing St John's wort, *Hypericum humifusum,* described as a common but attractive garden weed, and the neat moss campion, *Silene acaulis,* are two other examples of plants that sit comfortably on a gravelly base. The latter plant seldom flowers in the garden as freely as one wishes, but it does better on a well-drained gravel.

Plants for walls

When I think of plants for walls, I recall a narrow road winding through the hills in Ireland where for miles the bordering walls were rosy-topped with *Saxifraga* × *urbicum* in bloom. How odd, I thought, that this plant should be called *London* pride. The leafy rosettes made a dense cap and hung briefly over the edge, glistening under the film of ever-present mist. One is reminded that so many of the plants which will grow on rock gardens will also grow on walls so long as there is no danger of their drying out at the roots. Tufted, cushiony rock plants should grow well on wall tops or in crevices which are backed by good soil.

Some of them, like the saxifrage described, need to be planted on the shady rather than on the sunny side. Here also some of the little wall ferns can be grown. (See pages 89-90.)

On the other hand, there are many which will revel in the sunshine, the various stonecrops for instance, none of which are more glorious than the wall pepper, *Sedum acre.* Others include thick-leaved, English, white, rock and hairy stonecrops, and the native *Sedum ternatum.* A close relative of these is *Sempervivum tectorum,* the houseleek, sometimes to be seen growing on roofs. The adventuresome might try western American Lewisias.

The alpine rock cress, *Arabis alpina,* from which many garden varieties have come, makes neat leaf rosettes, while the round-leaved cranesbill, *Geranium rotundifolium,* behaves like herb robert, *G. robertianum* (also good for walls), by presenting us with attractive leaf and stem coloring as it ages.

LEFT *A wall top, especially if it is at a convenient height both for working and viewing, is a good environment for most of the species known as rock plants. Where crevices or apertures between the stones are very small it may be best to sow seed or prick out tiny seedlings. In time, the plants will clothe the wall top and cascade prettily over the edges, like the* Dianthus *in the background.*

BELOW *Like most other stonecrops,* Sedum album *is seen at its best when it grows on walls which it drapes so attractively. This species prefers limestone rocks.*

GARDEN AND PLANT CARE

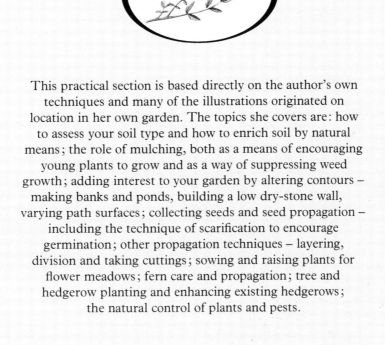

This practical section is based directly on the author's own techniques and many of the illustrations originated on location in her own garden. The topics she covers are: how to assess your soil type and how to enrich soil by natural means; the role of mulching, both as a means of encouraging young plants to grow and as a way of suppressing weed growth; adding interest to your garden by altering contours – making banks and ponds, building a low dry-stone wall, varying path surfaces; collecting seeds and seed propagation – including the technique of scarification to encourage germination; other propagation techniques – layering, division and taking cuttings; sowing and raising plants for flower meadows; fern care and propagation; tree and hedgerow planting and enhancing existing hedgerows; the natural control of plants and pests.

THE SOIL

All types of soil will support some kind of flora. Where this is monotonous, it may be possible to introduce plants, even foreign plants, suited to that particular soil type. Rather than try to change the soil, remember that the most successful wild plant gardener will be the one who accepts the soil in his garden and finds plants to suit it (see also charts, pages 142-157, and pages 158-159).

A great number of species accept a neutral, or neutral-to-slightly acid soil, which fortunately suits many gardens. There are a few species which seem happy to accept either a slightly acid or a slightly alkaline soil. The soil in a garden may vary and this can be used to advantage, to widen the range of species that can be grown.

TESTING SOIL

Determining basic acidity or alkalinity of soil is quite simple. Soil testing kits can be bought from garden centers and through mail order catalogs.

Take a trowelful of soil from several different parts of the garden. Keep these samples separate and clearly labeled, indicating the exact spot from where the sample was taken. The samples are then treated with the chemicals supplied and the resulting colors compared with those on a chart, to give the measure of acidity or alkalinity as a figure on the pH scale: 7.0 indicates a neutral soil; numbers higher than this indicate the degree of alkalinity, lower the degree of acidity. Generally, garden soils vary between pH 6.0 and 7.0.

SOIL ASSESSMENT

This method gives a good indication of the type of soil in your garden, and provides a guide to what you may grow. Take several trowelfuls of soil, one from each part of the garden, digging to a depth of 25cm/10in. Mix these thoroughly in a bucket, and then add a couple of tablespoons of the mixture to a jar of water. Shake this vigorously and leave to settle for half an hour. Organic matter will float to the surface, with the minerals settling in layers at the bottom.

Clay
Soil that has a high proportion of clay feels smooth and sticky when wet. Although it supports prolific plant growth, it is often hard to handle, being very heavy when wet, and sets hard in drought. It can also be very acid, badly aerated and poor to drain.

1 Organic matter
2 Clay
3 Sand
4 Gravel

Sand
Soil with a high sand content feels gritty when wet. Unlike clay, it does not bind together in a dry state. Often lacking organic matter, it tends to be infertile unless treated with compost or humus.

1 Organic matter
2 Clay
3 Sand
4 Gravel

Loam
Loamy soils contain plenty of organic matter, but vary from light to heavy, depending on the mineral contents. Loamy soil feels slightly gritty, and holds together when it dries. It is considered 'good soil', supporting rich plant growth.

1 Organic matter
2 Clay
3 Sand
4 Gravel

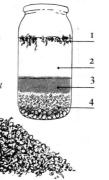

Limestone
Limestone soils are low in humus and are alkaline. With the incorporation of organic matter and the use of fertilizers, limestone will support a good growth of lime-tolerant plants.

1 Organic matter
2 Clay
3 Sand
4 Limestone and gravel

Humus-rich
Humusy soil will tend to be light, depending on the amount and type of mineral content. Woodland soil is rich in humus; so is soil to which liberal amounts of compost or leafmold have been added.

1 Organic matter
2 Clay
3 Sand
4 Gravel

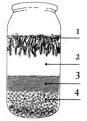

ADDING HUMUS

If the local soil is poor, it is possible to make it acceptable to a wider range of plants by improving it with the addition of humus-rich materials. Humus is decayed organic material, something that is abundant in the wild. Animal manure, leaves, grass, peat, kitchen vegetable refuse and seaweed are all a source of humus.

One of the quickest and simplest means of providing soil with humus is to treat it with generous quantities of homemade compost. This is so easy to make, and the resulting organic substance, if properly made, should be almost as good as farmyard manure – and a lot cheaper.

Humus is not to be confused with fertilizer, which is an immediate source of food for plants. Plant foods are released slowly from humus by the action of bacteria. However, humus of all types and from all sources should be regarded as a way of treating soil to enable it to become rich and fecund rather than a soil enricher itself. It creates the right atmosphere and texture for the bacteria to multiply and so leads to a more useful soil.

Soils which drain too rapidly and constantly lose essential plant foods by leaching (particularly sandy or light soils) will be improved by the addition of humus which holds water and provides healthy soil bacteria.

On the other hand, heavy clay soils are sour and unworkable because they retain water and lack air. Here again humus does the trick, for it will lighten the soil by opening it up, providing more air spaces and improving its texture. Healthy soil is lively soil and, like all living things, needs air. Soil bacteria cannot live without it, which is why waterlogged soil is such an unsatisfactory medium.

COMPOSTING

There are several methods for composting, but basically composts are made by mixing various soft-tissued vegetable materials together in a pile where the natural heating up of the pile and bacterial activity will transform the materials to a dark, sweet-smelling, crumbly, soillike matter,

pleasant enough to handle. If a chemical accelerator is used, it will speed the decomposition so that it is possible to get two 'crops' a year from the compost pile, rather than a more probable one.

If the garden area is very small, or where a compost pile would be an eyesore, it is possible to make compost, albeit of lesser quality, in black plastic bags. The materials are treated in the same way as illustrated below, and the bag securely sealed, after which the surfaces are punctured to allow air to enter. These sacks should not lie in full sun or the heat generated will be too much for the bacteria to develop properly.

All leafy plant materials, soft hedge clippings,

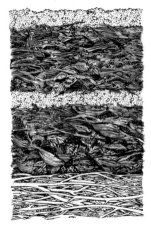

The compost pile
BELOW *Two compost boxes are useful as one pile can be left to rot. Also, as the center of the compost usually rots more quickly than the outside, the compost can be turned as it is moved to the second pile. Otherwise, the outside unrotted portion can be set aside and used to start the next pile. The sides should be sufficiently open to allow the passage of air – they can be made of wood, wire, plastic or metal. It is convenient to have one side that can be opened or removed.*

LEFT *Cross-section through a well-made compost pile. Twiggy material is put at the base (not part of the compost) to allow air to enter from below, and prevent water collecting in time of heavy rains. Screening can be used instead. Layers of vegetable material, 15–23cm/6–9in deep, are laid and covered with soil 5cm/2.5in deep, which helps weigh down the vegetable matter and spreads the movement of bacteria through the pile. In dry periods, water the pile well; keep it covered during rainy ones.*

lawn cuttings, vegetable refuse (including peelings), fallen leaves and the top growth of such perennial 'weeds' as nettles, dock and dandelion can be used. Tough, hard or diseased matter should be burnt first and the ashes, purified by fire, can then be added to the pile.

MULCHING

Mulching is a method of covering the soil with a thick layer either of organic substances, such as compost, peat, leafmold, spent hops, grass cuttings or chopped tree bark, or inorganic or other kinds of stone. Mulches play an important role by keeping the moisture in the soil down near the roots of the plant.

When organic mulches are used, they do in time disintegrate and become incorporated into the soil, thus enriching it, and making it more open and friable. Inorganic mulches will remain intact for a long time, but may eventually need renewing as they, too, will disappear into the soil.

Mulches have a secondary, important role in that they will suppress unwanted seedlings (for my own method, see page 138). But there are many other situations when mulches will prove useful. Ferns, shrubs and trees are likely to grow much better if after planting they are kept mulched with an organic substance until they are seen to be growing well. A mulched soil seldom freezes.

Proper composting breaks down the acidity of organic materials. Where fresh uncomposted materials, such as lawn cuttings, are used as a mulch, these are likely to add a degree of acidity to the soil. The more they are used the more acid the soil will become – a good reason for using lawn cuttings as a mulch around heathers, which is what I do. Elsewhere, a little liming from time to time will check the tendency to acidity.

LEAFMOLD

Leafmold is one of the best and most versatile mulches. It is also of great value when used in potting mixes or soil mixtures. Those who hope to raise many of their own seedlings would be well advised to build up a supply for the year ahead.

Almost any kind of leaves can be used, but some – beech, oak and birch, for example – rot down more quickly than others. Leaves from evergreens and all similar tough leaves are not suitable as they take much longer to decompose. How quickly leaves decompose also depends on how much moisture and heat there is. Generally speaking, however, those leaves stacked one autumn should be ready for use a year later. To test if the pile is ready, check that no complete leaves remain. The leafmold should be flaky, easy to crumble between the fingers and hardly recognizable as leaves.

BELOW *After planting shrubs and tree seedlings, keep the ground around them mulched with chopped bark or other coarse mulch throughout the first two growing seasons. Fine mulches such as peat tend to absorb moisture and provide a rooting ground for wind-blown seeds.*

Mulching young plants

BELOW *When raising young woodland plants, it is particularly helpful to simulate the soil conditions found in a wood. A mulch of leafmold, dead leaves or chopped bark will help keep the roots moist and prevent competition from unwanted seedlings.*

Leafmold

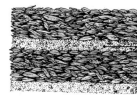

RIGHT *Make a neat rectangular pile of leaves some 15cm/6in deep. Cover with a layer of soil deep enough to hide the surface of the leaves. Repeat the layers of leaves and soil until the pile is 60-90cm/24-36in high.*

soil layer
rotting leaves

ALTERING CONTOURS

Any garden can be given interest by changing contours here and there. This need not involve great earthworks, but just some modest 'landscaping': adding banks and terraces, making a small pond which will instantly attract wildlife, building a wall for plants to grow on, or simply letting a path meander around the garden.

MAKING A BANK

The quickest way to make a bank is to import soil or use that excavated when making a garden pond. The method we use, though much slower, makes a richer soil, suitable for ferns or herbs, for example. We begin with dumping hedge cuttings and all plant refuse that is not easily compostable. Since there is also a vegetable and a nonwild garden to maintain, there are the inevitable wheelbarrow-loads of spent stems. These are then covered by what lawn cuttings can be spared, fallen fruit and leaves swept up from the drive which are not suitable for leafmold, the occasional load of bought in peat or soil. Like most else in a wild garden, such banks need not be made in a hurry. My own have taken years, and one made this way is now some 9m/30ft long and 1m/3ft high in places. It is planted as an informal herb garden (see page 99), mostly with native or naturalized species.

Another mound, this time running from north to south, was made to serve two purposes: to screen the kitchen garden which had been situated fairly near the house; and to accommodate those calcifuges we might wish to grow, placing those which needed it most on the sunny, south side.

For this purpose, quantities of both loose peat and peat blocks were brought in. Some of the latter were used as a 'wall' at ground level to stop

BELOW *Soak the blocks for an hour before they are laid. This not only makes them much heavier and therefore much easier to put into place, but it also helps them retain any moisture in the atmosphere. The more they swell the more effective the 'wall' will be. Once swollen, the blocks should stay this way except during a drought when they should be watered as often as possible preferably with soft rainwater, but not with limy or alkaline water.*

Using peat blocks for a terrace

BELOW *Do not leave any gaps between the blocks open to the drying air. Bank the peat or humusy-rich soil right up to the blocks. Once plants are established, the peat blocks should soon be disguised.*

An 'organic' bank

The bank shown here is made almost entirely from garden waste. The method, though slow, utilizes pruned branches at the base, then layers of plant refuse, windfall fruit, leaves and soil or peat, as available, on top.

soil/peat top layer

plant and garden refuse

rotted apples in among branches

the loose peat packed behind them from washing away. Elsewhere on the mound, small areas of peat, held in curving walls of blocks, were made to hold shrubs and give them adequate rooting room. The peat here was later regularly covered with a mulch of lawn cuttings.

As the years pass, the blocks gradually merge into the peaty soil they support. Moss, ferns and seedlings grow between and upon them attractively.

BUILDING A DRY-STONE WALL

Dry walls in which no bonding is used offer hollows and crevices as shelter for wildlife, and spaces for the roots of plants. They are not difficult to build, but certain rules apply. Some excavation will be needed to make a firm, level base.

Unlike bonded walls, dry-stone walls are normally 'battered', that is, they incline so that the top is slightly narrower than the base. A banked wall needs to incline more, to prevent it bulging.

Wherever possible, use regular-sized pieces of local stone that harmonizes with the garden as a whole. Rough stones, however, such as those put aside when they crop up in the garden, are seldom sufficiently even-sized. Grade the stones before you begin building, because different sizes are used variously in the construction.

Allow a little extra space between stones every so often, as a drainage hole and for adding plants as the wall is being built; this is the best planting method, because the roots can be covered with sufficient soil, more can be provided behind and below for them to spread into. As each course of stones is laid, spread a thin layer of slightly moist soil over it, both for plant roots and to help the next course to sit more securely.

A dry-stone retaining wall

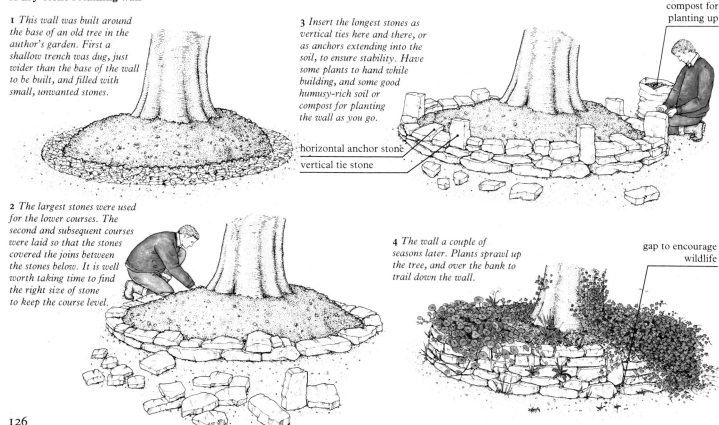

1 *This wall was built around the base of an old tree in the author's garden. First a shallow trench was dug, just wider than the base of the wall to be built, and filled with small, unwanted stones.*

3 *Insert the longest stones as vertical ties here and there, or as anchors extending into the soil, to ensure stability. Have some plants to hand while building, and some good humusy-rich soil or compost for planting the wall as you go.*

humus or compost for planting up

horizontal anchor stone

vertical tie stone

2 *The largest stones were used for the lower courses. The second and subsequent courses were laid so that the stones covered the joins between the stones below. It is well worth taking time to find the right size of stone to keep the course level.*

4 *The wall a couple of seasons later. Plants sprawl up the tree, and over the bank to trail down the wall.*

gap to encourage wildlife

MAKING A GARDEN POND

Concrete is seen to have too many disadvantages for use as a pond lining nowadays. The options are either a flexible sheeting material which will mold itself to the shape excavated, or a rigid, pre-molded container, placed into a hole dug to its exact dimensions. The latter is largely a question of trial and error; start by marking out the circumference as accurately as possible, using string to guide you.

The heavier the plastic sheeting the better; butyl or artificial rubber with a nylon fabric base is probably best. It can be bought by the square meter, and the quantity required is the maximum length of the pool times the maximum width, times twice the maximum depth. This material will stretch enough to mold itself closely to the pond's contours. Take care that no stones or projecting roots remain to puncture the sheet; it is best to line the hole with peat or sand first. The sheet should then be stretched over the hole and weighted down around the edges; folds and tucks will hardly show if the liner is dark. Water trickled gently into the center of the sheeting will push the sheet down, eventually pressing it closely against the base and sides. Smooth out any wrinkles as the water pressure reveals them.

Plastic sheeting

Unlike the preformed pond lining, flexible sheeting gives you a free hand in design of the pond. Do not make the slopes too steep, which might cause the plastic to slip at the sides. Leave shallow shelves all round, at a depth of 20cm/8in or so for marginal plants.

water lilies in position

marginal plants

sand or peat layer

heavy, rich soil at bottom

WINTER CARE OF THE POND

Remove all leaves from the pond, certainly before early spring when frogs and toads visit the pond to breed. Better still, stretch small-gauge plastic network tautly over the surface of the pond to catch and hold the leaves and other debris.

In winter, if the surface ices over, damaging gases build up, especially if there are any leaves in the water. These gases may kill wildlife, so the ice must be punctured or melted to allow them to escape. Never break ice forcibly, as the shock waves produced may damage fish and other creatures.

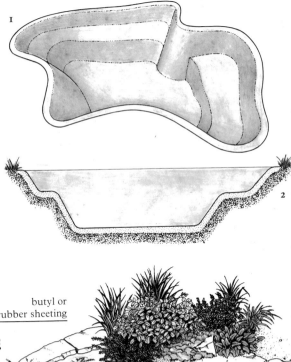

butyl or rubber sheeting

Preformed pond

1 *Fiberglass ponds come in various shapes and sizes, priced (not cheaply) according to size and complexity. The overall depth will vary considerably.*

2 *The hole dug for this type of pond must be an exact fit, for the fiberglass must be supported in all places, and the rim must be level with the ground so that when the pond is filled, the water does not appear to slope! Watch particularly the angle of slope of the sides, the depth of the shelves and the levels on the bottom. It is best to dig out too much soil and then fill in.*

The pond edges

For both types of pond, the best way of finishing off the sides is to surround them with pavements. This will hide the rim or the edges of the sheeting while holding it firmly in place.

PATH DESIGN AND CONSTRUCTION

Where your wild garden paths require a more substantial surface, you should consider carefully the form and materials that will blend in best. Harsh concrete or colored pavements will upset the natural effect of the scene. Straight lines should be avoided; any permanent surface should curve gently. By keeping the path narrow, but bearing in mind the kind of traffic that will use it (wheelbarrows, tricycles, etc.), you should be able to keep it a discreet feature of the garden. This could be helped by using several different surfaces, and not continuing any one of them for any great length (see plans on pages 31, 73 and 116). The surface could perhaps change according to the character of the different parts of the garden that the path links. Carpeting or mat-forming plants are useful as a link between one type of surface and another, and help make the transition gradual.

The path along the length of my herb bank, where I need to walk in all weathers, is a mixture of pale gray pavement slabs set well apart, with the space between well-graveled and planted with creeping thymes and pennyroyal – one species, or variety, per space. These plants have gradually formed leafy mats, which can be trodden on, and they trail prettily over the edges of the stones, softening their appearance.

An unusual surface that would suit a sitting area by a pond, or in a cool shady fern garden, or wooded area, is made from short lengths of wood – elm or other hardwood – bedded in gravel. This helps keep the wood well-drained and prevents slipperiness. A path through a damp area, or perhaps adjacent to a lawn or meadow area, could be graveled, using thin poles of alder or birch as edging to contain the stones. On a slope the path could be terraced, using the poles, almost buried, across the path to edge the steps.

Stepping stones, set in grass or across a pond or marshy area, are useful and look attractive. If set in grass, they should be level with the ground. If set in a pond, they will need to be well-founded on piers of brick or stone.

A gravel path
Poles embedded both along and across a sloping gravel path help contain the gravel.

A log path
1 An informal path constructed with pieces of sawn log about 20cm/8in thick.
2 They should be set in coarse sand or gravel with a base of larger stones or rubble. The gaps between the stones and the base will ensure good drainage.

Pavements and gravel with interplanting
Gravel planted with fragrant herbs that withstand crushing and soften the edges of the hard paving stones. A rubble base is essential; the stones would sit even more securely set in light cement.

A stepping-stone path for a pond or marshy area
Stepping stones across a natural or cement-based pond provide easier access for cleaning. The piers, which can be brick or stone, should be firmly set in strong cement. Make sure that the stones do not appear more than a few inches above the optimum water level.

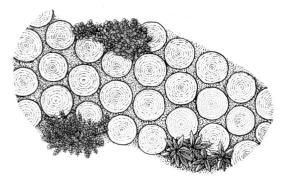

PLANT CULTIVATION

Earlier in this book I suggested that the successful wild gardener is one who adopts a different philosophy from those who intensively cultivate and tidy their gardens. Nowhere is this more true than in the matter of seeding plants.

SEED COLLECTION AND STORAGE

In traditional gardening practice, once herbaceous plants have finished flowering, most of their number are soon tidied by the removal of spent stems. In the wild, these stems remain so that the seed may ripen properly and then be dispersed in whatever manner is characteristic of the plant. This is a sequence which should also be allowed in the wild garden. Obviously it cannot be possible that all seed produced by a plant develops into another plant and it is quite likely that by allowing your plants to seed themselves there will be sufficient seedlings produced to suit your demands. Should too many grow then hand-weeding is called for. On the other hand, if you wish to establish quickly a colony of one kind of plant, it would be best to collect the seed and sow it more carefully so that each little seedling can be saved. Perhaps the plants you would like do not grow in your garden yet and you wish to collect some from the wild. Although there are 839 native plants classified as 'endangered' in the USA alone, these represent only 4.2 percent of the total and there are

Poppy seed heads
If you wish to save poppy seed, cut the seed stems as soon as they are ripe, otherwise some animal will be there before you to ea the oily seeds. Hold them upright for transport. When ripe, seeds fall readily when the stem is shaken.

many others which you can propagate.

My own method is to collect the seed stems, slipping them into a polyethylene bag so that no seed is wasted on the journey home, then to spread them out in a dry place for two weeks or so to ripen thoroughly. Since the plant was itself ready to shed its seed, I follow its example and sow seed in autumn in a nursery bed, where it can be subjected to weather in a natural manner.

If you do want to store seed, it should be in dry, cool conditions to maintain its viability: a plastic container in a refrigerator at about 2°C is ideal. Place a small packet of silica gel in the container to remove any moisture from the air and so prevent mold developing.

Stratifying berries
Berries and hard-coated seeds can be softened and so induced to germinate by stratifying them. They should be laid on sand, covered with more sand and left to over-winter outdoors.

Self-seeding parsley
This method is used in my own garden for parsley, which is always lush and plentiful. Allow some plants to flower and form seed. When the stems turn yellow, uproot and lay them along the ground. The dropped seed is then protected by the stems which are left until seedlings are visible.

Drying seed stems
Where seed vessels are small and numerous, lay the ripe stems well spaced apart on newspaper in a dry place away from draughts. When the stems are dry, shake out the seed.

PROPAGATION

The traditional methods of plant propagation – seed sowing, plant division, cuttings and layering – may be used just as effectively for wild plants. Seeds, however, do not all germinate at the same rate or under the same conditions, and gardeners who are used to the prompt and easy response of well-bred cultivars are likely to be put off by the frequently delayed behavior of some wild plant seed. Germination of some once common plants, such as mertensia, remains unpredictable, which must be baffling to those who know how abundantly this plant once grew.

It is most likely that there are substances in the soil which act on some seeds to soften their outer coats. It may be that germination is long delayed if these substances are absent at the time of sowing.

SEED SOWING

The basic method of seed sowing is extremely simple. The seed is broadcast on soil made ready by first clearing, forking and finally raking to get a fine tilth. Once the seed is cast, gently rake the surface to cover it. The ground can then be lightly trodden to anchor the seeds and to dissuade birds from using the fine tilth as a dust bath.

Spacing seeds
A simple method for ensuring that seeds do not cluster too thickly so they are wasted. Empty a few seeds into a folded slip of paper and gently flick them, using a pencil tip or other pointed object, into their required position.

The other method is to sow the seeds in seed potting mix in containers or in a specially prepared seed or nursery bed. Once the seedlings have grown large enough to handle easily, they can be lifted, carefully separated and individually transplanted, so that they are well-spaced. Then, as they grow large enough, they can be planted out in their permanent positions.

Watering seedlings
To avoid seedlings being disturbed or knocked over by a flow of water, use a plant spray. An alternative method for seedlings in containers or disposable pots is to stand the container or pots in some water for half an hour or so.

HASTENING GERMINATION

In the wild, most seeds lie on the soil surface where they are subjected to rough treatment. They become frozen, soaked by rain, and blown back and forth. Thus it often helps germination if these conditions are simulated by artificial means, particularly for those seeds which are sown undercover. Some tough seed coats can be nicked with a sharp knife so that moisture can enter and start the seed swelling. Other seed, such as that of most members of the pea family as well as meadow cranesbill and

Avoiding taproot damage
Plants with fibrous root systems are easy to transplant, but particular care must be taken with taproots because, if their growing points are damaged, growth will cease. Avoid this by sowing the seed in small disposable pots which break down in the soil and are planted direct into the ground. The developing root need suffer no check in growing if the pot is planted out before the root tip protrudes through it. The units must be kept moist. Peat pots in particular become very tough if they dry out.

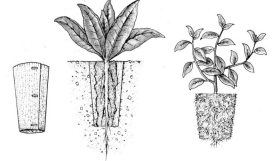

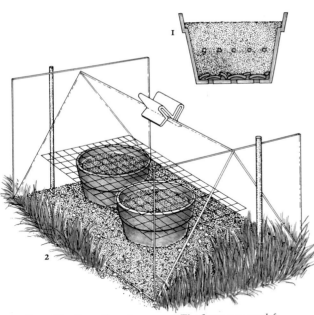

Stratification of seed

1 *The seed is placed on a layer of sand over a base of drainage material. More sand covers the seed to fill the pot.*

2 *The flower pots are left outside over the winter for the weathering process. Here they are half-buried and protected from rain by cloches.*

Helianthemum, should be rubbed between sheets of coarse abrasive paper to scarify their coats so that moisture can again enter and the seed swell. Other treatments include heat, refrigeration in sealed bags, or stratification.

Germination of many kinds of berries and hard-coated seeds can be speeded up by stratification (see illustration). Use separate flower pots for each type of seed – I prefer to use earthenware pots, though this is not essential. A layer of suitable drainage material – shingle or broken flower pot crocks, for instance – is laid at the bottom, for it is important that water should not linger and cause the seed to rot. Over this, spread a layer of sand, half filling the pot. Space the large seeds, or sprinkle smaller kinds, on the surface of the sand. Cover with more sand. More than one layer of seeds can be made, but one is usually easier to deal with. Stand the pots in a cold place outdoors, either half-buried in open ground or placed in a frame or box

of sand. To prevent mice from raiding the pots, secure fine mesh wire network over the pots or the box, and cover with a cloche or piece of clear plastic. If this is done in midautumn, the seeds will be ready for sowing in potting mix in peat pots in early spring.

A quicker alternative to stratification for some seeds or berries is to mix them with damp sand and place inside a polyethylene bag in a refrigerator, generally for a month or two before they are sown. There are some plants, usually alpines, which are said to respond after just 24 hours cold storage, and it is certainly useful to experiment.

Seed from berries can be sown directly, but as a rule germination does not take place until the second year after sowing. When the berries are ripe, the seeds are removed and sown at once in containers in a 50:50 mixture of moist peat and sharp grit, at a depth of just a little deeper than the seed's own thickness. The soil should never be allowed to dry out, and after the seeds have received one winter's natural 'vernalization', they are left to grow in these containers until the following winter when they can be transplanted into individual pots or planted in rows in the open ground. It is a good way to raise hedging plants.

NURSERY BEDS

We are warned by seed merchants that seed simply cast into rough grass or onto unprepared ground is most likely to be wasted. The method that is particularly suited to wildflowers for a meadow area is to propagate the seedlings in a nursery bed, and then to let them mature there before transplanting to the meadow area.

The bed is better drained and warmer if it is raised a little above ground level, 8-10cm/3-4in will do. Keep it narrow, 1-1.2m/3-4ft, so that you can reach the center from one side or another without treading on the soil. After preparing the soil by forking and raking, some gardeners add a top layer of specially prepared potting mix, about 2.5cm/1in deep. This is helpful but not essential, and it serves to give the seedlings a good start.

Nursery bed

A special nursery bed is well worth making and maintaining. Keep it filled most of the time. Here the seed is sown directly into a patch of good soil. Later, the crowded seedlings are carefully lifted and transplanted into rows spaced a few inches apart each way. There they stay until they touch or are ready to go into their permanent places.

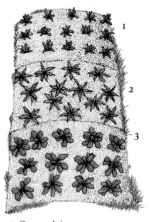

1 Oxeye daisy
2 Knapweed
3 Meadow clary

LAYERING

The illustration shows one method of layering heaths. Another one, which can be used for most other members of the Ericaceae while the plants are dormant, is as follows. Spread out the stem or stems of low-growing types, or bend down those of more upright plants until some part of the stem other than the tip touches the soil. If necessary, use a strong twig, forked or bent hairpin-wise, to straddle the stem and pin it in place. Pile a mixture of peat and sand over the stem at the point where it touches the soil so that it is well covered.

When layering dianthus, make a horizontal cut on the underside of each stem at the point where it touches the soil. Do not sever the stem. Place a little heap of sand and soil mixture under the cut stem and push the cut portion into it so that the cut opens. Place more soil over the stem to hold it down. The roots should form in a few weeks. Heaths take longer – six months or so – the more shrubby the plant, the longer it takes to root. To transplant, after the layer has formed roots, detach it from the parent plant with pruners. Then lift it from the soil carefully and replant.

Layering heathers

1 Test to determine how far the heath stem will reach when spread out comfortably. At this point, scoop out a slight depression around the plant. Make sure that you do not dig so deeply that roots are damaged.

2 If several stems are to be layered, take each singly and space them well apart so that none are crossed. Bend the stem a little so that it touches the soil at the bottom of the depression. Anchor it in place with a large stone.

TAKING CUTTINGS

Some plants take root easily in water – for example willow and shrub dogwood – though you could also experiment with others. If a good example is available, such as a shrub dogwood with particularly brilliant colored bark, follow the method shown below. The cutting should be left to stand outdoors, sheltered from the wind. See that the level of water in the vessel does not drop to less than 15cm/6in from the bottom of the stem. The speed of root production varies with the time of year, but may take two to three months in spring.

When a good mass of roots has been formed, a mixture of sand and potting mix can be added to the container as shown. When you can see the roots growing out to the edges of the potting mix, the root ball can be lifted out and transplanted in a larger pot. Once the roots have filled this, it can be planted in the open ground.

Taking a willow cutting

1 Stand the cutting in a wide-mouthed jar or container placed inside a bucket so that the stem is supported and held steady. Fill the jar with rain-water, immersing about 10cm/4in of the stem.

2 When a root mass has formed, pour sand into the container to settle in a 3cm/1½in layer at the bottom. In a few days, add a layer of potting mix and gradually build up the layers until the roots are covered. Transplant into a proper flower pot.

Using forks to divide plants

1 Some plants are easily pulled apart by hand, but old, usually tough specimens need more force. The usual method is to use two forks. Here a garden fork is used with a small handfork.

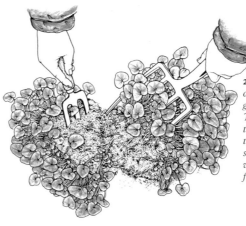

2 Find the center of the plant or some part into which a garden fork will go easily. Take another fork, place the two back-to-back and wrench them apart, bringing the separated halves of the plant with them. Divide these farther in the same manner.

PLANT DIVISION

An excellent way of obtaining more plants of the same kind is by taking a well-grown specimen, lifting it with as large a root mass as possible, and then separating, or dividing, it into many smaller, vigorous, well-rooted pieces. This technique is also useful for checking the spread of plants, for example herbs, that are beginning to occupy too much space. Suitable subjects are fibrous-rooted perennials and small, bushy shrubs. Very compact or tough roots – some ferns, for instance – can be cut with a sharp knife while others are best pulled apart in some way, by hand or with the aid of garden forks (see illustration). Discard obviously aged and spent portions. Rhizomatous plants may also be divided, the most healthy-looking or youngest rhizomes being pulled off from the mass. Do not replant these deeply: most of the top half of the rhizome should be above the soil surface.

Division should be carried out in autumn, even in a mild winter, when the plants are dormant or in spring, before they have started into growth.

INTRODUCING POT-GROWN MEADOW FLOWERS INTO TURF

Bulb planters (originally designed for planting bulbs into lawns or rough grass) provide an easy way of introducing pot-grown plants into existing grass. The seed is first sown in seed flats in the normal way, and pricked out into disposable pots when at first or second true leaf. Use a soil-based potting mix rather than a peat one, to ensure that shrinkage does not occur when pots are planted out. Plants should be grown on in the pots until roots begin to show at the bottom.

Pressing the bulb planter into the turf, a core of soil is removed as the planter is taken out. The disposable pot with the plant, which should be the same size as the bulb planter, is given a good soaking before being inserted into the hole. Press gently around the edge with the heel of your boot. Do not replace any turf, but add a little soil around the plant if necessary to keep the ground level.

Water the plant well if rain does not follow within seven days. It is best to introduce pot-grown plants into turf either in early spring or in autumn, though summer plantings can be successful if water is available.

Bulb planters are not advised in stony soil, but work well in most garden soils. The advantage of planting pot-grown plants is that they will often flower within a year of planting.

Bulb planter

This device was designed for planting bulbs in grass. By pushing the corer into the soil, a plug of soil is removed as the corer is withdrawn. The bulb is placed in the hole as shown, and the plug of soil tipped out of the corer (use a stick to push if the soil is sticky clay), replaced over the bulb and firmed in. The method is also successful for planting pot-grown plants.

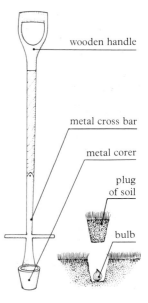

wooden handle

metal cross bar

metal corer

plug of soil

bulb

SOWING WILDFLOWER SEED IN LAWNS

An alternative to introducing pot-grown plants into turf (see page 133) is to sow seed. Scattering seed onto the turf itself, however, is a waste of time. It is essential to 'scarify' the turf first, in order to make bare batches of soil into which the seed can be sown. The turf is ripped out with a rake exposing the soil and at the same time dead grass and unwanted plants should be removed. It is easier if the grass has not been long established so that there are gaps in the sward. The poorer the soil, the more chance of successful germination, but this depends also on soil type and seasonal conditions. If the soil is at all rich and the weather wet, grasses will soon swamp the seedlings, unless controlled in some way. If the seed is sown in autumn, the gaps are less likely to close over quickly, though, in the right conditions, seed can also be sown in spring. Choosing species to suit your soil type is very important (see page 159). It is worth sowing seed of 20 species and hope for perhaps half of them to germinate and grow.

A NEW FLOWER LAWN FROM SEED

You should not be put off by the idea of starting a flower meadow from scratch. The secret of success is ground preparation, and a low-fertile, clean soil

Scarification
This is the technique of ripping patches of turf from lawn or meadow with a rake to expose bare soil. It is essential
that the meadow flower seed makes good contact with the soil in order to germinate.

Introducing species-rich turves into lawns
A method that has met with success among some conservation bodies, and could be tried whenever the opportunity arises, is to take whole turves from threatened meadows (perhaps where roads are being widened or made), or by
kind permission of the owner. The benefit of this method is that a community of plants and insects can be transplanted (and perhaps saved), thus spreading and increasing their stock.

with no drainage problems. Avoid topsoil altogether. The site should preferably be sunny, as few meadow species will tolerate shade.

In order to clear the site sufficiently of all unwanted perennials (docks, thistles etc.), it may well be necessary to use a herbicide. After spraying, it is a good idea to leave the site, say for a couple of months during the summer to clear any weeds that grow over this period before the meadow flower and grass mixture is sown.

The best time for sowing, again, is early autumn. Midspring is the alternative, though some species will then not germinate until the following year. (For examples of seed mixes for soil types, see page 159. See also pages 142-3 and 145.) Even distribution of seed is vital. Because seed varies so much in size, it is important that it is well-mixed. Adding sand or fine sawdust to it to increase the bulk helps spread the seed more evenly, and the light color helps you see where seed has been spread. Over a small surface, lightly rake the soil and tread the seed in well. Over a larger surface use a roller to keep the surface firm.

Sowing grasses and planting wildflowers
The method shown below is a combination of sown meadow grasses and pot-grown meadow flowers. The grass seed is sown in circular drills, and pot plants (a bulb planter could be used, see page 133) interplanted in the gaps the following spring.

circular drill
pot plant

PLANTING AND CARING FOR FERNS

In Victorian times, it was fashionable to grow ferns in a purpose-built place made much like a rockery, or sometimes even on a steep, rocky slope attached to the north wall of a house. Usually this was done to ensure that the site was well drained, and this is important. Although some ferns need moisture, they do not grow well in sour, wet soil. The better the soil the more luxuriantly the ferns will grow, although some species do well in little soil on walls. The method traditionally used is good.

Make a potting mix of 2-parts fibrous turf, 1-part half-rotted leafmold and 1-part coarse silver (i.e. horticultural) sand. Builders' sand, unless washed, may contain harmful substances. Make planting holes at least twice as wide and deep as the root ball of the fern. After planting and watering in, mulch the soil surface with either leafmold or homemade potting mix, or, failing that, with a mixture of peat and soil. As the years go by, keep the soil surface well mulched, preferably with leafmold, to help retain the soil moisture. In a dry season, water the ferns from time to time. Try not to splash the fronds in hot, dry weather and certainly not if the sun shines on them or they may become spotted or marked in some way. Dusty ferns can be gently hosed in the evenings in summer, but as a rule rain showers keep them clean and unmarked.

The faded fronds should be left on deciduous ferns, for they help to protect the crown of the plant; an important point, especially in districts or seasons where the winter is hard.

PROPAGATING FERNS

Ferns that form several crowns as they age can be lifted and divided, pulled or even cut apart, in early spring. Those which are rhizomatous are best propagated by detaching rooted pieces from the parent, and immediately planting these in the ground. The method is more reliable if the pieces are layered into small pots of soil sunk in the ground next to the parent plant so that their rhizomes can grow before they are severed from the parent. This can be done at almost any time of year.

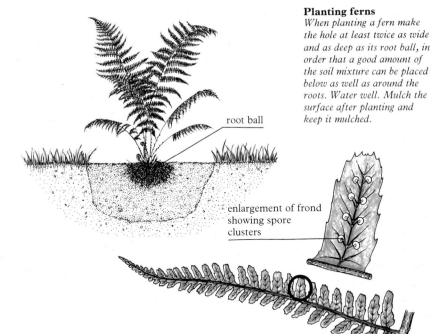

Planting ferns
When planting a fern make the hole at least twice as wide and as deep as its root ball, in order that a good amount of the soil mixture can be placed below as well as around the roots. Water well. Mulch the surface after planting and keep it mulched.

root ball

enlargement of frond showing spore clusters

Fern spores
Fern spores, arranged in small round clusters, or sori, are found on the under surface of fertile fronds. These must be ripe for propagation to be successful. The fronds which bear them should be examined frequently so that the spores can be taken as soon as they are ready, and before they have a chance to disperse.

Experts are agreed that the best way to raise a stock of ferns is from spores, a delicate process needing patience. The spore-cases are ripe when they are a light-brown color. Collect a few pieces from a fertile frond, place them in an envelope and allow to dry for 48 hours or so in a warm place.

When the spores are released, they will be found as a fine dust – brown, yellow or green, according to species – in the bottom of the envelope.

Make a mix of equal parts of sand, peat and leafmold, place in a crocked pot and sterilize by pouring boiling water over. Allow to drain and cool. Scatter the spore dust into the pot and cover with glass or enclose in a polyethylene bag. Stand in a warm place out of direct sunlight, and do not allow to dry out.

Germination and fertilization may take several weeks, even a few months, depending on species. The first sign will be a green tinge to the potting mix. Later the first fronds will begin to show, and these can be pricked off into individual pots as soon as they are large enough to be handled. The pots must be kept moist continually.

TREE PLANTING

Whether planting individual trees, or laying out a small coppice, the wild gardener should ideally choose tree seedlings, either grown himself from seed or bought from nurseries, rather than buy pricy standard trees, which will look inappropriate in an informal setting. Two-year old saplings cost a fraction of the price of standard trees. Normally they will not need staking, and within two or three years should have overtaken the standards.

If you are establishing a coppice, the poorer the soil the better as the seedlings will not be smothered by competitors, such as couch grass, *Agropyron repens*, which often happens if trees are planted in topsoil. It is essential that all plants that might compete with the seedlings are eliminated, and though this can be done by using herbicide to prepare the ground first, my own method is to use a newspaper mulch (see page 138). If the ground is already clear, mulches such as chopped bark will prevent germination of the wealth of dormant weed seeds disturbed in the planting.

The method I use for planting trees in grass is as follows. A roughly rectangular area is cut with the spade and a deep turf lifted. The soil at the bottom of the hole is forked and well-broken. Some good, humusy soil is then laid over it, and the plant's roots placed on this. A cane or stake, both as a marker and support, may be set in place at the same time. Soil is then taken from the underside of the lifted turf (or turves) and used to cover the roots. The plant is firmed into position and the remains of the turves turned over (tucking any long grass under) and placed around the plant.

CARE OF SHRUBS AND TREES

The danger period for shrubs and trees is the first few months after planting. Make sure that they are never allowed to dry out, and water daily if the weather is hot, and when drying winds blow. Spray the foliage with clean water, rainwater preferably. An initial heavy watering followed by the application of a thick mulch will keep the roots from drying out over a long period.

After periods of heavy wind, examine young trees and shrubs to make sure that they have not been rocked. If this happens, a hollow area may form round their roots which will fill with water

Staking a tree in a very exposed position
Where strong winds prevail it is prudent to stake newly planted trees. Where there are adequate windbreaks one stake should be sufficient. Otherwise a tripod of stakes can prove most effective. Inspect ties regularly to ensure that they are not weakening nor so tight that they cut into the tree bark.

Planting a tree using a stake

stick to indicate soil level

1 *Make the planting hole wider than the tree's root spread and/or deeper than the root ball. Pile the excavated soil on a plastic sheet nearby. Into this, mix compost, leaf soil or peat and general garden fertilizer. Insert stake.*

2 *Place the stem near the stake. To ensure that the tree's roots will be at the same depth as they were growing at before transplanting, place a stick across the hole.*

3 *A clearly visible soil-level mark will be seen on the stem a little above the roots. Cover these with the new soil, firming it thoroughly so that no air pockets exist. Water the area thoroughly.*

4 *Fasten the tree to the stake using a tree tie.*

and induce rotting. Hold the plant upright again and tread the soil, firming it around the roots and the stem base once again. If the tree is in a particularly exposed situation, it may need staking.

PLANTING A WILD HEDGEROW

Hedgerows bordering roads and fields have been in sharp decline in recent years, and their loss has meant a severe decrease in the stock of wild plants and wildlife that enjoyed the hedgerow habitat. A hedge of native plant species as a feature of the wild garden is an important aid to conservation.

Hedges are best planted in the autumn. Clear a strip of ground some 1.2m/4ft wide, and dig the soil deeply before incorporating plenty of organic matter. Using a garden line or length of string down the center of the prepared ground, plant two-year-old seedlings (obtainable from nurseries). Do not alternate them singly but plant in runs of threes or fives of a kind. Mix the species so that they set one another off. You could follow this sequence: hawthorn, arrow-wood, holly, black haw, hornbeam, wild plum – then repeat it. The mixture can be as varied as there are plants available; my own ancient hedge has guelder rose, hazel, willow, buckthorn, beech, oak and elm.

ADDING PLANTS TO A HEDGE

This method can be used for repairing a gappy hedge, enlivening a single-species hedge, or introducing climbers into a newly established hedge.

Grow the seedlings to be introduced in plastic or fiber pots. It is much easier to establish a pot than to dig out a large planting hole in the base of the hedge. Crack or split plastic pots at the bottom so that, when the root is ready, it can grow out into the soil. Remove some soil at the spot where the seedling is to grow, so that the pot stands secure, half-buried. Keep the seedling well-watered, remembering that the cracked pot will lose water quickly.

Filling a gap in an old hedge
Have a seedling ready in a plastic or fiber pot, and dig a hole where the plant is to grow in the hedgerow. Leave the plant in the half-buried pot, which is split apart at the bottom so that the roots of the seedling can grow into the soil below. The pot can be removed later, or covered with soil.

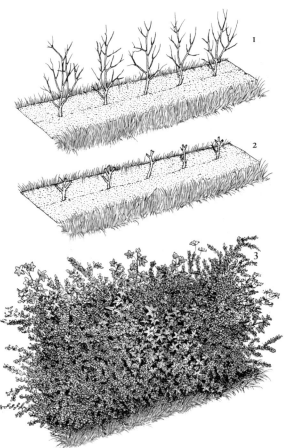

Planting a hedgerow

1 The two-year-old seedlings placed closely together, about 50cm/20in apart. After planting, the ground must be well-mulched to keep roots moist and suppress weeds.

2 Once the seedlings are established, it is advisable to cut some species back hard in the spring after planting to encourage bushy basal growth. Evergreen species should merely be tipped, so, if the hedge is very mixed, it may be necessary to prune some plants and not others. Beech, hornbeam, holly and hemlock are best left uncut for two years. Use pruners rather than loppers in the early years.

3 After four or five years, the hedge will be ready for clipping into shape, or for traditional 'laying'. However, precise clipping and shaping will not be desirable for the wild garden, neither will it suit any climbers growing in the hedge.

PLANT AND PEST CONTROL

In the wild garden, we need to avoid using chemical sprays to control plants, although there are times, for example when clearing larger areas of poor undergrowth, when selective weedkillers are necessary, and, indeed, are recommended by some conservation bodies. In this latter case, once the area has been cut down or mown, those species that cannot be successfully hand-pulled or cut out may be treated with a gel-based nonselective systemic contact herbicide such as glyphosate. Once the planting is underway or the garden established, all herbicides should be avoided.

MULCHING AS A WEED INHIBITOR

One of the simplest inhibitors of weed growth is a heavy mulch of some kind. This will not only keep down other seedlings in the soil around a planted patch, but will maintain moisture at the plant's roots (see mulching, page 124). This method will take longer than an application of herbicide, but it is effective, less unsightly and is beneficial to the soil, as long as organic materials are used. (Black plastic or purpose-made plastic mulch sheets can be used, but, unless they are covered with thin soil to disguise them, they look unsightly and are not recommended for the wild garden.)

In my own garden, where space for a coppice is being cleared in rough grassland, the following method is being used successfully. Whenever a plant, such as a small tree seedling, is added to the design (see page 136), several overlapping sheets of newspaper are laid on the ground around the plant, and the grass, together with other unwanted plants, pressed down as flat as possible under the paper. This is then covered and weighted with some organic material. As this mulch is laid down at each planting, gradually all the space between the introduced plants is covered, and the ground will eventually be ready for field layer plants.

Unplanted areas or spaces between rows of plants (such as in the nursery bed) can also be treated this way, to suppress new weed growth. The vegetation underneath the newspaper is so deprived of light that it gradually rots and eventually both paper and covering are drawn into the soil. The time this takes depends on the vitality and

Newspaper mulch as a weed suppressor

1 Overlapping double or triple sheets of newspaper should be laid around a shrub, tree seedling or any other plant, leaving it free but closely covering all growth around it. If necessary, weight down the papers as they are being laid.

2 The grass and weeds are pressed flat under the paper, which is then weighted and covered with a layer at least 5cm/2½in deep of some organic material such as lawn cuttings, chopped bark, peat (moistened to prevent it from blowing away), chopped spent bracken, fallen leaves, compost, or whatever comes to hand.

population of the soil: if many worms are present, it may take a couple of months only. So far, the only plants that have managed to penetrate this newspaper and mulch cover have been a very few thistles, which are easy enough to pull up as they appear. If unwanted grasses appear, the process will be repeated so that a thicker mat is formed.

It is worth noting that in many countries there are certain plants which are listed as being undesirable to plant or for which planting is prohibited. Some may have become too invasive, some may be host plants of pests of important agricultural or horticultural plants.

In the United States and in some other countries, the common berberis has been eradicated and its cultivation prohibited because the plant acts as an intermediate host for black rust, a fungus which attacks wheat. Other species of berberis do not appear to be attacked by this fungus. In the UK, cultivation of the beautiful ragwort is discouraged.

COPPICING

Coppicing is the term used when a tree is grown as a 'stool' rather than as a trunk, the stool throwing out many young growths from ground level which can be cut and used as poles etc. In the first instance the main trunk is cut; buds are then produced at or just above ground level. Subsequently the thicket of young growths is cut back almost to ground level. Coppicing is done on a

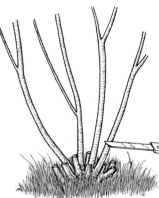

Coppicing hazel
This is usually carried out in late autumn or winter, in the plant's dormant period. Once the main stem has been cut at ground level, buds are produced which grow into stems or poles. These are then cropped roughly every seven to twelve years, or as required.

Pruning buddleia
Once, goldfinches nested among the old seedy tips of the buddleias in my own garden, so now only half of them are pruned, the other half left till the following year. Although not essential, pruning in spring encourages good, strong, flowering stems which produce heavy racemes of flowers for butterflies and others. Simply cut back last year's flowering stems back to a good pair of fat buds.

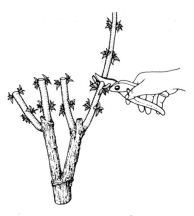

regular cycle, ranging from about seven to twelve years, depending on the size of timber required. Hazels were once widely coppiced because their poles were required for horticultural and agricultural purposes. Coppicing is a good method of keeping down those species which as full-grown, seed-bearing trees might become invasive.

POLLARDING

This is done to restrict the growth of large, deciduous trees. The tree is severed at about 2m/6ft 6in from ground level. New growth sprouts from this point. Pollarded trees most often include willow, sycamore and linden.

CONTROLLING NETTLES

When nettles are growing vigorously it is difficult to lift the massed net of thick, thonglike ocher colored roots from the soil. A tip from Gertrude Jekyll is useful for those who do not wish to use herbicides. Simply thrash the plants down with a stick whenever they have grown tall. If this is done three times during the year, the roots will become weakened and they will loosen their hold on the soil. They can then easily be forked out. Remember that butterflies will only lay their eggs on young, soft nettle growth, so nettles should be cut back in late summer to promote this new growth, ready for late broods. Use loppers and a rake for this. Do not waste the stalks – remember that they are good material for the compost pile.

CONTROLLING BRAMBLES

The various brambles around my own garden are easily controlled as they are cut back when the farmer cuts the hedges each year. However, birds still feed from their fruits and spread the seed, so bramble seedlings abound as they will do where the blackberry grows locally. It is important that the bramble seedlings are pulled up when young, so search regularly for them. They soon develop long, anchoring roots and their young stems also root at their tips, thus further entrenching them.

Plants allowed to grow as naturally as possible, instead of being trained against a flat surface or along wires as is customary when cultivated varieties are grown, can be restricted in size if old stems are cut down to ground level in the autumn. But if the plant is grown mainly for the benefit of wildlife, pruning can be delayed until spring, so that it affords good cover during winter, but be sure to do this before the nesting season begins.

PEST CONTROL

It is well known that ladybugs and their larvae are useful in combating some garden pests: they feed voraciously on aphids and their relatives. Lacewing and syrphid also have larvae that feed on aphids, and one way to encourage these insects is to have a ready supply of nectar and pollen for the adults – they in any case make attractive insect visitors. For syrphids, grow flat open flowers, especially those of the families Compositae and Umbelliferae.

One of the secrets of a healthy garden is a large range of plants and habitats. Planting native flowers, shrubs and trees will encourage a rich insect life. The more niches available for nesting birds, the greater the chance there is of encouraging these birds to stay and feed over a season and not just pass through your garden. Thrushes will tackle your surplus snail population and titmice and warblers will keep buds and foliage clear of greenfly and small caterpillars.

There really is no need to use pesticides in a wild garden. If the plants are well diversified, and

Bramble tip-root cutting
The tip of a bramble in contact with the soil will produce roots and grow into the ground. Later it can be detached, lifted and transplanted.

no one species of a kind massed together, there should be enough predators in the form of insects, and the odd toad and bird visitor, to deal with an aphid epidemic or a plague of caterpillars.

Yet sometimes, usually because of forces beyond control, some creatures increase so rapidly that they become a nuisance. The so-called 'garden pests' are in this category and it is not always the absence of predators that explains their great numbers. Sometimes, as in the case of the cabbage white butterfly, whose caterpillars eat brassica crops, it is more to do with the fact that in a garden (or on a farm) their host plants are concentrated in greater numbers than they would be in the wild. Or, in the case of hybrid roses, the plant's growth is softer and more succulent than that of a wild species and so more attractive to insects and animals.

The introduction of ash trees is our garden had an unexpected result. Although the bullfinches were welcome for their beauty, we regretted that they destroyed so much blossom. But once the ash bore seeds, the birds turned their attention to the 'keys'. Thus the once denuded trees are again as beautiful as they should be.

APPENDICES

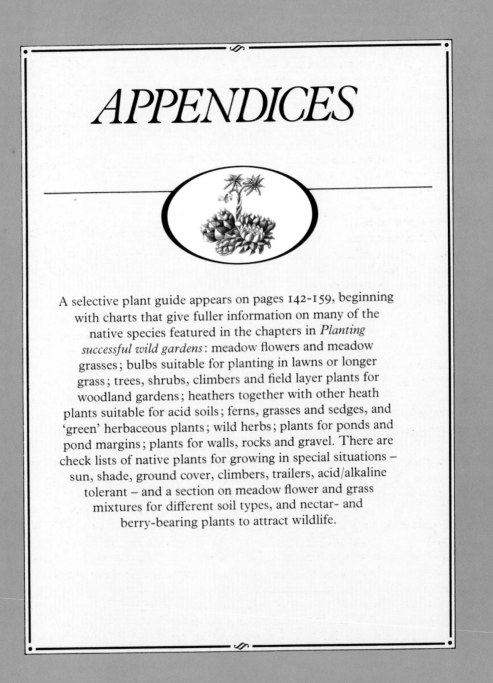

A selective plant guide appears on pages 142-159, beginning with charts that give fuller information on many of the native species featured in the chapters in *Planting successful wild gardens*: meadow flowers and meadow grasses; bulbs suitable for planting in lawns or longer grass; trees, shrubs, climbers and field layer plants for woodland gardens; heathers together with other heath plants suitable for acid soils; ferns, grasses and sedges, and 'green' herbaceous plants; wild herbs; plants for ponds and pond margins; plants for walls, rocks and gravel. There are check lists of native plants for growing in special situations – sun, shade, ground cover, climbers, trailers, acid/alkaline tolerant – and a section on meadow flower and grass mixtures for different soil types, and nectar- and berry-bearing plants to attract wildlife.

MEADOW FLOWERS

A selection of colorful wildflowers, suitable for a variety of soil and moisture conditions. They will enhance an existing lawn, or form the basis of a spring or summer meadow area in the garden. All these species can be obtained from specialist seed merchants (see pages 167-8). For a guide to flower and grass seed mixtures for three soil types, see page 159.

SL = Spring lawn   FL = Flower lawn
M = Summer meadow

	Habit H = height	Flowers Nos = months 1-12	Propagation	Suitability for SL, FL, M	Cultivation
Achillea millefolium Yarrow	Downy, aromatic, perennial; H 10-70cm.	White rose-forms; 6-9.	Seed.	FL, SL, or best in M.	Grows on most soils except the most acid. Tolerates some shade.
Anemone canadensis Canada anemone	Clumping perennial from rhizomes; H 20-70cm.	Large, white; 5-6.	Seed or division of rhizomes.	SL, M.	Damp soil, calcareous or alluvial, sun or light shade.
Anemone caroliniana Carolina anemone	Bushy perennial from tuber; H 5-30cm.	White, 3-4cm across; 4-5.	Seed; division of tubers.	FL, SL, M.	Calcareous, sandy or gravel soils. Often a prairie plant in the wild.
Anemone virginiana Thimbleflower	Hairy perennial from a stout root; H 40-80cm.	Yellowish or greenish white, sometimes tinged red; 6-8.	Seed (easy); seedhead elongated and thimble-like.	FL, M	Will take light shade. Likes drier soil than *A. canadensis*.
Asclepias incarnata Swamp milkweed	Upright perennial; H 30-120cm.	Dusky-rose to white, flat clusters; 6-8.	Seed. Germinates easily.	M.	Will grow in very damp soil, but takes drier conditions.
Asclepias tuberosa Butterflyweed	Spreading perennial with arching branches from root; H 25-75cm.	Brilliant orange, heavy, deep in compound clusters; 6-9.	Seed. Easy and blooms first or second year.	M; also heath in full sun.	Found on acid, sandy or gravelly soil in wild; adaptable to all but heavy clay. Needs drainage.
Bellis perennis Daisy	Low perennial with a rosette of basal leaves; H 3-20cm.	White or pink with yellow centers; 3-10.	Seed. Avoid cultivated double forms.	Best in FL (where it is often a 'weed') or in SL.	All soils and moisture conditions. Will tolerate some shade.
Cardamine pratensis Cuckoo flower	Graceful perennial with pinnate leaves; H 15-60cm.	Lilac or white; 4-6.	Seed or as pot grown plants.	Only suitable for wet areas in FL, SL, or M.	Does best in damp meadows, by ponds or streams on most soil types.
Centaurea nigra Common knapweed	Downy perennial with stiff ribbed stems; H 15-90cm.	Pale purple-red to dark purple; 6-9.	Seed, or as pot grown plant.	Because of its stature best in M.	Will grow on all but the most acid soils. Suitable for all moisture conditions.
Chrysanthemum leucanthemum Oxeye daisy	Large daisy, a perennial with small glossy green leaves; H 20-70cm.	White with yellow centers; 6-8.	Seed. Germination usually 90% plus.	Essential for all meadows and easy to grow.	On all but the most acid clays or sands. Tolerates a wide range of moisture.
Claytonia virginica Spring beauty	Delicate perennial from a deep-seated corm; H 4-20cm.	White, with fine pink lines; 4-5.	Seed.	FL, SL.	Will grow in almost any soil, in sun or deep shade; looks well with *Bellis*.
Daucus carota Queen Anne's lace	Hairy biennial with stiff sold stems; umbellifer; H 30-100cm.	White; 6-8.	Seed. Sow in autumn.	M. Cut late if this is to survive.	Has a preference for dry calcareous soils.
Galium verum Lady's bedstraw	Sprawling perennial; smells of new-mown hay; H 15-100cm.	Bright yellow; 7-9.	Seed.	Can survive in mown lawns, but best in M.	In grassland on all but the most acid soils. Will grow in hedgebanks. A scrambler.
Geranium maculatum	Erect perennial with handsome leaves; H 20-55cm.	Rose, lavender or white, to 5cm; 5-6.	Seed, but slow.	SL.	Prefers moist, neutral or slightly acid soil. Will grow in shade.

	Habit H = height	Flowers Nos = months 1-12	Propagation	Suitability for SL, FL, M	Cultivation
Heliopsis helianthoides False-sunflower	Branched perennial; H 30-150cm.	Composite, orange-yellow, sunflower-like, 6-8cm across; 6-9 (long-lasting).	Seed.	M.	Will grow in almost any soil, but best in slightly acid or neutral soil with plenty of moisture.
Hypochaeris radicata Cat's-ear	Erect tufted perennial with round-toothed leaves in basal rosette; H 20-60cm.	Bright yellow, gray violet beneath; 6-9.	Easy from seed or as pot grown plant.	Common as 'weed' on many lawns, but also good for M.	Will grow in all soils and moisture conditions. Tolerant of some shade.
Lotus corniculatus Common birdsfoot-trefoil	Prostrate perennial with trifoliate leaves, highly variable; H 10-70cm.	Yellow often streaked with red; 6-9.	Seed. Scarification enhances germination.	Strains suitable for FL, SL and M. Beware vigorous agricultural strains.	A highly variable species which will grow on all but the most acid soils. Suitable for all moisture conditions.
Lychnis flos-cuculi Ragged robin	Slender perennial with pointed leaves; H 30-75cm.	Rose-red, rarely white; 5-7.	Seed or as pot grown plants. Seed very small.	SL or M. Damp areas only.	Damp or wet soils. Good for edges of ponds, marshes, stream banks.
Malva moschata Musk mallow	Graceful hairy perennial; H 30-85cm.	Rose-pink, also a white form; 7-8.	Seed or as pot grown plants.	M or shady ride in wood.	On most moderately fertile soils. Tolerates shade.
Medicago lupulina Black medick	Low prostrate downy annual; H 5-30cm.	Yellow; 4-8.	Seed.	Does well in FL. Also suitable for SL and M.	All soils and will grow in dry places. Often short-lived but replaces itself by seeding.
Prunella vulgaris Self-heal	Short creeping downy perennial; H 5-30cm.	Violet to pink; 6-9.	Seed.	FL, SL or M.	Prefers basic or neutral soils under a wide range of moisture and light conditions.
Ranunculus acris Meadow buttercup	Hairy perennial with deeply cut palmate leaves; H 15-100cm.	Bright yellow, glossy; 5-7.	Seed or as pot grown plants.	SL or better in M.	Best in damp grassland on neutral or calcareous soils.
Ranunculus bubosus Bulbous buttercup	Hairy perennial with marked swollen base to stem; H 15-45cm.	Bright yellow underside shiny; 4-6.	Seed or as pot grown plants.	Common 'weed' of many lawns, but good for M.	Dry soils, with a marked preference for calcareous or neutral.
Rudbeckia triloba Brown-eyed Susan	Short-lived perennial, much branched; H 30-90cm.	Composite, yellow with dark brown central cone; 6-10.	Seed; abundant and easy, blooms first year.	M.	Will take some shade; prefers moisture-retentive soil.
Sanguisorba canadensis Canadian burnet	Upright perennial; H 30cm to 2m.	White flowers, tinged pink, in cylindric spikes, 5-20cm long; 8-10.	Seed.	Wet M, bog.	Will grow in acid or alkaline soils as long as they are moist.
Trifolium dubium Lesser trefoil	Low annual, often goes purplish; H 5-25cm.	Yellow turning brown; 5-10.	Seed.	Excellent in mown lawns and survives by seeding.	Grows best in open vegetation on all soil types. Completes life-cycle quickly.
Trifolium pratense Red clover	Slightly downy perennial; H 10-60cm.	Pink-purple; 5-9.	Seed. Scarification enhances germination.	SL, or M.	Tolerates all but the most acid soils. Avoid vigorous cultivars.
Veronica chamaedrys Germander speedwell	Weak hairy perennial; H 10-40cm.	Bright blue with white eye; 3-7.	Seed. Germination usually low and erratic.	FL, SL or M.	Will grow in most soils and will tolerate shade, e.g. suitable for woodland paths.
Viola sororia (V. papilionacea) Meadow violet	Clumping rhizomatous perennial; H 6-25cm.	Violet-blue, sometimes white or reddish-purple; 4-5.	Seed, abundantly produced; easy.	FL, SL, M.	Beautiful in flower, but may be too invasive for some FL.

143

BULBS AND MEADOW GRASSES

Closely mown lawns give one no idea of how beautiful grasses can be when allowed
to flower nor how attractive they are to many forms of wildlife. It is so easy to
add to existing kinds by sowing seed. In short grass in spring or autumn,
little drifts of bulbous plants, bought from bulb merchants, will provide
a succession of enchanting flowers.

	Habit H = height	Foliage	Flowers Nos = months 1-12	Natural habitat	Cultivation
BULBS & CORMS					
Allium cernuum Nodding onion	Hardy bulbous perennial; H 10-30cm.	Grasslike, green or glaucous.	Small, nodding rose-pink to white, in globose clusters; 5-7.	NY to BC, south to Ga. and Tex.	Alpine meadows, rocky slopes.
Camassia quamash (*C. esculenta*) Common camash	Hardy bulbous perennial; H 35-50cm.	Basal, strap-shaped, blue-green.	Racemes deep violet-blue, irregular in shape otherwise squill-like; 5-6.	BC and Alberta south to Idaho and Oregon.	Moist meadows, river bottoms; soil neutral or acid; intolerant of drought.
Claytonia virginica Spring beauty	Delicate perennial from deep corm; H 8-15cm.	Fleshy, narrow.	Starry, white or pink, 1cm; 3-5.	Common throughout much of US.	Grows best in acid or neutral moist soils, sun or shade.
Colchicum autumnale Meadow saffron	Variable perennial which produces flowers in the autumn and leaves the following spring; H 20-25cm.	Bright green; 3-8, large and lanceolate.	Rosy-mauve, rarely white, crocus like with long orange anthers; 8-10.	In damp meadows and woods, Europe.	Prefers damp, neutral or basic soils; good by pond.
Erythronium grandiflorum Glacier lily	Hardy bulbous perennial; H 15-20cm.	Basal, tuliplike, olive-green.	Yellow, with recurved segments (like turkscap lily) 1-5 per scape; 4-5.	BC and Mont. south to Ga. and Tex.	Alpine meadows, moist, acid soils.
Galanthus nivalis Snowdrop	Vary variable perennial; H 10-20cm.	Grey-green, linear, usually 2.	White, streaked green; drooping; 1-3.	Naturalized in damp woods, on banks and old dwelling sites.	Grows well in short grass
Leucojum aestivum Summer snowflake	Perennial; H 60cm.	Mid-green; linear.	Pure white, green-tipped in clusters of 4-8; 4-5.	Naturalized especially along waterways in US.	Easily grown in ordinary soil.
Muscari racemosum Grape hyacinth	Perennial; H 20cm.	Long, narrow and limp.	Dark-blue tipped with white: small; egg-shaped; in dense raceme: musk-like scent; 4-5.	In sandy dry grass-land.	In short grass.
Narcissus majalis Pheasant's eye	Distinctive perennial; H 25-45cm.	Erect, smooth	Outer petals white; eye-like corona, short with red rim; fragrant; 3-5.	Possibly naturalized; a feature of meadows in the South of France.	Almost anywhere in or out of grass.
Narcissus pseudo-narcissus Wild daffodil	Very variable species, parent of many garden varieties; H 20-35cm.	Erect, glaucous.	Bright yellow, somewhat drooping trumpet, petals paler; scented; 3-4.	Damp meadows, riversides, lakesides.	In fairly moist soil.
Ornithogalum umbellatum Nodding star-of-Bethlehem	Hardy, bulbous perennial; H 35-40cm.	Dark green, rather broad, tuliplike.	Flowers in a raceme, hyacinthlike, 2.5cm across, white with green reverse.	In grassy places mainly in East Anglia in England.	Good for grassy woodland borders.

	Habit H = height	Foliage	Flower head Nos = months 1-12	Natural habitat	Cultivation
MEADOW GRASSES					
Agrostis canina Brown bent	Tufted perennial spreading by rhizomes or stolons; H 10-60cm.	Narrow and flattened.	Purple-brown, contracted at first but spreading later.	Damp and dry grassland; E. Canada and US.	Best on more acid soil; useful in a mixture, never alone.
Agrostis tenuis Fine bent, Rhode I. bent	Tufted perennial forming a loose or dense tuft; H to 20cm.	Flat and fine.	Purple; on loose and spreading flower heads.	Acid soils; naturalized throughout US.	Useful for dry acid soils but will also grow on clays and sands.
Alopecurus pratensis Meadow foxtail	Loosely tufted perennial, rarely forming dense patches; H 30-90cm.	Roughish; upper sheaths inflated.	Gray-purple; on long cylindrical flower head.	Common in meadows and by roadsides.	For low-lying moist to wet areas on clay and alluvial soils.
Andropogon scoparius Little bluestem	Clumping perennial; H 40-100cm.	Narrow, glaucous; culms stiff and hard. Whole plant turns bright orange in winter.	Spikelets axillary in leaf bases.	Dry prairies, barrens, shores.	Dry, acid soils.
Anthoxanthum odoratum Sweet vernal grass	Slender tufted perennial; rarely forms a turf; H 20-50cm.	Flat.	Purplish, on slightly branched, egg-shaped flower head.	Common in grassland and in woods.	Suitable for a wide range of soils; a 'must' for most mixtures.
Briza minor Lesser quaking grass	Annual, never forms dense tufts in mixtures; H 10-40cm.	Broad, rough, finely pointed.	Loose and open flower head, nods in the wind.	Open land and waste places, naturalized from Europe.	Sometimes difficult to grow from seed, often better pot grown.
Festuca ovina Sheep's fescue	Densely tufted perennial; very variable; H 10-50cm.	Stiff and narrow, almost hair-like, often waxy-green.	Greenish or purplish; small and variable.	Drier grassland on chalk and limestone.	Suited to poor, well-drained soil; withstands close-cutting.
Festuca rubra Red fescue	Slightly hairy perennial, usually short, creeping; very variable; H 10-60cm.	Inrolled, wire-like and pointed.	Usually with a purplish tinge; variable.	Widespread in all grassy places worldwide.	Varieties for all soil conditions; cultivars are too vigorous.
Festuca saximontana Mountain fescue	Densely tufted perennial; tough and wiry; H 15-60cm.	Bright green to dark green.	Yellow-green on erect cylindrical flower head.	Dry slopes and plains, Alaska and Newfoundland; south in mountains.	Useful for 'difficult' situations; fairly drought-resistant.
Helictotrichon pubescens Downy oat-grass	An attractive loose-tufted perennial; not vigorous; H 30-70cm.	Flat and downy.	Green-purple; branched and spreading.	In rough grass and on dunes.	On damp calcareous soils in milder situations.
Holcus lanatus Yorkshire fog	Gray, softly downy perennial with tough creeping rhizomes; H 20-60cm.	Gray-green; downy; narrowed to fine point.	Whitish then pale-pink to purple; on downy flower head.	Widespread through whole of US; naturalized from Europe.	Too vigorous for lawns but good for meadows; shade-tolerant.
Hordeum jubatum Squirrel-tail grass	Annual or biennial; H 30-70cm.	Gray-green or green, rough, hairy.	Green to purple, nodding, forms dense spike with bristles.	In meadows and pastures.	Does best in heavy soils; worth including for its inflorescence.
Poa pratensis Kentucky bluegrass	Stiff stocky creeping perennial; forms compact turf or tufts; H 15-80cm.	Green or slight bluish or grayish; blunt-tipped.	Purplish; flower head often triangular in outline.	Drier grassy places	On well-drained soil; will tolerate some shade.
Poa trivialis Rough meadow-grass	Loosely tufted perennial with creeping stolons, vigorous; H 20-60cm.	Pale and flat.	Green, purplish or reddish; in erect, dense panicles.	In moist and often shaded grassy places.	Useful for damp soils, green in winter.
Sorghastrum nutans Indian grass	Clumping perennial; H 80-200cm.	Glaucous, persistent when dried (winter).	Panicle slender cylindrical, to 50cm; pale straw color; fawn colored hairs.	Dry, sterile fields, railroad banks, barrens.	Best in dry, acid soils.
Trisetum flavescens Yellow-oat-grass	Pale, slender loosely tufted perennial with few basal leaves; H 20-50cm.	Narrow and flat.	Shining yellow; on spreading flower head.	Fields and roadsides, naturalized from Europe.	Best on calcareous soils, drought resistant; not highly competitive.

TREES AND WOODLAND PLANTS

These trees and shrubs can be bought as mature plants, in which case they may take two or three years to become properly established. Those grown more cheaply from seed mature surprisingly quickly and soon outpace the others. The field layer flowering species can be bought as plants, roots or seed from garden centers and specialists.

Z = hardiness zones	Habit Height = H; Spread = S	Foliage.	Flowers Nos = months 1-12	Fruit	Cultivation
TREES					
Acer saccharum Sugar maple Z 4-7	Tall, roundheaded tree; H 22m; S 18m.	Large, 5-lobed, brilliant deep golden to orange red in autumn.	Small, pale yellow in clusters; early spring.	Keys green turning brown.	Well drained, fertile soil. Intolerant of poor drainage, salt and air pollution.
Betula papyrifera White, paper, or canoe birch Z 3-7	Tall, handsome tree; snowy bark, red brown on young trees.	Oval, pointed; clear yellow in autumn.	Catkins.	Small, brown seeds eaten by finches and small mammals.	Well-drained soil. Does best where summers are cool.
Carpinus caroliniana Ironwood, American hornbeam Z 4-9	Small, graceful tree; trunk smooth, gray, sinewy in appearance; H 10m; S 10m.	Toothed, prominently veined, oval, bright green turning yellow.	Catkins.	Hoplike clusters of nutlets, each with a leafy bract.	Understory tree. Grows easily in most soils.
Cornus florida Flowering dogwood Z 6-8	Rounded tree, with tiered branches; H 10m; S 10m.	Ovate, pointed, glaucous green, turning deep claret in autumn.	White or pink, in clusters tended by 4 showy bracts, covering tree; 4-5.	Scarlet, in tight clusters. (Excellent food for birds, squirrels, etc.)	No woodland complete without dogwood. Needs rich, humusy soil and moisture.
Crataegus viridis Green hawthorn Z 5-9	Roundheaded tree; H 10m; S 10m.	Toothed, bright green; very lustrous.	Like pear blossom, white, in flat clusters, strongly odorous; 5.	Red, about 8mm across, lasting much of winter. (Good wildlife food.)	Will grow in wet or dry soils; var. 'Winter King' selected for large, long-lasting fruits.
Ilex opaca American holly Z 6-9	Dense, upright evergreen tree; H 12m; S 8m.	Ovate-oblong, dull green, bristle-toothed. May wind-burn bronzy in winter.	Small, greenish white, fragrant; sexes on different plants. Good bee plant.	On female trees only, red, in clusters. (Eaten by birds.)	Will grow in wet acid soil. In north may need protection from winds.
Malus coronaria Wild crab apple Z 5-7	Small, spreading tree; H 8m; S 8m.	Rather large, downy, oval; lobed on young branches.	Large (5cm) clear pink, fragrant; early May.	Flattened, yellow-green apples, hard and sour, 3-5cm.	Understory tree, good in rich, well drained soil.
Prunus serotina Rum or black cherry Z 4-9	Tall, handsome, open tree with dark typically cherry bark; H 25m; S 15m.	Oval or oblong, lustrous, dark green, turning yellow or orange.	Small, white, in fragrant, pendulous racemes in late spring.	Small, bitter purple-black cherries in late summer. (Excellent bird food.)	One of the most disease-resistant cherries.
SHRUBS					
Cornus sericea Red-osier dogwood Z 3-8	Dense, rounded deciduous shrub; bright red (or yellow) twigs in winter; H 3m; S 3m.	Pointed, oval, medium green turning dark red in fall.	Small, white, in flat clusters, early summer.	Clusters, pale blue to white, quickly eaten by birds.	Adaptable to any soil, acid or alkaline, wet or dry.
Corylus americana American hazel Z 3-8	Thicket forming shrub; H 3m; S 2m.	Oval, rounded or heart-shaped at base, to 12cm long; yellow in autumn.	Catkins, the male golden yellow, 7-8cm long; early spring.	Filbert or hazel nut. (Edible to man and a variety of animals.)	Any soil, even sterile gravels.
Prunus americanus American wild plum Z 4-9	Roundheaded, suckering shrubby tree with black bark and often thorny branches; H 7m.	Small, oval, pointed; orange yellow in fall.	Abundant, snowy white on black branches in earliest spring.	Red or yellow, sweet, 5cm long.	Grows in most soils. Soon becomes a dense thicket from root suckers.

Z = hardiness zones	Habit Height = H; Spread = S	Foliage	Flowers Nos = months 1-12	Fruit	Cultivation
Rhamnus caroliniana Carolina buckthorn Indian cherry Z 6-9	Upright shrub; H to 10m.	Lustrous, bright green, narrow; yellow in fall.	Clustered, greenish, inconspicuous.	Cherrylike, sweet, red turning black. (Good for wildlife.)	Easy and adaptable.
Rosa virginiana Virginia rose Z 5-8	Thicket-forming shrub, twigs red; H to 1.5m.	Small, compound, dark green and very glossy. Orange red in fall.	Deep rose, 5-petaled, 6cm across; 6-8.	Small, red hips, 1.5cm across.	Will grow in most soils including beach sands. Needs some sun for flowering.
Viburnum trilobum High-bush cranberry Z 2-7	Upright, bushy; H 4m; S 3m.	Maplelike, turning flame red.	White, flat-topped, with outer ring of much larger flowers.	Translucent scarlet berries persist well into winter. (Valuable for wildlife.)	Moist soil and some shade.
CLIMBERS					
Clematis virginiana American virgin's bower Z 4-8	Woody vine; H to 6m.	Ternate or pinnate, opposite, deciduous.	Creamy white in fragrant panicles; 7-8.	Conspicuous hairy seedheads like grayish shaving brushes.	Adaptable to soil pH. Needs moisture.
Lonicera sempervirens Trumpet honeysuckle Z 4-9	Twining vine; H 4-6m.	Evergreen, large oval-oblong, glaucous, 7cm long.	Tubular, scarlet in clusters; 5cm long (hummingbird flower); 6-7.	Succulent, coral red, clustered.	Does well in moist soil, acid or neutral.
Rosa setigera Prairie rose Z 4-9	Shrub with long trailing stems; H to 5m.	Leaflets 3-5.	Flowers 5cm across, clustered, pink, fading paler; scentless; 6-7.	Globose, small (8mm), red.	Robust plant, parent of many hybrids.
Smilax walteri Red-berried greenbrier Z 6-9	Deciduous vine, older stems prickly, climbing by tendrils; H to 6m.	Lance-ovate to oblong, glossy, to 10cm long.	Greenish, in axillary clusters.	Bright red, showy.	Often grows in wet acid places in wild.
FIELD LAYER					
Anemone quinquifolia Wood anemone	Slender, horizontal rootstocks; H 7-15cm.	Ternate, but toothed so as to look like 5 leaves – hence Latin name.	White with many yellow anthers, 2.5-3.5cm; 4-5.	None.	In groups under trees or shrubs, especially conifers and rhododendrons. Wet, acid soil.
Anemonella thalictroidis Rue anemone	Delicate perennial from cluster of tuberous roots; H 10-30cm.	Columbinelike, blue-green, abundant, persisting most of summer.	Anemonelike, white or pink, 2.5-3cm; 4-5.	None.	Upland woods, in rocky or loose humusy soil. Acid or slightly acid soil.
Convallaria montana American lily-of-the-valley	Creeping rootstock; H 15-20cm.	Broad, oblong or elliptical.	White, bell-like in raceme; richly fragrant; 5-6.	Bright red berries in summer.	Needs humus-rich soil and moisture at roots; does well in light shade.
Mertensia Virginia cowslip or bluebell	Smooth, glaucous perennial from thick, tuberous root; H 20-50cm.	Large, smooth untoothed, not persisting in summer.	Sky-blue from pink buds, trumpet-shaped, 2.5-3cm, gracefully pendulous clusters; 4-5.	None.	River bottoms. Rich soil, acid to neutral, with abundant moisture, at least in spring.
Trillium grandiflorum Large-flowered trillium, wake-robin	Handsome, herbaceous perennial from tuberous rootstock; H 15-45cm.	In 3s, green, pointed, oval to nearly orbicular at tip of a stout stem.	Petals (3) white, showy; flowers 7-10cm wide, fading pink; 4-5.	None.	Rich soil, moderately acid to neutral. Plenty of humus essential.
Viola conspersa American dog violet	Stemmed perennial; H 5-20cm.	Toothed, heart-shaped.	Blue-violet or white; short spur.	None.	Rich deciduous woods, often on limestone. Best in fertile soil, slightly acid to neutral.
Viola pubescens Downy yellow violet	White-villous stems; H 10-45cm.	Thick, hairy, heart-shaped and pale green.	Yellow with purple veins; 4-5.	None.	As *V. conspersa*.

PINE BARREN AND HEATH PLANTS

Many acid-loving plants are evergreen. Most of them are long-lived. They are also excellent ground covers, spreading out attractively over the soil, merging one with another. Almost all of those described here have been in cultivation for many years. Some can be bought from garden centers, others from specialist nurseries.

	Habit H = height; S = spread	Foliage	Flowers Nos = months 1-12	Natural habitat	Cultivation
Andromeda polifolia Bog rosemary	Straggly evergreen shrub; H 30-60cm.	Linear, shiny grey-green above, glaucous below.	Bell-like, small and nodding, pink or white; 5-6.	Peat bogs in North.	Peaty soil with adequate moisture; preferably in sun or partial shade.
Arctostaphylos uva-ursi Bearberry	Prostrate evergreen shrub of rapidly spreading habit; H 90-15cm; S 1.2m.	Mid-dark green, leathery, glossy.	Small, globular, pink or white, in small, pendant, terminal racemes; 5-6.	Common on stony moors and mountains in North.	Well-drained, light, lime-free peaty soil in woodland borders.
Aster specabilis Showy aster	Perennial, spreading slowly by stolons; H to 90cm.	Oval, grayish green, mostly basal.	Rich purple, yellow-centered; 9.	Coastal barrens, pine woods.	Sandy, acid soil.
Calluna vulgaris Scotch heather	Evergreen upright bushy shrub; H 15-45cm; S 30-45cm.	Linear, minute, numerous in four longitudinal overlapping rows.	Pale-purple in racemes 5-8cm long; 7-9.	Heaths and moors in Europe and N. Asia.	On acid peaty soil in open position.
Cytisus scoparius Common broom	Deciduous, erect much-branched shrub with stiff, wiry, green angled branches; H 0.3-2.4m.	Three-foliate at lower ends of shoots; pubescent when young.	Rich yellow, sometimes tinged red, solitary or in pairs; 5-6.	Pine barrens, road-sides; from Europe.	Well-drained soil; does best in sand and gravel.
Daboecia cantabrica St Dabeoc's heath	Evergreen heath-like shrub; H to 1m.	Narrow, ovate-lanceolate, white, tomatose beneath.	Rosy-purple or white egg-shaped, in upright terminal racemes 8-15cm long; 5 onwards.	Heaths in Ireland and Spain.	Good for woodland fringes; needs protection from cold winds and drought.
Epigaea repens Trailing arbutus	Prostrate, creeping evergreen.	Leathery, pale green.	White or pink, in clusters, fragrant; 3-5.	Sandy or rocky woodland.	Sandy, acid soil.
Erica cinerea Twisted heather	Neat, very varied branching, evergreen shrub with downy, young wood; H 23-60cm.	Dark green, short; linear with rolled margins, usually in threes.	Crimson-purple in terminal umbels or racemes, fading to russet brown bells;	Common on drier heaths and moors, Europe; naturalized New England.	Well-drained deep peaty cool moist (never water-logged) soil.
Erica tetralix Cross-leaved heath	Spreading, downy evergreen shrub; H 30-45cm.	Four in a whorl or cross; green, short; hairy, white beneath.	In terminal racemes of 4-8; waxy rose-pink, small and drooping; 6-8.	Common on boggy heaths.	Cool moist peaty soil or leafy loam.
Erica vagans Cornish heath	Symmetrical evergreen shrub, bushier than other heathers; H up to 2.4m; S 30-60cm.	In a whorl of 4-5, short, linear smooth, glossy, heathers	In terminal racemes 7.5-20cm long; pale pink or lilac with chocolate anthers; 7-9.	Wet bogs in mild situations.	Vigorous; will tolerate ordinary garden soil. Easily grown, pollution-tolerant.
Gaultheria procumbens Wintergreen, teaberry	Stoloniferous shrublet; H 5-15cm.	Dark green, glossy, smells of wintergreen.	White, bell-shaped; 7-8.	Woods and clearings.	Moist acid soil.
Kalmia latifolia Mountain laurel	Shrub or small tree; H to 4.5m.	Evergreen leathery, deep green, pointed at both ends.	Pink or white, in bowl-shaped clusters; 5-7.	Rocky woods.	Sandy soil with some peat, partial shade.
Ledum groenlandicum Labrador tea	Evergreen upright shrub with rusty tomentose young wood; H 20-100cm.	Variously shaped, rusty tomentose beneath.	Creamy-white in terminal clusters; 5-6.	Peat bogs in North.	Moist peaty soil or lime-free loam.

	Habit H = height; S = spread	Foliage	Flowers Nos = months 1-12	Natural habitat	Cultivation
Leiophyllum buxifolium Sand myrtle	Low, mounded shrub; H 10-20cm.	Small, dark green, persistent.	White, in large, umbel-like clusters; 3-5.	Sandy pine barrens.	Lime-free soil.
Linnaea borealis Twinflower	Trailing, sub-shrubby, evergreen perennial; H 5-8cm; S to 60cm.	Rounded or small, ovate, slightly hairy.	Pink, trumpet-shaped, pendulous on slender stems; fragrant; 6-8.	Northern forest and cold bogs.	Shade; cool peaty or leafy soil.
Lupinis perennis Sundial lupine	Clumping perennial; H 20-60cm.	Gray-green, palmately divided, long stalked, handsome.	Deep purple-blue on long racemes; 4-6.	Dry sandy woods and banks.	Slightly acid soil, well-drained, in full sun.
Mitchella repens Partridgeberry	Trailing perennial; stems 15-45cm long.	Roundish, shining, evergreen.	White, paired;	Woods.	Soil with peat, some shade.
Moneses uniflora One-flowered pyrola	Single species of its genera, dwarf perennial; H 8-15cm.	Radical, vaguely spoon-shaped, leathery and toothed.	Fragrant, waxy-white, or pink, solitary and drooping; 6-7.	Open moist mossy places in coniferous forest.	Edge of woodland in light peaty soil, or in partial shade in rock gardens.
Myrica gale Bog myrtle	Small tufted deciduous, resinous shrub with reddish-brown twigs; fragrant; H 60-120cm.	Oblanceolate, dark glossy green above; paler or downy underneath.	Males on orange stalkless catkins; females small, closely packed and resinous.	Bogs and wet acid soils in North.	Only grows well on acid loam or peat soils.
Pyrola minor Lesser pyrola	Slender, creeping, dwarf, hardy, glabrous perennial; H 8cm.	Roundish.	Waxy white tinged with rose in many-flowered racemes.	Cool woods.	As for *Moneses*.
Rhododendron calendulaceum Flame azalea	Shrub; H to 3.6m.	Hairy, light green, deciduous.	Brilliant orange, yellow or red, trumpet-shaped; 5-6.	Mountain woodland, balds.	Peaty, well-drained soil.
Rhododendron catawbiense Catawba rhododendron	Dense and spreading evergreen shrub; H to 3m.	Glossy, dark green.	Lavender or white (white very lovely); 5-6.	Mountain woodland.	Rich, moist, well-drained, acid soil, partial shade.
Rhododendron maximum Great laurel, rosebay	Large evergreen shrub or small tree; H 1.5-12.5m.	Glossy green, woolly beneath.	Pink to white, from pink buds, in compact clusters; 6-7.	Damp woods and swamps.	Rich, moist well-drained acid soil, shade.
Rhododendron periclymenoides Pink azalea	Deciduous shrub; H to 3m.	Hairy, light green.	Bright pink; 5-6.	Woods, barrens, roadsides.	Acid, well-drained soil.
Trientalis europaea Chickweed wintergreen	Perennial with erect stem, creeping rhizome; H 10cm.	Shining rigid, mostly broad lanceolate 5-7 in a whorl at top of stem or below the flowers.	White or pale pink, few on long stem, 6-7.	High moors and coniferous woods in North, Europe, North Asia.	Light, rich soil, plenty of leafmold; shady site.
Vaccinium myrtillus Bilberry, blaeberry, whortleberry	Deciduous dwarf shrub with angled green twigs; H 15-45cm; S 30-45cm.	Bright green, oval, turning dull purple and gold; pointed, downy on veins beneath.	Pink, almost round attractively lobed; 4-7.	Common on heaths and moors.	Moist rock or heather garden; acid soils, more tolerant of exposure and shade than *Calluna*.
Vaccinium oxycoccus Small cranberry	Creeping, straggling evergreen shrub with wiry ascending stems.	Dark green above, glaucous below sparse and alternate.	Pink, usually solitary or 2-4 urn-shaped; 6-8.	In bogs with sphagnum moss.	Moist rock or heather garden; acid soil.
Vaccinium uliginosum Bog bilberry	Deciduous, stiff, much-branched low broad bush with glbrous young shoots.	Blue-green waxy round, glaucous beneath.	Pink, usually solitary or 2-4 urn-shaped; 5-7.	Wet moors.	As above.
Viola pedata Birdsfoot violet	Dwarf, clumping perennial; H 10-25cm.	Finely divided, larkspurlike.	Blue-violet, large and showy; 4-6.	Sandy acid barrens.	Sandy soil in full sun.

FERNS AND FOLIAGE PLANTS

Because, for some years, flower arrangers have been interested in growing
and gathering leaves and grasses as much as they have been in blooms,
most nurseries and garden centers offer a fine range of green flowers, ferns, plants
with handsome foliage and grasses in great variety. At the same time,
many of the species listed here can be raised from seeds.

	Habit H = height	Foliage	Flowerhead Nos = months 1-12	Natural habitat	Cultivation
FERNS					
Asplenium trichomanes Maidenhair spleenwort	Small and delicate forming dense tufts; H to 20cm.	Long, with oval or oblong leaflets narrowing at base.	None.	Moist, moss-covered cliffs, rocks and walls.	Lime-loving; well-drained site.
Athyrum filix-femina Lady fern	Large, showy, lacy-cut; H 15-150cm.	Fresh green; fronds divided into lesser fronds.	None.	Damp woods, rocks, hedge banks.	Leafy soil or loamy peat; moist; in semishade.
Blechnum spicant Deer fern	Extremely variable, evergreen, sturdy; grows in a tuft; H to 50cm.	Dark green, lanceolate; barren fronds shorter and narrower than fertile fronds.	None.	In woods and among rocks from Calif. to Alaska; on acid soil.	Ideal for moist shady nooks; dislikes lime.
Dryopteris filix-mas Male fern	Extremely hardy and very variable; almost evergreen; H 60-120cm.	Broad fronds with pinnae; 10-15cm long.	None.	Wooded and rocky areas.	Prefers a light sandy loam to stiff clay; prefers shade.
Phyllitis scolopendrium Hartstongue	Tufted evergreen; H 45-60cm.	Undivided, strap-shaped, wavy.	None.	On rocks and hedge-banks.	Leafy well-drained soil.
Polypodium dryopteris Oak fern	Graceful with creeping rootstock; H 15-30cm.	Emerald green.	None.	Damp woods and rocky screes.	Peaty soil, well-drained.
Polypodium vulgare Common polypody	Small vigorous evergreen; mat-forming; H 15-35cm.	Broad, green, deep-cut, wavy, oblong-lanceolate fronds, sometimes lustrous-golden above.	None.	In woods elevated on trees, stumps, moist banks and walls.	Most luxuriant in almost any position except marsh; will take sun and drought.
Polystichum aculeatum Hard shield fern	Variable, bold, handsome tufted with long-stalked fronds; H to 1.2m.	Broad, leathery, ovate-lanceolate.	None.	Hedge banks, wood margins and thickets.	Best in shade; should be watered freely.
GRASSES & SEDGES					
Briza maxima Pearl grass	Annual; forms small tuft of erect smooth stems; H 38-50cm.	Bright green, narrow and pointed with rough upper-sides.	Panicle nodding with about 8 large, green, ovate spikelets.	Much cultivated in gardens. Locally introduced from Europe.	Well-drained soil in sunny position.
Briza media Quaking grass	Slow-creeping rhizomatous perennial with erect, slender smooth stems; H 23-45cm.	Light green, flat and tapering with rough margins.	Panicle 15cm long, small purple-brown heart-shaped spikelets.	On sunny well-drained grassland. Naturalized from Europe.	As above.
Carex pendula Drooping sedge	Graceful tufted perennial, 3-angled solid stems; H 90-150cm.	Pale glossy, green, broad.	Very long, drooping spikes.	Damp woods and shady places.	Suitable for watersides also.
Eriophorum polystachion Common cotton grass	Perennial untufted sedge; H 15-60cm.	Grooved, grass-like, triquetrous.	Brown-green; terminal drooping cymes.	Bogs.	Suitable for pool margins and boggy places.
Festuca arundinacea Tall fescue	Grows as large coarse tussocks; H to 1.5m.	Long, flat, coarse with hairy sheaths.	Graceful panicle with opposite branches.	Dry grassy places on clay.	Any meadow garden.
Glyceria grandis Reed meadow grass	Stout, reedlike perennial that can form large patches; H 90-150cm.	1.5cm broad, rather smooth.	Open, loose with several flowered purplish spikelets.	Margins of fresh and brackish water.	Useful for waterside gardens, also on moist soil.

	Habit H = height	Foliage	Flowerhead Nos = months 1-12	Natural habitat	Cultivation
Melica mutica Wood melick	Common, graceful, slender-stemmed perennial; H 40-90cm.	Limp, flat and downy, pointed leaf sheath often hairy.	Open panicle with branches of purplish-brown, egg-shaped spikelets.	Woods and shady hedge banks, especially on calcareous soils.	In leafy soil.
Phalaris canariensis Canary grass	Tufted annual; H 25-90cm.	Flat.	Large green and white plumes.	Naturalized from Mediterranean.	Ordinary soil; full sun.
Triodia flava Purple-top	Clumping perennial; H 60-120cm.	Broad, pale green, becoming pale straw yellow in winter.	Large, open to 45cm long; spikelets deep bronzy purple.	Roadsides, meadows, wood edges.	On well-drained soil in sun.

GREEN HERBACEOUS PLANTS

	Habit H = height	Foliage	Flowerhead Nos = months 1-12	Natural habitat	Cultivation
Alchemilla vulgaris Lady's mantle	Hardy perennial with short, stout, black rootstock; H 16-46cm.	Hairy above, green beneath; numerous, wide, and kidney-shaped on long stalks.	Yellow-green; in foamy racemes or panicles; 6-8.	Grassland.	Ordinary soil well-drained.
Arum italicum Cuckoo pint	A variable plant similar to *A. maculatum* (below); H 25-70cm.	More triangular than *A. maculatum* with creamy, patterned veins; on long stalks.	Light-green drooping spathe with yellow-orange spadix; 5-6.	Woodland.	Sheltered shaded site.
Arum maculstum Cuckoo pint	Tuberous perennial with handsome foliage; H 25-40cm.	Dark-green often spotted purplish-black; large, bluntly arrow-shaped leaves in spring.	Arum-like, green spathe, often with purple margin and veining; 4-5.	Hedgerows and woods.	Any rich, moist, partially shaded site.
Daphne laureola Spurge laurel	Smooth erect evergreen shrub; H 60-90cm.	Dark-green, glossy, leathery, broad-lanceolate.	Green, small, fragrant, in racemes of 5-10; 3-4.	In woods on limestone.	In limy soil in partial shade.
Eryngium maritimum Sea holly	Very glaucous, spiny, umbelliferous perennial; H 30-45cm.	Leathery, white glaucous; basal, heart-shaped, upper stem-clasping palmately lobed.	Powder blue and mauve, globular; surrounded by broad, spiny bracts.	On sand and short turf by the sea.	Gravel gardens in light sandy soil and sunny position.
Euphorbia lathyrus Caper spurge	Handsome, glaucous, waxy, erect, annual or biennial; H 90cm.	Lower leaves lanceolate, upper ones broad.	Small yellow-green on long-stalked umbels.	In woods on limestone.	Self-seeds freely.
Helleborus foetidus Stinking hellebore	Leafy, glabrous evergreen sub-shrub.	Dark shining green; leathery; palmate with 7-10 lanceolate toothed segments.	Yellow-green; cup-shaped; crowded panicles of bracts and flowers; 3-5.	In woods and scrub on limestone.	Ordinary soil, deep but well-drained, in shade.
Helleborus viridis Green hellebore	Glabrous, deciduous.	Dull green above, paler with prominent veins beneath; 7-11 segments on long stem.	Bright green; cup-shaped; scentless; few flowers on each stem; 3-5.	In woods on limestone.	As above.
Iris foetidissima Gladdon	Hardy perennial, grows in thick tufts; H 50cm.	Dark evergreen; glossy; acrid and highly fetid when crushed.	Slate gray-purple in lateral clusters; small; short-lived; 6.	In dry woods, thickets and hedge banks on dry calcareous soils.	In shade in rich humus.
Petasites fragrans Winter heliotrope	Naturalized perennial with deep rhizomes.	Very large, cordate, coming just after flowers emerge.	White or pale lilac, vanilla-scented, 6-8 heads per stem; 1-2.	Banks and roadsides.	Effective by watersides. Good on banks; can become invasive so should be isolated.
Polygonatum multiflorum Solomon's seal	Graceful hardy perennial with round, arching stems; H 60-120cm.	Oblong; alternate; stem-clasping.	Greenish-white; in small hanging clusters; 5-6.	In woods.	Ideal for naturalizing in woods and shady borders.

HERBS

Herbs are among the easiest of all plants to grow. Most settle down as happily in a
garden environment as in their natural habitats. None seems to be rare.
Most are easily raised from seed and have been propagated this way for centuries.
Alternatively, you can often find plants on sale, or beg one or two from
a kind gardener who is willing to share them.

	Habit H = height	Foliage	Flowers Nos = months 1-12	Habitat in the wild	Cultivation
Allium schoenoprasum Chives	Hardy, tufted perennial; narrow bulb covered with crimson sheath; H 8-30cm.	Hollow, cylindrical, glaucous green; fine-pointed.	Rosy-violet, rose in a dense umbel; 6-7.	Rare in the wild; on limestone cliffs in N. Europe, Asia, N. USA.	Ordinary soil in sun or semi-shade.
Angelica archangelica Angelica	Statuesque hardy biennial with a stout hollow stem; aromatic; H 2m.	Bright green compound with terminal leaflet in 3 parts, 0.6-1m wide.	White or green in large compound umbels; 7-8.	Naturalized on some river banks, wet woods and damp grass.	In deep moist soil, in sun or partial shade; keep moist.
Anthemis nobilis Chamomile	Procumbent aromatic perennial; H to 25cm.	Finely-cut 2 pinnate linear; a little downy.	Daisylike rays, white disc, yellow solitary; 6-7.	Sandy soil; grassy and heathy places.	Tolerant of acid soils and some shade.
Anthriscus cerefolium Garden chervil	Free-seeding hardy annual; with furrowed, pubescent stalks; H 60cm.	2 pinnately-cut, delicate; anise-scented.	White in small slightly radiate umbels; 5-6.	Naturalized in some waste places.	Ordinary soil in dappled shade.
Artemisia absinthium Common wormwood	Herbaceous perennial with a woody rootstock; H 1m.	2 or 3 pinnate, silky both sides; bitter-scented.	Downy, yellow; globose; borne in slender leafy panicles 40-45cm long; 7-8.	Waste ground, road-sides and coastal.	Well-drained soil in sunny position.
Artemisia maritima Sea wormwood	Downy subshrub with woody, branched root-stock and herbaceous stems; H 40-60cm.	Pinnate, covered with white down.	Tiny yellow or red, in leafy panicles; 8-9.	Sandy seashores and seasides.	Ordinary soil.
Borago officinalis Borage	Naturalized, stout, roughly hairy annual; H 30-60cm.	Large, ovate, young leaves taste and smell of cucumber.	Panicles of bright blue, star-shaped, drooping; 6-9.	Waste places in the South.	In ordinary dryish soil in sunny position.
Calamintha nepeta Lesser catmint	Branched, downy, gray tufted perennial; H 20-30cm.	Small and hairy, pungently scented..	Pale lilac in loose whorls on leafy stem; 7-8.	Rare; mainly in S. England.	Light soil, in sunny position; will grow on gravel.
Carum carvi Caraway	Biennial with strong tap-root and hollow furrowed and branched stem; H 30-60cm.	2-pinnate, narrow, deeply-cut, much-divided and feathery.	Irregular white umbel and outer flowers; 6-7.	Naturalized but rare.	Ordinary, well-drained soil in full sun.
Foeniculum vulgare Fennel	Short-lived but free-seeding perennial with stout erect stems; H 90-150cm.	3-4 pinnate with very fine segments; beautifully feathery.	Yellow in large umbels; 8-10.	Sea cliffs, waste-ground, motorway verges.	Any type of well-drained soil in sunny open position.
Hypericum androsaemum Tutsan	A medicinal sub-shrub with angled or winged shoots; H 1m.	Broad-oval, pale beneath, resinous.	Yellow in terminal cymes of 3-9; 6-9.	Grass in damp hedge-rows, thickets and ditches.	Almost any soil and situation.
Ligusticum scoticum Lovage	Glabrous perennial with stiff, ribbed, purple stems; H 22-45cm.	Pinnate, bright-green, leathery, glossy; smelling of celery.	12-20 rayed umbels of white or tinged pink flowers; 6-7.	On northern rocky coasts.	Will grow in any ordinary soil.
Marrubium vulgare White horehound	Hoary or woolly perennial with short stout rootstock; H 35-45cm.	Ovate, wrinkled with rounded teeth, in opposite pairs at right angles to each other.	Off-white crowded in axillary whorls; 7-10.	On downs and chalk cliffs.	Well-drained sunny position.

	Habit H = height	Foliage	Flowers Nos = months 1-12	Habitat in the wild	Cultivation
Melissa officinalis Balm	Hardy perennial with erect branched stems; H 30-60cm.	Lemon-scented when bruised; yellow-green, oval, pointed.	White, small and narrow, in whorls on leafy stem; 6-10.	Naturalized; native to Central and South Europe.	Well-drained soil in full sun.
Mentha arvensis Corn mint	Perennial with sprawling leafy stems; H 7-45cm.	Oval, pointed and toothed.	Small, lilac, in tight axillary whorls; 6.	In arable fields and grassland.	Ordinary soil in sun.
Mentha pulegium Pennyroyal	Prostrate, much-branched perennial; H 5-25cm.	Long-stalked, small, oval; scented.	Pale purple in dense, well-spaced whorls; 7-8.	Damp, sandy places.	Light soil with sand added.
Mentha rotundifolia Round-leaved mint	Stout, erect, hairy perennial; taller than most other mints.	Strongly-scented round-ovate, hairy and wrinkled above.	Purple-white in dense conical-cylindrical spikes; 8-9.	In damp and watery places.	Ordinary soil; sun or shade but prefers cool soil.
Mentha spicata Spearmint	Erect perennial with creeping rootstock; H 30-60cm.	Ovate-lanceolate almost sessile; strong mint smell when crushed.	Lilac flowers in whorls on a narrow, loose, interrupted spike; 8-9.	Naturalized, widespread.	Best in fairly moist soil in partial shade.
Myrrhis odorata Sweet cicely	Hairy perennial with hollow, furrowed stem; H 1.5m.	Pale green, finely divided or 3-pinnate, smelling of licorice and anise seed.	White compound umbel with only outer flowers fertile; 5-6.	In grass and hedge-rows in N. England and Scotland.	Thrives in almost all soils.
Nepeta cataria Cat nip	Single species of its genus; erect, hoary, leafy-stemmed perennial; H 30-60cm.	Heart-shaped, deeply lobed at base, white and hairy beneath.	White with dark pink spots; in dense, many-flowered whorls forming broad heads; 7-11.	Open hedge banks roadsides.	Ordinary soil.
Origanum vulgare Marjoram	Strongly aromatic perennial with softly hairy crimson stems; H to 60cm.	Oval, blunt, slightly toothed.	Dark purple buds opening to pale purple, in loose corymbs; 7-8.	Common on calcareous soils.	Well-drained soil in sunny position.
Papaver somniferum Opium poppy	Glaucous, erect annual; very variable; H 45-120cm.	Large (8-12cm) with wavy margins.	Lilac with purple blotch at base; 6-9.	Widespread, naturalized weed of cultivation.	Any soil type in sunny position.
Poterium sanguisorba Salad burnet	Perennial; H 45cm.	Pinnate leaflets in pairs; smell of cucumber when crushed.	Unisexual, green, tiny and petal-less. 5-8.	Grassy places on chalk and limestone.	Well-drained soil in sunny position.
Rumex acetosa Sorrel	Succulent perennial; H 15-60cm.	Arrow-shaped, long stalked, alternate.	Female in greenish erect panicle; male in dense 4-8 flowered clusters; 5-7.	Dry pastures.	Ordinary soil.
Tanacetum vulgare Tansy	Stiff stout aromatic perennial with grooved stems; H to 60cm.	Pinnate with numerous leaflets, deeply toothed.	Golden-yellow; buttonlike; many in stout corymbs; 8-9.	Riversides, grassy verges, waste places and hedge banks.	Ordinary soil; can be invasive.
Thymus drucei Creeping thyme	Extremely variable prostrate mat-forming faintly aromatic perennial; H 5cm.	Oval, very small.	Reddish-purple in roundish heads on erect stems; 6-8.	Dry grassland, heaths and dunes.	Well-drained soil; sunny position.
Thymus pulegiodes Large wild thyme	Spreading, bushy sub-shrub with mostly ascending shoots; H 10-30cm.	Very variable in shape.	Purple, mauve, white or crimson; stems 4-sided; 7-9.	Calcareous dry soils and grassland.	Light, well-drained soil on sunny site.
Valeriana officinalis Common valerian	Hardy perennial, with grooved stems; H 1.5m.	Pinnate, the lower stalked, the leaflets toothed.	Pale pink, darker in bud; small; in numerous corymbs.	Common in ditches, damp woods.	Usually on damp soils; prefers calcareous.

WATER PLANTS

The ever-growing interest in garden pools, and now in larger ponds, has meant that there exists a good selection of aquatic plants on sale, some in a separate department of a garden center, others from aquatic specialists. Although there are many exotics on offer, fortunately native species will also be found which are both handsome and hardy.

	Habit H = height	Foliage	Flowers Nos = months 1-12	Natural habitat	Cultivation
Acorus calamus Sweet flag	Aquatic perennial with creeping rootstock; H 60-90cm.	Long and swordlike, wavy-edged; emits strong aroma when bruised.	Green; densely packed on a spadix; 6-7.	Margins of ponds.	Shallow water and loamy soil.
Alisma-plantago aquatica Great water plantain	Stout aquatic perennial; H 30-60cm.	Long-stalked, ovate, arising from roots.	Pale-rose; small and 3-petalled on whorl-branched spikes; 6-8.	Pond margin and shallow water on silt; seldom on limestone.	In water up to 30cm deep.
Butomus umbellatus Flowering rush	Tall perennial with thick creeping rootstock; H 90-120cm.	Bronze-purple when young; long, linear triquetrous.	Rose-pink; borne on large umbel; 7-9.	By ponds and ditches; especially on clay.	Pond margin.
Caltha palustris Marsh marigold	Perennial with fat, hollow stem and creeping rootstock; H 30-60cm.	Green, glossy, often with purplish sheen; heart-and-kidney-shaped; large, up to 25cm by the summer.	Glossy yellow; large; 4-6.	Marshy places; common.	Pond margin.
Cyperus strigosus Umbrella sedge	Strong-growing hardy perennial with tough, rhizomatous rootstock; H 50-100cm.	Soft, flat and arching.	Golden-brown; in spikelets that form a loose, graceful spray; 8-10.	Ponds, ditches and wet pastures; very local.	Water depth up to 45cm; can be invasive.
Epilobium hirsutum Great willow-herb	Tall downy perennial; H 90-180cm.	Ovate-lanceolate: sessile.	Purplish-pink in leafy corymbs; 7-9.	Ditches and streams; naturalized in E. US.	Pond margin up to 15cm; apt to be invasive.
Eupatorium fistulosum Tall Joe-Pye weed	Tall perennial; stem often reddish, spotted; H 60-120cm.	Short stalked and lanceolate.	Pink, reddish, or nearly white; in close corymbs; 7-9.	Ditches, streamsides and moist ground; common.	Easily grown in ordinary soil; will not grow in water; tolerates some shade.
Filipendula ulmaria Meadowsweet	Stiff-stemmed perennial; H to 120cm.	Pinnate, silvery beneath; stem often purplish.	Cream-colored, in small, fragrant clusters; 6-8.	Wet meadows and ditches.	Moist soil and partial shade.
Hottonia palustris Water violet	Graceful pale-green aquatic perennial with long trailing rhizome; H 30-60cm.	Submerged, in basal rosette; pinnate and finely-lobed.	Pale-lilac with yellow throat; project above. surface; 5-6.	In ditches and ponds.	Will grow in water at least 30cm deep.
Iris pseudacorus Yellow flag	Perennial with thick horizontal rootstock; H 60-90cm.	Blue-green or glaucous, sword-like.	Bright yellow, borne on branching, shiny stems; 6-8.	Common in wet fields and marshes.	Pond margin; needs full sun to flower.
Lysimachia nummularia Creeping jenny	Prostrate evergreen perennial; stems about 30cm long or more.	Opposite; glabrous; rounded.	Bright yellow; cup-shaped in leaf axils; 6-8.	Moist banks.	Pond margin.
Lysimachia vulgaris Yellow loosestrife	Downy perennial; H 60-90cm.	Ovate-lanceolate; whorled or opposite.	Yellow, dotted orange, in leafy terminal clusters; 7-8.	In wet herbage by rivers, ponds and fens.	Pondsides and moist, places, but not in water-logged conditions.
Lythrum salicaria Purple loosestrife	Variable perennial with square stems; H 60-150cm.	Lanceolate, cordate at base.	Bright red-purple on spike-like raceme; 6-7.	River banks, ditches, marshes, commons.	Pond margin; moist soil.

	Habit H = height	Foliage	Flowers Nos = months 1-12	Natural habitat	Cultivation
Mentha aquatica Water mint	Hairy, often purplish perennial with stiff stems; H 22-60cm.	Oval, serrated, becoming smaller at top of stem.	Lilac or reddish in a dense, terminal head, rounded in 2-3 whorls; 7-9.	Damp meadows and river banks.	Moist soil.
Menyanthes trifoliata Bogbean	Distinctive aquatic perennial with procumbent stem and dense mat of roots; H 25cm.	Olive green, smooth, trifoliate.	White, pink in reverse fimbriate, in conspicuous spikes; fragrant; 7-9.	Common in watery bogs.	Will grow in or out of water in a moist site.
Mimulus guttata Monkey flower	Attractive hollow-stemmed perennial; H 10-60cm.	Ovate or oblong, toothed, opposite.	Yellow with 2 dark-red marks at mouth; 6-9.	By shallow streams; Western N. America.	Moist soil.
Myosotis scorpioides Water forget-me-not	Creeping perennial; H 15-30cm.	Bright glossy green, oblong.	Cobalt blue with yellow eyes; often in paired racemes; 4-7.	Ditches, streams and pond margins.	Likes a heavy fertile loam, waterlogged or to depth of 7cm; in full sun.
Narthecium americanum Bog asphodel	Short creeping perennial; H 15-30cm.	Often green, small, flattened, sword-shaped.	Yellow with orange anthers; starlike; in a continuous raceme; 7-8.	Sphagnum bogs.	Boggy, acid soil, turf.
Nuphar microphyllum Small splatter-dock	Aquatic perennial.	Oval and lobed at base.	Yellow 1-4cm across; 6-10.	Ponds and lakes in Canada and NE USA.	As for *Nymphaea odorata*, below.
Nymphaea odorata White water lily	Aquatic perennial with thick fleshy rootstock.	Rounded, floating on long stalks.	White with yellow stamens, floating; fragrant; 6-8.	Sheltered freshwater.	In a fertile loam, 20-30cm deep, in full sun.
Nymphoides peltata Fringed water lily	Long-branching, stemmed aquatic perennial.	Almost orbicular; purple below.	Yellow, 5-lobed in umbels; buds submerged but rise up before opening; 7-9.	Ponds and slow streams.	Will grow in deep water to 2m deep.
Osmunda regalis Royal fern	Graceful and striking perennial with erect fronds, coloured in autumn; H to 180cm.	Pale green; 2-pinnate; long and broad.	Fertile pinnules form an attractive velvety panicle; 6-8.	Lake sides	Moist peat, naturalized in turfy loam.
Portaderia cordata Pickerel weed	Compact aquatic perennial with rigid stems; H 45-75cm.	Bright glossy-green often with maroon patches; heart-shaped and thick.	Sky-blue or white with yellow eye, closely set in terminal spike; 8-9.	Ponds and marshes.	Pond margin; in loam at edge of pool to depth of 30cm; full sun.
Ranunculus aquatilis Water crowfoot	Variable aquatic perennial; stems trailing or creeping.	2 sets: small and floating and submerged, variously cut.	White buttercuplike, solitary on stem, often in masses; 5-6.	Ponds and streams.	Can be invasive.
Ranunculus lingua Greater spearwort	Hollow-stemmed perennial with densely fibrous roots; H 60-90cm.	Very large; lanceolate; half-stem clasping.	Yellow, twice as large as meadow buttercup; 7-9.	Marshes, ditches and fens.	For damp places; good marginal.
Sagittaria latifolia Arrowhead	Aquatic perennial with stoloniferous swollen rootstock; H 60-90cm.	3 sets of leaves; earliest submerged, then spearlike; later aerial arrow-shaped, on long stalks.	White petals with dark center, in whorls of 3-5 on long stalk; 7-8.	In mud by streams and ponds.	Wet loamy soil.
Scutellaria epilobiifolia Common skullcap	Slender-stemmed perennial; H 15-45cm.	Tinged purple on underside; variable shape, oblong to ovate, and cordate; crenately toothed.	Bright-blue with white marking within; in pairs in leaf axils; 6-9.	Edges of ponds and streams.	Good marginal plant; moist soil or water up to 5cm deep.

ROCK PLANTS

Many a gardener spends a lifetime in search of the rarest rock plants. As one would expect, some are found in specialist nurseries, but others are discovered in out of the way places, or on market stalls in small towns.
Many are easily raised from seed, that offered by garden seedsmen as well as by wildflower firms.

	Habit H = height	Foliage	Flowers Nos = months 1-12	Natural habitat	Cultivation
Antennaria plantaginifolia Pussy toes	Short neat perennial; forms a dense creeping mat; H 6-30cm.	Spoon-shaped; woolly-white beneath.	Male white and spreading, female, pink, erect; borne on different plants; 5-6.	Heaths, dry pastures and mountain slopes.	Light, well-drained soil in sunny position.
Aquilegia canadensis Wild columbine	Tufted perennial; H 10-50cm.	Finely divided, blue-green.	Red and yellow, spurred; Hummingbird plant; 4-5.	Rocky ledges on acid or neutral soil, Eastern US and Canada.	Grow in poor soil to keep stature low.
Arenaria stricta Rock sandwort	Tufted, sprawling perennial; H to 15cm.	Mossy, dark green, needlelike.	White on slender stalks; 5-7.	Dry outcrops usually limestone or serpentine; Que. and Ont. south to SC and Ark.	Well-drained soil.
Campanula divaricata Southern harebell	Perennial with branched stems; H 12-60cm.	Narrowly ovate, pointed, toothed.	Small, blue bells; 7-9.	Rocky slopes of southeastern mountains.	Grows in poor soil, sun or shade.
Campanula rotundifolia Harebell	Slender creeping perennial; H 15-50cm.	Small and heart-shaped; basal leaves wither early.	Slate-blue to bluepurple; bell-shaped and nodding; 6-9.	Dry grassland.	Light, well-drained soil; open position.
Corydalis flavula Yellow harlequin	Tufted perennial with succulent stems; H 12-35cm.	Finely divided, pale green with whitish bloom.	Pale yellow, single spurred, clustered; 4-5.	Rocky slopes south to La. and Kan.	Grows in dry rock clefts.
Corydalis lutea Yellow corydalis	Tufted perennial; H 15-20cm.	Fernlike; slight glaucous.	Rich yellow in short spikes; 4-11.	In hilly districts and as garden escape on walls.	Best on walls and between paving stones.
Cymbalaria muralis Ivy-leaved toadflax	Trailing perennial; H 5-10cm.	Ivy-shaped; long-stalked.	Short-spurred, snapdragonlike; lilac, with yellow on lower lip; 4-10.	Shady rocks and woods; prefers limestone; garden escape on walls.	Ordinary soil in some sun; good trailing plant.
Dryas octopetala Mountain avens	Creeping woody perennial; forms extensive mats; H 15-30cm.	Shiny; mid to deep green; downy-white beneath.	White with many gold stamens; anemonelike; 5-6.	Rocky limestone ledges.	Well-drained sunny site; prefers limestone. Do not disturb roots.
Helianthemum canadense Frostweed	Tufted subshrub; H 8-16cm.	Small, narrow, oblong.	Yellow, solitary; 5-7.	Dry, gravelly slopes and acid barrens, E. Can. and US.	Dry, sand or gravel.
Helianthemum nummularium Rock rose	Low, open, often prostrate semi-shrubby plant. H 10-15cm.	Narrow, oblong; green above, downy beneath.	Yellow, 5-petaled; 5-9.	Grassy places on limestone.	Well-drained soil in a sunny position.
Hypericum buckleyi Buckley's St John's wort	Prostrate shrub; H to 25cm.	Obovate, light green.	Yellow; 5-7.	Rocky cliffs and slopes, only in mountains of Carolinas and Ga.	Well-drained soil in sun.
Lewisia rediviva Bitter root	Deep-rooted perennial; H 6cm.	In rosettes, fleshy, narrow, dying away in summer.	Pink or white, many petaled; 6-7.	Boulders and gravelly slopes from Rocky Mts to Pacific.	Grow in vertical cleft to prevent root rot.
Lewisia tweedyi Lewisia	Deep-rooted perennial; H to 10cm.	In rosettes, evergreen, spatulate, leathery.	Creamy-yellow with apricot tips, many petaled, in clusters; 5-6.	On decayed granite slopes of Mts of central Washington.	As preceding; they need a rich acid or neutral soil and a gravel collar.

	Habit H = height	Foliage	Flowers Nos = months 1-12	Natural habitat	Cultivation
Maianthemum bifolium May lily	Perennial with slender creeping rootstock; mat-forming; H 10-20cm.	Two, thickly-veined, shiny and heart-shaped.	Fragrant, white with prominent stamens in a 12-30 flowered raceme; 5-6.	Woodland; very rare in the wild.	Ideal ground cover for cool, moist (not wet) places.
Penstemon pinifolius Scarlet beard-tongue	Sprawling shrubby perennial; H to 30cm.	Narrow, needlelike, evergreen.	Scarlet, tubular. Hummingbird plant; 6-9.	Mts of south N. Mex. and Ariz.	Hardy, if given sharp drainage in winter.
Phlox bifida Prairie phlox	Sprawling evergreen, forms mats to 50cm.	Narrow, needlelike.	Lavendar blue or white, petal tips deeply-notched.	Dry, rocky or gravelly soils throughout Midwest.	Full sun in well-drained soil.
Phlox nivalis Tufted phlox	Tufted decumbent evergreen; H 15cm.	Juniperlike.	Purple, pink or white; petals sometimes notched; 4-5.	Sandy or gravelly places, Va. to Fla. and Ala.	Will grow in any soil.
Potentilla tabernaemontani Spring cinquefoil	Prostrate, bristly ever-green perennial; mat-forming; H 5-7.5cm.	Basal, stalked and palmate.	Yellow, on ascending, slender stalks; 4-5, and often again in summer.	Dry chalk and lime-stone rocks and grass.	Full sun in well-drained soil.
Potentilla tridentata Three-toothed cinquefoil	Creeping subshrub; H 5-20cm.	Thrice-divided, glossy evergreen, some turning crimson in autumn.	White, small, with prominent stamens; 6-10.	Cliffs and rocky peaks Greenland to Minn. south to mts. of Ga.	Indifferent to lime but said to develop better autumn leaf color in acid soils.
Primula farinosa Birdseye primrose	Small perennial; rosette of leaves; H 10-15cm.	Pale green; narrow and oblanceolate.	Lilac-pink with yellow eye; in umbel; 5-6.	Banks and slopes on limestone outcrops in north.	On soil enriched with peat or leaf mould.
Primula farinosa ssp. *laurentia*	Stoutish perennial.	Rosette, narrow lanceolate; mealy on undersides.	Pink-light purple, in an umbel; 5-8.	North of the St. Lawrence.	Soil enriched with peat.
Pulsatilla occidentalis Mountain pasqueflower	Low perennial, thick rootstock; H 20-40cm.	Much divided, hairy.	Pure white, chalice shaped; 4-5.	Rocky areas in mts. of the West.	Needs perfect drainage.
Pulsatilla vulgaris Pasque flower	Variable tufted perennial with thick black fibrous rootstock; H 15cm.	Feathery, deeply divided and hairy.	Rich violet with golden anthers, silky outside; 4-5.	Limestone slopes.	Open sites and well-drained soil.
Sedum album White stonecrop	Mat-forming glabrous evergreen; H 3.5-15cm.	Oblong; cylindrical; alternate.	White; borne pro-fusely in loose clusters; 7.	Limestone rocks and walls.	Suitable for walls and for ground over stones.
Sedum nevii	Low, mounded succulent; H 10cm.	Spatulate on nonflowering shoots; linear on flowering shoots.	White, starry, with purple anthers; 5-6.	Limestone or shale outcrops in the Southeast.	Will take some shade.
Sedum ternatum	Procumbent mat-forming perennial.	Oval, in threes.	White, starshaped, in cymes;	In rocky woods of southeastern mountains.	Rich, well-drained soil.
Silene caroliniana Wild pink	Tufted perennial, from a deep root; H to 20cm.	Spatulate, hairy.	Deep pink-white, in clusters; 4-6.	Sandy or rocky places in the eastern US.	Well-drained acid soil.
Silene virginica Fire pink	Erect perennial with short rootstock and branching stems; H 20-70cm.	Basal leaves in an over-wintering rosette; stem leaves small and narrow.	Brilliant scarlet in loose heads, petals deeply notched; 4-6.	Sandy or gravelly out-crops in acid soil.	In sun or light shade.
Zauschneria californica California fuschia	Branching perennial or subshrub; H 20-50cm.	Small, narrow, fuzzy and gray.	Bright red, trumpet-shaped. Hummingbird flower; 7-10.	Coastal Calif.	Hardy only if grown in gritty, neutral or slightly acid soil, in full sun.

PLANTS TO ATTRACT WILDLIFE

Native plants for a hummingbird garden

(*nos refer to flowering months, 1-12*)

Aquilegia canadensis,
 wild columbine (4-5)
A. formosa, western columbine (4-5)
Bignonia capreolata, crossvine (6-7)
Campsis radicans, trumpetvine (6-8)
Castilleja coccinea,
 Indian paintbrush (5-7)
Clinopodium coccineum,
 red savory (6-7)
Delphinium cardinale,
 scarlet larkspur (5-7)
D. nudicaule, canyon larkspur (5-7)
Dichelostemma ida-maia,
 firecracker flower (5-7)
Fritillaria recurva,
 scarlet fritillary (5-7)
Hibiscus coccineus,
 scarlet rosemallow (7-9)
Impatiens capensis, jewelweed (7-8)
Ipomoea coccinea,
 scarlet morning glory (7-9)
I. quamoclit, cypress vine (7-9)

Ipomopsis aggregata,
 sky rocket (6-9)
I. rubra, standing cypress (6-9)
Lilium grayi, roan lily (6-7)
Lobelia cardinalis,
 cardinalflower (7-8)
Lonicera sempervirens,
 trumpet honeysuckle (7-8)
Mimulus aurantiacus,
 bush monkeyflower (5-9)
M. cardinalis,
 scarlet monkeyflower (5-9)
Monarda didyma,
 bee balm, Oswego tea (6-8)
Penstemon centranthifolius,
 scarlet bugler (5-7)
Rhododendron flammeum,
 Oconee azalea (5-6)
R. calendulaceum,
 flame azalea (6)
R. prunifolium,
 plumleaf azalea (7-8)
Silene regia, royal catchfly (5-7)
S. virginica, fire pink (5-7)
Spigelia marilandica,
 Indian pink (5-7)

PLANTS FOR SPECIAL SITUATIONS

Trees and shrubs tolerant of acid soils

Acer rubrum, red maple
Aronia arbutifolia, red chokeberry
Chamaecyparis thyoides,
 Atlantic white-cedar
Kalmia latifolia, mountain laurel
Pinus rigida, pitch pine
P. virginiana, scrub pine
Quercus alba, white oak
Q. falcata, Spanish oak
Q. prinus, chestnut oak
Rhododendron maximum, rose bay
R. viscosum, swamp azalea

Trees and shrubs tolerant of alkaline soils

Celtis occidentalis, backberry
Fraxinus americana, white
 ash
Juniperus virginiana,
 eastern red-cedar
Lindera benzoin, spicebush
Quercus macrocarpa,
 mossy-cup oak
Q. muehlenbergii, yellow oak

Thuja occidentalis,
 eastern arborvitae
Ulmus rubra, slippery elm
Zanthoxylum americanum,
 toothache tree

Native plants for sunny places

Arenaria spp., sandworts
Asclepias tuberosa, butterfly weed
Aster spp., frostweeds, starworts
Chrysopsis villosa,
 hairy golden-aster
Eschscholzia californica,
 California poppy
Geranium robertianum, herb robert
Helenium spp., sneezeweeds
Helianthemum spp.,
 frostweeds, rock roses
Helianthus spp., sunflowers
Iris versicolor, blue flag
Liatris spicata, gay feather
Manfreda virginica, false aloe,
 rattlesnake master
Opuntia humifusa,
 prickly-pear cactus
Phlox subulata, moss phlox
Thermopsis caroliniana,
 Carolina lupine
Vernonia noveboracensis,
 New York ironweed
Viola pedata, birdsfoot violet
Yucca glauca, soapweed

Some native plants for shady places

Anemonella thalictroides,
 rue anemone
Asarum canadense, wild ginger
Clintonia umbellulata,
 speckled beadlily
Cynoglossum virginianum,
 wild comfrey
Delphinium tricorne,
 dwarf larkspur
Dicentra cucullaria,
 Dutchman's breeches
Dodecatheon meadia,
 shooting star
Jeffersonia diphylla, twinleaf
Mertensia virginica,
 Virginia bluebell
Oxalis acetellosa, wood sorrel
Podophyllum peltatum, may-apple
Polemonium reptans,
 Jacob's ladder

Seed- and fruit-producing plants for birds and other creatures

Alnus spp.	alders	seeds (fall-winter)	winter finches, small mammals
Amelanchier spp.	shad bushes	fruits (early summer)	birds, small mammals
Aronia spp.	choke-berries	fruits (fall-winter)	birds, small mammals
Betula spp.	birches	seeds (fall-winter)	winter finches, small mammals
Cirsium spp.	thistles	seeds (summer-fall)	goldfinches etc.
Cornus spp.	dogwoods	fruits (autumn)	migrating birds etc.
Corylus spp.	hazels	nuts (autumn)	many birds and mammals
Crataegus spp.	hawthorns	nuts (autumn)	many birds and mammals
Gaylussacia frondosa	huckleberry	fruits (summer)	many birds and mammals
Helianthus spp.	sunflowers	seeds (summer-fall)	goldfinches etc.
Ilex opaca	American holly	fruits (winter)	many migrating birds
Lindera benzoin	spice bush	fruits (autumn)	birds; spice bush swallowtail
Lonicera spp.	honeysuckles	fruits (summer-autumn)	many birds and mammals
Morus rubra	red mulberry	fruits (summer)	many birds and mammals
Oenothera biennis	evening primrose	seeds (fall-winter)	goldfinches etc.
Pinus spp.	pines	seeds (fall-winter)	winter finches, esp. crossbills; squirrels etc.
Polygonum pensylvanicum	Pennsylvania lady's thumb	seeds (fall-winter)	winter finches and small mammals
Prunus spp.	cherries, plums	fruits (summer-autumn)	many birds and mammals
Rhus typhina	staghorn sumas	fruits (summer-autumn)	esp. good for migrating birds
Rubus odoratus	flowering raspberry	fruits (summer)	birds, insects
Quercus spp.	oaks	nuts (autumn-winter)	many birds and animals

WILDFLOWER AND MEADOW GRASS SEED MIXTURES

Polygonatum biflorum,
    Solomon's seal
Sanguinaria canadensis, bloodroot
Smilacina racemosa,
    Solomon's plume
Stylophorum diphyllum,
    golden wood poppy
Tiarella cordifolia,
    Allegheny foamflower
Tillium cuneatum,
    whippoorwill flower
Uvularia grandiflora,
    large-flowered bellwort
Viola rotundifolia,
    round-leaf yellow violet

Native climbers and trailers

Arctostaphyos uva-ursi, bearberry
Bignonia capreolata, crossvine
Campsis radicans, trumpetvine
Clematis viorna, leather flower
Cocculus carolinus, snailseed
Echinocystis lobata, balsam apple,
    wild cucumber
Ipomoea pandurata,
    man-of-the-earth
Menispermum canadense, moonseed
Mitchella repens, partridgeberry
Parthenocissus quinquefolia,
    Virginia creeper
Passiflora incarnata,
    maypops, apricot vine
Smilax laurifolia, bamboo vine
Wisteria frutescens

Wildflowers and grasses for limestone

% GRASS SPECIES

35.0 *Poa pratensis,*
        Kentucky blue grass
23.0 *Festuca rubra,* red fescue
20.0 *Cyanosurus cristatus,*
        crested dogstail
 5.0 *Bouteloua curtipendula,*
        side-oats grama
 2.0 *Uniola latifolia,* wild oats

% WILDFLOWERS

 2.0 *Heuchera americana,*
        alumroot
 1.0 *Anemone caroliniana,*
EACH Carolina windflower;
        A. multifida,
        Argentine windflower;
        *Chrysanthemum
        leucanthemum,* oxeye daisy;
        Draba glabella,
        smooth whitlow-grass;
        Parnassia palustris,
        grass-of-Parnassus;
        Plantago media,
        hoary plantain;
        Prunella vulgaris, self-heal;
        Stylophorum diphyllum,
        gold poppy
 0.5 *Astragalus canadensis,*
EACH milk vetch;
        Campanula rotundifolia,
        harebell; *Dryas integrifolia,*
        mountain avens;
        Galium verum,
        lady's bedstraw;
        Hieracium pilosella,
        mouse-ear hawkweed;
        Leontodon hispidus,
        greater hawkbit;
        Origanum vulgare,
        marjoram;
        Primula mistassinica,
        bird's-eye primrose;
        Saxifraga cespitosa,
        tufted saxifrage;
        Saxifraga oppositifolia,
        purple mountain saxifrage

Wildflowers and grasses for loam and alluvial soils

% GRASS SPECIES

20.0 *Festuca rubra,* red fescue
30.0 *Setaria geniculata,*
        perennial foxtail millet;
        Calamagrostis canadensis,
        blue-joint;
        Phalaris arundinacea,
        reed canary grass;
        Calamagrostis cinnoides,
        wood reed; *Panicum anceps,*
        two-edged panic grass;
        Panicum virgatum,
        switch grass
10.0 *Agrostis alba,* red top;
EACH *Poa trivialis,*
        rough-stalked meadow grass;
        Triodia flava, purple top;

% WILDFLOWERS

 8.0 *Aster novae-angliae,*
        New England aster;
        Solidago canadensis,
        Canada goldenrod
 6.0 *Ranunculus acris,*
        meadow buttercup;
        Senecio aureus,
        golden ragwort
 4.0 *Liatris spicata,*
        spiked gayfeather;
        Oenothera tetragona, sundrops;
        Penstemon digitalis,
        foxglove beardtongue;
        Rudbeckia fulgida,
        showy coneflower;
 2.0 *Aster pilosus,* frostweed;
        Cirsium discolor, field thistle;
        Helianthus giganteus,
        tall sunflower;
        Lobelia siphilitica,
        great blue lobelia;
        Lilium canadense,
        meadow lily;
        Tragopogon pratense,
        goatsbeard;
        Verbena hastata,
        blue vervain;
        Vernonia crinita,
        ironweed;
        Viola sororia (papilionacea),
        meadow violet

Wildflowers and grasses for clay soils

% GRASS SPECIES

40.0 *Festuca rubra,* red fescue;
EACH *Andropogon virginicus* var.
        abbreviatus (A. glomeratus),
        broomsedge
 3.0 *Holcus lanatus,* velvet grass
 2.0 *Anthoxanthum odoratum,*
        sweet vernal grass

% WILDFLOWERS

 2.0 *Hedyotis caerulea*
        (Houstonia c.), Bluets
 1.5 *Rhexia mariana,*
EACH Meadow beauty
        Viola primulaefolia,
        primrose-leaved violet
 1.0 *Chrysanthemum*
EACH *leucanthemum,* oxeye daisy;
        Galium verum,
        lady's bedstraw;
        Gentiana andrewsii,
        close gentian; *G. saponaria,*
        bottle gentian;
        Medicago lupulina,
        black medick;
        Prunella vulgaris, self-heal;
        Spigelia marilandica,
        Indian pink
 0.5 *Achillea millefolium,* yarrow;
EACH *Asclepias incarnata,*
        swamp milkweed;
        Erigeron pulchellus,
        Robin's plantain;
        Leontodon autumnalis,
        fall dandelion;
        Linaria vulgaris,
        butter-and-eggs;
        Ranunculus repens,
        creeping buttercup

GLOSSARY

Acid Term applied to soils with a pH lower than 7.0.

Acuminate Term applied to a leaf which tapers to a long, narrow point.

Alkaline Term applied to soils with a pH higher than 7.0, normally with a comparatively high lime content.

Alpine A plant that grows naturally on mountain slopes; a plant suitable for a rock garden.

Annual A plant that germinates, grows, flowers, seeds and dies within the space of 12 months.

Anther The terminal part of a stamen containing the pollen.

Aquatic Term applied to a plant of any genera living mainly in water.

Axil The upper angle formed by the union of the leaf and the stem.

Axis The part of a plant around which the organs are developed.

Bedding plant Any flowering annual used for seasonal display in the traditional garden.

Biennial A plant that germinates, grows, flowers, seeds and dies within two years.

Bog Wet land of an acid nature but not so wet that plants are constantly under water, nor so dry that the roots dry out.

Broadcast To sow or scatter seeds over an area of soil instead of in marked rows or drills.

Bulb A storage organ with fleshy scales or a swollen leaf base containing food for a resting period.

Bulbils Small bulbs that grow on some plants and can be detached and grown into full-sized bulbs.

Calcareous Term applied to soil containing lime.

Calcifuge A lime-hating plant that will not grow well if there is lime in the soil.

Clay Term applied to a soil mixture of very fine sand and alumina which is moisture-retentive, heavy and sticky but usually fertile if treated.

Composite Term applied to a plant in which the flowerhead consists of separate florets.

Compost The product of rotted vegetable matter.

Coppicing Term applied to practice of chopping first the main stem of a tree, and, in subsequent years, the young growths, to ground level.

Corm A storage organ comprising a thickened underground stem.

Corymb A flat head of stalked flowers ranged at different levels.

Cottage garden A garden in which the needs of a family are catered for – with a mixture of vegetables, herbs and flowers grown together rather than separately.

Crown Top of the rootstock from which new shoots orginate.

Cultivar Cultivated *variety* (q.v.) either bred purposely or developing spontaneously, but incapable of exact reproduction by seeds.

Deciduous Term applied to a plant that drops its leaves in winter.

Dentate Term applied to a leaf with toothed edges.

Dormant A condition of inactivity in plants usually occasioned by low temperatures.

Evergreen Term applied to a plant that drops its leaves gradually and replaces them through the year.

Exotic A plant not indigenous to the country in which it is growing, and which is unable to naturalize.

Falls Those petals that hang down, such as those of an iris flowerhead.

Fimbriate With a fringed margin.

Glabrous Smooth; devoid of hair.

Ground cover Thickly growing low shrubs or herbaceous plants that closely cover the soil which supports them.

Habit General appearance or manner of growth of a plant, e.g. upright, sprawling, creeping, etc.

Habitat Natural home or living area of a plant.

Half-hardy Term applied to a plant that needs protection in winter. some say with bank and/or ditch.

Herbaceous Term applied to a plant with soft or sappy, instead of woody, growth.

Humus Decayed organic matter- a soil conditioner rather than a fertilizer.

Hybrid Product of a cross between plants of different species, sometimes indicated by a cross, e.g. *Erica × darleyens.*

Lanceolate Term applied to a lance-shaped leaf, longer than its width and tapering at both ends.

Laying The process of hedge-making in which saplings are bent over almost horizontally and staked.

Limestone Underlying rock formation usually associated with a surface soil of high pH.

Linear Slender.

Loam Rotted turf; normally a soil mixture of sand, clay and humus but with no precise definition.

Marginal Term applied to a plant that grows in shallow water at the margin or edge of a pool or pond – 'emergent' to the botanist.

Marsh Land that is watery at all times.

Moraine A bed of small stones or grit, usually for growing alpines and usually watered from below, unlike a *scree* (q.v.).

Native Term applied to a plant or animal that is indigenous to a locality or country.

Naturalize To grow plants under conditions that are as nearly natural as possible; naturalized plants are those that were originally imported but have subsequently reseeded themselves in the wild.

Ovate Term applied to a leaf that is egg-shaped.

Oxygenating Term applied to a plant that grows in or under water, and which produces oxygen.

Palmate Term applied to a leaf shaped like a hand.

Panicle Flower cluster of several separate branches, each carrying numerous stalked flowers.

Peat Soil from boggy or swampy land. Moss peat comes mainly from decomposed sphagnum moss, whereas sedge peat comes from the roots and leaves of sedges.

Pedunculate Having a flower stalk.

Peltate Term applied to a shield-shaped leaf with a central stalk.

Perennial Any plant that lives and flowers for a number of years.

Pinnate Term applied to a feather-like leaf having several leaflets on each side of a common stalk.

Pinnule A secondary division of a pinnate leaf.

Pubescent Covered with fine hairs.

Raceme An unbranched inflorescence with flowers carried on equal-length stalks.

Radical Growing from the root.

Rhizome An underground stem that usually grows horizontally, producing shoots some distance from the parent plant.

Root ball A cluster of roots embedded in the soil.

Runner A shoot that roots at intervals along its length.

Scree Similar to a **moraine** (q.v.), but usually watered from above.

Sessile Without a stalk.

Species A group of plants that resemble each other, breed together and maintain the same constant distinctive character.

Stolon A creeping stem that roots at intervals.

Taproot A straight root, thicker at its top than its base, from which subsidiary rootlets spring.

Tomentose Hairy, having a dense covering of short hairs.

Trickle irrigation A system using flexible small-bore tubing to drip or trickle water to adjustable nozzles to specific plants or pots.

Trifoliate Having three leaflets.

Triquetrous Triangular and acutely angled.

Umbel Flower clusters where the flower stalks all rise from the top of the main flower stem.

Variegation White or yellow spots, blotches or streaks on green leaves, arising from mutation, a benign virus or mineral deficiency.

Variety A group of plants within a species; any plant with distinctive characteristics but not worthy of specific rank.

Vernalization The exposure of a plant or bulb to low temperature to encourage early flowering.

GENERAL INDEX

PLANT INDEX

BIBLIOGRAPHY AND ADDRESSES

Ayensu, Edward S. and Robert A. DeFilipps, *Endangered and Threatened Plants of the United States*, Washington, DC: Smithsonian Institution and World Wildlife Fund, Inc., 1978

Bell, C. Ritchie and Bryan J. Taylor, *Florida Wild Flowers and Roadside Plants*, Chapel Hill: Laurel Hill Press, 1982

Bruce, Hal, *How to Grow Wildflowers and Wild Shrubs and Trees in Your Own Garden*, New York: Alfred A. Knopf, 1976; Van Noxtrand Reinhold Company, 1982

Currah, R., A. Smreciu and M. Van Dyk, *Prairie Wildflowers*, Edmonton, Alberta: Friends of the Devonian Botanic Garden, University of Alberta, 1983

Dana, Mrs William Starr, *How to Know the Wild Flowers*, New York: Dover Publications, Inc., 1963

du Pont, Elizabeth N, *Landscaping With Native Plants In the Middle-Atlantic Region*, Chadds Ford, PA: Brandywine Conservancy, 1978

Fernald, Merritt Lyndon, *Gray's Manual of Botany*, New York: American Book Company, 1950

Foster, H. Lincoln, *Rock Gardening*, Boston: Houghton Mifflin Company, 1968

Frederick, William H., Jr., *100 Great Garden Plants*, New York: Alfred A. Knopf, 1975

Newcomb, Lawrence, *Newcomb's Wildflower Guide*, Boston: Little, Brown and Company, 1977

Niehaus, Theodore F., and C. L. Ripper, *A Field Guide to Pacific States Wildflowers*, Boston: Houghton Mifflin Company, 1976

Pyle, Robert Michael, *The Audubon Society Field Guide to North American Butterflies*

Radford, Albert E., Harry E. Ahles, and C. Ritchie Bell, *Manual of the Vascular Flora of the Carolinas*, Chapel Hill: The University of North Carolina Press, 1968

Rickett, Harold William, *The Northeastern States*. Vol. 1 of *Wild Flowers of the United States*; *The Southeastern States*, Vol. 2 of *Wild Flowers of the United States*, New York: McGraw-Hill Company, 1966

Robbins, Chandler S., Bertel Bruun, and Herbert S. Zim, *Birds of North America*, New York: Golden Press, 1966

Taylor, K. S., and Stephen F. Hamblin, *Handbook of Wild Flower Cultivation*, New York: The Macmillan Company, 1963

Seed suppliers

Applewood Seed Co., 5380 Vivian St, Arrada, Co. 80002 USA

Arrow Seed Company, Ltd, Box 722, Broken Bow, Nebraska 68822 USA

Boehlke's Woodland Gardens, W 140 N 10829 Country Aire Rd, Germantown, Wisconsin 53022 USA

Christensen's Nursery Co., 935 Old County Rd, Belmont, Calif. 94002 USA

Clyde Robin Seed Co., Inc., Box 2855, Castro Valley, Calif. 94546 USA

Conley's Garden Center Inc, 145 Townsend Ave, Boothbay Harbor, Maine 04538 USA

Curtis & Curtis, Inc., Star Route Box 8A, Clovis, New Mexico 88130 USA

Dean Swift, PO Box B, Jaroso, Colorado 81138 USA

Environmental Seed Producers, PO Box 5904, El Monte, Calif. 91734 USA

Golden West Seeds, Ltd, 1108 6 Street SE, Calgary, Alberta T2G-2Y2 Canada

Horizon Seeds, Inc., 1600 Cornhusker Highway, PO Box 81823, Lincoln, Nebraska 68501 USA

Jacklin Seed Company, West 17300 Jacklin Ave, Post Falls, Idaho 83854 USA

Lafayette Home Nursery, Inc., Layfayette, Illinois 61449 USA

Little Valley Farm, RR 1, Box 287, Richland Center, Wisconsin 53581 USA

Midwest Wildflowers, Box 64, Rockton, Illinois 61072 USA

Natural Habitat Nursery, 4818 Terminal Road, McFarland, Wisconsin 53558 USA

Northplan Seed Producers NAPG Inc., PO Box 9107, Moscow, Idaho 83843 USA

Prairie Associates, 6328 Piping Rock Road, Madison, Wisconsin 53581 USA

Prairie Nursery (J. R. Smith), Rt. 1, Westfield, Wisconsin 53964 USA

Prairie Restoration, Inc., 990 Old Long Lake Road, Wayzata, Minnesota 55391 USA

Prairie Ridge Nursery (Joyce Powers), 9738 Overland Road, Rt. 2, Mt. Horeb, Wisconsin 53572 USA

Prairie Seed Source, Box 831, North Lake, Wisconsin 53064 USA

Prairie Seed Source, PO Box 1131, Des Moines, Idaho 50311 USA

Rocky Mountain Seed Service, Box 215, Golden BC, VOA 1HO Canada

Sharp Bros. Seed Company, Healy, Kansas 67850 USA

Stock Seed Farms Inc., RR Box 112, Murdock, Nebraska 68407 USA

Wildlife Nurseries, PO Box 2724, Oshkosh, Wisconsin 54903 USA

Windrift Prairie Nursery, Rt. 2, Oregon, Illinois 61061 USA

Plant suppliers

Woodlanders, Inc., 1128 Colleton Ave, Aiken, S.C. 29801 USA

We-Du Nursery, Route 5, Box 724, Marion, N.C. 28752 USA

ACKNOWLEDGMENTS

The publishers would like to thank the following people:

Mr Terry Wells of the Institute of Terrestrial Ecology (NERC), Monks Wood Experimental Station, for commenting most helpfully on the typescript, and in particular on the wildflower meadows chapter and the bulb planter technique.

Mrs A. H. Bauerman, Mrs M. Huiskamp, Mr George Innes, the Hon. Mrs Lyttleton, Mr Ian Mylles and Mr Peter Baistow for their kind permission to photograph their gardens.

For this edition, special thanks go to Mr Hal Bruce, Curator of Plants, Winterthur Museum, for his expert contributions, and also to Joanna Chisholm for editorial work.

Susan Berry for initial work on the book and for editorial work; Joanna Jellinek for editorial work; and Leslie Johns for compiling the index.

Project editor
Alison Freegard

Art editor
Steven Wooster

Editor
David Black

Designer
Claudine Meissner

General editor
Pippa Rubinstein

Picture researcher
Anne Fraser

Photographs
ARCAID/Richard Bryant: 10; ARDEA: 77T; Peter Baistow: 62T, 66; Karl-Dietrich Bühler: 13, 14, 15, 48, 57, 59, 85, 101T, 103; Robert César: 9; Geoff Dann, 4, 11, 18, 20, 22/23, 25, 29, 35, 37, 45, 54/55, 79, 82, 83, 87, 91, 95, 97, 100B, 109, 115, 120T, front and back cover; Henk Dijkman: 194, 113T; Inge Espen-Hansen: 1, 31, 34, 38, 49, 56, 96, 106B, 108, 110, 120B; Derek Fell: 19, 32, 61T, 68, 69, 72, 74, 114; Valerie Finnis: 7, 117; John Glover: 70, 76, 80, 119B; Jerry Harpur: 39L, 111; Pat Hunt: 40, 98, 100T, 119T; Jacqui Hurst: 12, 17, 21, 42, 47, 62B, 64, 65, 84, 86, 106T; Leslie Johns: author's photograph; Nature Photographers Ltd: 105T, 113B; Oxford Scientific Films/ Stephen Dalton: 101B; Harry Smith (Horticultural Photographic Collection): 30; Ron Sutherland: 2, 28, 36, 43, 63, 71, 77B, 89, 105 (BL and BR), 112; George Taloumis: 8, 39R; Steven Wooster: 61B; George Wright: 53, 90, 118.

Illustrations
Angela Beard: 33; Jeanne Colville: 52, 75; Jane Cradock-Watson: 122; Fiona B. Currie: 7, 19, 21, 24, 26, 29, 37, 43, 53, 72, 76, 78, 85, 90, 94, 98, 102, 111, 114, 118, 121, 141; Will Giles: 123-140; Vana Haggerty: 142; Ros Hewitt: 16, 17, 41, 58, 59, 65, 67; Sally Launder: 31, 60, 73, 81, 88, 99, 107, 116; Andrew Macdonald: 27; Shirley Wheeler: 50, 51, 92, 93.

Garden designs
Anthony Paul 107; Robin Williams 73, 88, 116.

Cover border
Michael Craig

Typesetting
Chambers Wallace, London

Reproduction
Hong Kong Graphic Arts Limited